TRASH AND LIMITS IN LATIN AMERICAN CULTURE

Trash and Limits in Latin American Culture

Micah McKay

UNIVERSITY OF FLORIDA PRESS

Gainesville

This book will be made open access within three years of publication thanks to Path to Open, a program developed in partnership between JSTOR, the American Council of Learned Societies (ACLS), University of Michigan Press, and The University of North Carolina Press to bring about equitable access and impact for the entire scholarly community, including authors, researchers, libraries, and university presses around the world. Learn more at https://about.jstor.org/path-to-open/

Publication of this work made possible by a Sustaining the Humanities through the American Rescue Plan grant from the National Endowment for the Humanities.

Copyright 2024 by Micah McKay
All rights reserved
Published in the United States of America

29 28 27 26 25 24   6 5 4 3 2 1

Library of Congress Cataloging-in-Publication Data
Names: McKay, Micah, author.
Title: Trash and limits in Latin American culture / Micah McKay.
Description: Gainesville : University of Florida Press, 2024. | Includes bibliographical references and index.
Identifiers: LCCN 2023039990 (print) | LCCN 2023039991 (ebook) | ISBN 9781683404057 (hardback) | ISBN 9781683404286 (paperback) | ISBN 9781683404163 (pdf) | ISBN 9781683404378 (ebook)
Subjects: LCSH: Latin American literature—History and criticism. | Refuse and refuse disposal in literature. | BISAC: LITERARY CRITICISM / Caribbean & Latin American | PERFORMING ARTS / Film / History & Criticism | LCGFT: Literary criticism.
Classification: LCC PN849.L29 M44 2024 (print) | LCC PN849.L29 (ebook) | DDC 860.9—dc23/eng/20231004
LC record available at https://lccn.loc.gov/2023039990
LC ebook record available at https://lccn.loc.gov/2023039991

University of Florida Press
2046 NE Waldo Road
Suite 2100
Gainesville, FL 32609
http://upress.ufl.edu

Contents

Acknowledgments vii

Introduction 1

1. Excess and Lack: Trash and the Limits of the Human 22
2. In and Out of the Dump: On the Limits of Community 53
3. Trash Works: On the Limits of Waste Management 73
4. Cleaning Up: On the Limits of Neoliberal Environmentalism 109

Conclusion 143

Notes 149

Works Cited 169

Index 179

Acknowledgments

One of the great pleasures of writing a book is sharing ideas with and receiving feedback from mentors, colleagues, and friends. Many of the people in my life who fit into one or more of those categories have given me generous and timely feedback on my work, and they deserve far more than the meager thanks I can express here. Glen Close dedicated much time and thought to my project at its earliest stage, and his keen insights inevitably helped me to improve my ideas. The same can be said for Severino Albuquerque, Kata Beilin, Ksenija Bilbija, and Víctor Goldgel Carballo, whose critical feedback and warm enthusiasm have left a mark on all the work I do.

The Department of Modern Languages and Classics at the University of Alabama has been a lovely place to work on this book. My colleagues in the Spanish section and across the department have shown unwavering support for my research and teaching, trash and all. In particular, I would like to thank the following former and current colleagues who gave valuable feedback on sections of this book in the department's Works in Progress seminar: Fabio Battista, Matthew Feminella, Jessica Goethals, Xabier Granja, Alessandra Montalbano, Alexandra Gozenbach Perkins, Kelly Shannon-Henderson, Gina Stamm, and Bill Worden. Also, my hearty thanks go to the students at UA who have taken my seminars on trash and the Anthropocene; they always delight me with their insights and excitement.

I am also grateful to those who invited me to present my research or talk to their students about trash and culture and to those who included me in panels at several different academic conferences: Anindita Banerjee, Debra Castillo, Nicolás Campisi, Odile Cisneros, Ali Kulez, Maryanne Leone, Shanna Lino, John Maddox, Tamara Mitchell, Sarah Moody, and Iñaki Prádanos. These interactions were invigorating and changed the course of my project for the better.

The process of publishing a monograph can be daunting and mysterious for a first-timer like me, but working with a fantastic editor like Stephanye

Hunter makes it a pleasure. Stephanye's enthusiasm for my project and her timely suggestions for improvements to the manuscript were key in making this book a reality. I appreciate the care with which she and her colleagues at the University of Florida Press guided me through the publication process. I would also like to thank the three anonymous reviewers whose generous, insightful comments and helpful suggestions invigorated me during the final stretch of working on this project.

While I was in graduate school at the University of Wisconsin, Nora Benedict, Eric Hartmann, and Joe Patteson became three of my best friends. Besides serving as important interlocutors on this project, they taught me many things about thinking, reading, writing, teaching, parenthood, and friendship. But the most important thing we learned together—over french fries and cheap drinks at the Library—is who Miguel de Cervantes really is.

If anyone is to blame for my reading habits, it's my dad, Jim McKay. I thank him for giving me access to books and for encouraging me to read and explore ideas from an early age. His love and support are constants in my life. In fact, I think that he's even more excited about this book becoming a reality than I am, which is saying quite a lot.

My daughter Hazel was born in 2014, just as I was starting the project that would become this book. Watching her grow has been a beautiful gift. For the past couple of years, she's been asking every few days if my book is out yet, and I'm so glad to be able to tell her that, yes, it finally is. My son Ellis came along in 2020, another beautiful gift to fill my life with joy. And through all of this and more, Alisha has been my love, my life, my friend. This book is for you. Sorry about all the trash.

Chapter 2 features revised material from "Trash and the Coming Community: Portrayals of Trash and Trash Workers in Argentina and Brazil," from *Environmental Cultural Studies Through Time: The Luso-Hispanic World*, edited by Katarzyna Beilin, Kathleen Connolly, and Micah McKay (*Hispanic Issues On Line*, vol. 24, 2019, pp. 45–64); and "On the Nature of the Border: Trash Thresholds in Luis Alberto Urrea's *By the Lake of Sleeping Children*," from *Latin American Literary Review* (vol. 48, no. 96, 2021, pp. 13–21). Chapter 3 includes revised portions of "The Littered City: Trash and Neoliberal Urban Space in *El aire, Bariloche*, and *La villa*," originally published in *Revista Canadiense de Estudios Hispánicos* (vol. 41, no. 3, 2017, pp. 597–620). Chapter 4 features revised sections of "Documenting Jardim Gramacho: *Estamira* (2004) and Waste Land (2009)," from *Luso-Brazilian Review* (vol. 53, no. 2, 2016, pp. 134–52; © 2016 by the Board of Regents of the

University of Wisconsin System); it is reprinted courtesy of the University of Wisconsin Press.

Support for this scholarly work was provided by the University of Alabama Office of Academic Affairs.

Introduction

People young and old cram onto a city train full of shopping carts that carry loads of cardboard. A woman digs through trash bags on a curbside while she explains the unwritten rules of who can pick recyclable goods on one block or another. A paper plant executive says that margins are tight and trash pickers can't be paid more. Teenagers from an environmental cooperative go door-to-door in a middle-class neighborhood asking residents to sort recyclable goods from the rest of their garbage. An artist explains how the sculptures he makes from scrap metal bear witness to bygone modes of industrial production. And *cartoneros*, the people who make a living from the cardboard, paper, metal, and plastic they pull from the trash, work and work and work. These are some of the images that Ernesto Livon-Grosman gives us in his 2006 documentary *Cartoneros*, an insightful exploration of neoliberalism's role in the dramatic increase in the number of trash pickers in Buenos Aires in the wake of Argentina's massive financial crisis at the turn of the twenty-first century. Peppered throughout the film is a curious series of sequences that suggests a connection between the circulation of trash and the articulation of discourses about modern urban space. First, at about the four-minute mark, Cristina Banegas's narration, reflecting on trash and contemporary social concerns in Buenos Aires, gives way to a brief mid-twentieth-century film clip extolling Buenos Aires as a paragon of modernity. With a jaunty, upbeat delivery, the film clip's narrator proclaims, "Buenos Aires, un refugio cosmopolita de América, un crisol de multitudes, una nueva y maravillosa capital del mundo. A la magnificencia de su arquitectura colosal aporta Buenos Aires un elemento nuevo: su fina espiritualidad y un cosmopolitismo que las supera a todas. Buenos Aires encierra un pequeño París, una pequeña Roma, un Londres, un Nueva York. Pero ni Nueva York, ni Londres, ni Roma, ni París encierran un pequeño Buenos Aires. Es que Buenos Aires está hecho en esencia con un poco de cada uno." (Buenos Aires, a cosmopolitan refuge in the Americas, a melting pot of multitudes, a new and marvelous world capital. Along with the magnificence of its colossal architecture, Buenos Aires contributes a new element: a refined spirituality and a cosmopolitanism that exceeds that of other cities. Buenos Aires contains a little Paris, a little Rome, a London, a New York. But neither New York, London, Rome, nor Paris contains a little Buenos Aires. Truly, Buenos Aires is made, in essence, of a little bit of each one.)

A montage of urban scenes accompanies and exemplifies the content of the voiceover: shots of city streets bustling with vehicle traffic, aerial views of the famous obelisk in the Plaza de la República and the Palacio del Congreso, and worm's-eye shots of elegant high-rise buildings seem to confirm Buenos Aires's place in the network of cosmopolitan centers, which, as the narrator asserts, are the constitutive ingredients of Argentina's capital. But as the film clip ends, Livon-Grosman makes a simple editing choice that subtly calls into question this triumphalist discourse: he cuts short the images from the film clip just enough so that the voiceover extends into the next shot of *Cartoneros*, which is a slow pan over a photo of men working in an open-air garbage dump. This image stands in sharp contrast to the ones in the film clip, and Livon-Grosman's decision to juxtapose it with the final words of the film clip's voiceover seems to be a way of asking how trash, the spaces where it is gathered, and the people who work with it fit into the idea that Buenos Aires is a "refugio cosmopolita" in an otherwise provincial continent.

About forty minutes further into *Cartoneros*, Livon-Grosman returns to the film clip to continue picking it apart, albeit with somewhat less subtlety. This time he lays the same triumphalist voiceover on top of a different montage of *escenas porteñas* (Buenos Aires scenes). As we hear the voice extol Buenos Aires's monumental architecture and impressive cosmopolitanism, we see what at first appears to be an updated, contemporary version of the black-and-white city scenes from the film clip. There are cars and people making their way through busy streets, images of high rises and skyscrapers, and even shots of the Palacio del Congreso and the Obelisco that remind us of the ones from earlier in the film. Soon enough, though, a presence for which the original film clip did not account makes its way into the frame: cartoneros, people who make a living scavenging trash all over the city for recyclable goods to sell. As traffic buzzes by on a busy street, we see several cartoneros riding in a horse-drawn cart slowly enter, then leave the frame. A different shot shows a cartonera navigating a shopping cart loaded with scavenged material through a jumble of pedestrians on a sidewalk. Still another shot shows a ramshackle truck, loaded with cartoneros and their haul, weaving in and out of traffic somewhere in the city.

Livon-Grosman returns to the film clip once again toward the end of *Cartoneros*. The final step in his critique involves an inversion of the previous one: instead of fusing together the original voiceover and contemporary images, he returns to the montage from the original film clip but rewrites the voiceover, which is now given by Banegas, the narrator of the film. As we view once again the images of a mid-twentieth-century Buenos Aires, Banegas proclaims, "Buenos Aires, un refugio europeo en América Latina, es también una de las grandes capitales del mundo. Con una población de más de 3 millones de habitantes, supera a muchas otras en varios miles de personas que llegan todos los días a la ciudad para revisar y clasificar la basura que los vecinos dejan en las calles. Buenos Aires tiene algo de México, de Bogotá, de Caracas y de Rio, y es que México, Bogotá, Caracas y Rio tienen en común que una parte de su población vive de la basura." (Buenos Aires, a European refuge in Latin America, is also one of the great world capitals. With a population of more than three million, it has several thousand more people than other cities who arrive daily to look through and sort trash that inhabitants leave on the streets. Buenos Aires has a bit of Mexico City, of Bogotá, of Caracas and Rio, because one thing Mexico City, Bogotá, Caracas, and Rio have in common is that a portion of their population lives on trash.)

The overall effect of incorporating the film clip into *Cartoneros* and then picking it apart by isolating the basic elements of its composition—sight and sound—and examining them in dialogue with Livon-Grosman's central concern—the cartonero phenomenon—is highly suggestive. Not only does Livon-Grosman manage to locate Buenos Aires within a cosmopolitan network that would undermine the city's status as the "Paris of the South," but also by foregrounding cartoneros and their work with trash (and by alluding to this phenomenon as one that is common throughout Latin America), he allows us to see the central role that garbage and the social practices that surround it play in contemporary Latin American life.

Trash and Limits in Latin American Culture explores the role of trash, waste, garbage, and detritus in a range of cultural texts produced across the region between the 1950s and 2010s, with a particular focus on texts from the 1980s onward, when the region experienced the full effect of neoliberalism. A documentary film like *Cartoneros* serves as one of what I (somewhat playfully) call a series of "pre-texts" for the critical task I undertake in the following pages: it is a relatively obscure scrap of culture, a creative treatment of trash-related themes that catalyzes my own analysis. It is a good excuse (a pretext) for delving into the topic, and placing it before my own intervention (a *pre*-text) both signals the critical path I will take and suggests that there are many rich texts for thinking about trash beyond the ones that receive sustained attention in this book. In a way that resonates with Livon-Grosman's suggestion that waste and waste work are key to understanding social processes like marginalization, political struggle, and the production of aesthetic value, I argue that by paying attention to trash in films, novels, short stories, nonfiction narratives, and environmental projects, we attain a sharper focus on important questions of our moment. More specifically, *Trash and Limits in Latin American Culture* contemplates the way trash signals a number of key limits that structure the ways we inhabit the planet and attempt to prolong that habitation in an era of increasing anxiety about the future. If Livon-Grosman focuses his camera on waste and the activities that surround it in order to signal the limits of the notion that Buenos Aires is the exception to the Latin American rule, then I train my critical gaze on trash to better understand how Latin American cultural texts help us to see the limits of normative notions of the human, community, waste management, and environmental activism. In this sense, trash does the work of what Jacques Derrida calls "limitrophy": it "sprouts or grows at the limit, around the limit, by maintaining the limit, but also what *feeds the limit,* generates it, raises it, and complicates it" (2002, 398). Trash, then, participates in enacting and reproducing these limits, but it also complicates them and gestures toward a space beyond the limits in question. The stakes of paying attention to the production and handling of waste are high, for trash—as a set of material objects and relations between humans and the material world—obliges us to consider what part individual and societal habits of consumption and disposal play in perpetuating or ameliorating the environmental crises that have come to define the contemporary world.

The Anthropocene: Living in an Age of Trash

The idea of the Anthropocene—a designation for a new geological epoch that would mark the end of the Holocene and frame human beings as a species that has made profound modifications to the Earth's geology and atmosphere—is gaining purchase both in and out of scientific circles. For all of us, this new label raises significant questions about our relationship with the Earth and its inhabitants. What is more, it unavoidably brings to the fore the notion of limits, in terms of both the boundary between the Holocene and the Anthropocene and the question of the limits of human power over the environment in view of the planet's limits in terms of carrying capacity and resilience. If we accept that human activity has wrought irrevocable changes on our planet and that those changes are not altogether salutary for human communities (not to mention other forms of life), it is imperative that we carefully examine the way we think about human activity in the "natural world" in order to determine the role that discourses about nature and culture have played in the advent of the crises that are unfolding before our very eyes. Until recently, our understanding of the passage from one segment of geological time to another has been marked by what we could call natural phenomena: shifts in plate tectonics, changes in glaciation, cataclysmic events like asteroid impacts, and the like. What does adding human activities like oil and coal extraction, deforestation, and large-scale urbanization and industrialization to that list of "natural" phenomena mean? If those human practices can change the Earth to the extent that our mark can now be found in every corner of the planet, does that make our practices into a force of nature?[1] In this context, are received ideas about the limits between culture and nature useful to us, or should we be rethinking those ideas? If such a reexamination is necessary, what tools are available to us in order to carry it out? What things should we focus on as we think about these issues?

The so-called linguistic turn of twentieth-century Western philosophy has, of late, given way to a newfound interest in materiality, in large part due to the perhaps overblown characterization of postmodern and poststructuralist thinking as modes of inquiry that dematerialize the world by reducing it to a series of social and linguistic constructions. Instead of focusing on the power of language and sociality at the expense of the material world, the thinking that is undertaken in what has been dubbed the "material turn" considers how those two spheres are mutually imbricated in ways that transcend traditional material/nonmaterial dualisms like the binary treatment of mind and body. In large part, "the reconsideration of materiality is associated with the twentieth-century developments in natural sciences and with the radical changes that have affected our environments in the last decades" (Iovino and Oppermann 2012, 75). Renewed interest in materiality allows us to rethink the relationships we have with things, and in the context of the Anthropocene and the light that such a concept sheds on the radical changes to our environments that are only becoming more noteworthy, this type of reassessment is very timely. There are many points of entry into critical inquiries of how humans and the material world shape each other; we could talk about soil, the built environment, wind, stones, animals, computer processors, minerals, books, drugs, microwave ovens, or any number of different things. We are, simply put, inhabitants of "an ineluctably material world" as well as being "ourselves composed of matter" (Coole and Frost 2010, 1). But of all the material that could serve as the basis for an inquiry into what it means to be human in an era of human-induced climate change and ecological destruction, there is one category that, for me, stands out from the rest: trash.

Trash has a central role to play in thinking about the Anthropocene and its reframing of the "cultural" and "natural" crises that human beings currently face. Trash is, as Myra Hird has claimed, "*the* signifier of the Anthropocene" in that it is an epoch defined by the traces of waste and detritus that modern industrial societies have scattered about the planet, whether it be carbon dioxide emissions from the burning of fossil fuels, plastic particles that overwhelm ocean ecosystems, nuclear waste that remains radioactive for tens of thousands of years, landfills of such enormous dimensions that they change the topography of the regions where they are located, or any number of manifestations of trash. And the waste produced by globalized, consumer-oriented, capitalist societies threatens to engulf those societies. Beyond the glut of discarded material that is impossible to ignore, trash defines our era because of the processes that bring it about, the "socio-ecological relations" that, through "sorting out what has value and what does not," create "wasted people and wasted places" (Armiero 2021, 10).

Needless to say, all the trash produced in consumer societies must be dealt with: it is thrown away, consigned to some other space. For Gay Hawkins, disposal practices in consumer culture are facilitated by "the ethos of disposability," the social investment in the capacity to readily and constantly replace consumer goods that entails the need for people to discard their possessions with ease (2001, 9). What effect does this have on people? What are the implications of the cycle of production, consumption, and disposal for human relationships with material objects? Hawkins posits that contemporary regimes of commodity production that make it easy to throw things away without a second thought reconfigure the problem of waste as a technical one with technical solutions and bypass ethical concerns for what happens to the places where trash ends up and the people who come into contact with those discards. This classic neoliberal gesture of framing social and environmental problems as ones that technocrats will take care of through innovation fosters the false sense that when we throw something away it truly *goes away*, and as long as we maintain our spaces safe and clean, broader ethical concerns regarding waste do not matter. Moreover, the regime of disposability that is bolstered by (supposedly) apolitical technification both naturalizes wasting as an unavoidable part of modern life and reinforces the notion that we who discard are in control, we are masters of our own spaces who neutralize the threat that garbage poses to our bodily and social integrity (Hawkins 2001, 10).

The stakes of the ethos of disposability are clear. On a human level, the ability to dispose of trash with complete ease and comfort allows us to ignore the ontological dilemma that trash presents to those of us who produce it: What does this stuff, this material substance that we throw away have to say to and about us, we who are also fundamentally material beings? And from an environmental perspective, the fantasy of human separation from and mastery over the material world engendered by the ethos of disposability has dire implications. However, if the growing prominence of the idea of the Anthropocene can be characterized as the realization that the waste we produce is more rebellious and uncontrollable than we thought, then this fantasy deserves serious critical attention. And such attention is especially timely given the seemingly unchecked advance of the consumption of disposable commodities all across the globe.

Perhaps the best way to start thinking about trash is to ask what exactly it is. Beyond the biological universalism of certain processes of waste production, when we talk about trash, we are always talking about a historically determined, culturally constructed category. Like many contemporary scholars of trash, I take its culturally constructed nature to be the starting point of a definition of the term.[2] The simplest way to define trash is as excess matter that is discarded or expelled. Despite this definition's apparent simplicity, each of its terms prompts further inquiry. "Matter" certainly does not help us to narrow down the field of possible candidates that fit into the category of trash; rather, it indicates that all of physical substance is susceptible to becoming trash. And while the qualifying adjective "excess" attempts to delimit a more manageable field than the entire physical universe, it conceals a value judgment: What is the threshold between sufficiency and excess and how is it determined? Finally, the passive verbal construction "is discarded or expelled" pulls our attention away from the active subject—who is it that discards or expels?—and raises questions of space and movement: Where (both *to* and *from*) is this excess matter discarded or expelled? All of this underscores the fact that a category that is so seemingly simple and naturalized (everybody everywhere throws away trash and has done so forever, right?) is in fact an important site of contestation and negotiation that reveals a great deal about what it is that a society values.

Pulling apart a simple definition of trash shows that there are social and political structures at the heart of the production and management of waste. Such an exercise also highlights the key role that language plays in ascribing value to things, for value is a function of discourse, a determination of the meaning of a thing within a system of other things. And, just as a trying to pin down a definition of trash suggests, there is a great deal of unclarity underlying the seemingly rigid divisions posited by systems of meaning. In this sense, one of the most powerful ways in which trash's unclarity manifests itself is in its ability to call attention to and call into question the divisions between various sets of things that give structures of meaning their apparent solidity. What trash manages to do is to shift "our attention to the absent parts of our worldmaking," because "garbage is neither one thing nor another, but instead is the remainder of such neatness" (Scanlan 2005, 15–16).

This characterization of trash as a third element that troubles the parceling work of binary structures resonates with Julia Kristeva's theorization of the abject, which is "on the borderline" and therefore "calls into question borders and threatens identity" (Oliver 2002, 225). As unruly matter that exceeds containment, trash, like the abject, foregrounds "the in-between, the ambiguous, the composite" (Kristeva 1982, 4). Just as the abject calls into question the construction of identity based on a supposed absolute distinction between Self and Other or subject and object (3), trash complicates normative or accepted ways of delineating experience. It is not simply inert material that we deal with, but rather it is part of who we are because it "*constitutes* the self in the habits and embodied practices through which we decide what is connected to us and what isn't" (Hawkins 2005, 4). And the self that is predicated on the "carefree" consumption of convenient, disposable goods is, as Greg Kennedy observes, simultaneously—and paradoxically—more and less human. On the one hand, this disposing self is more human in the sense that disposable commodities "disburden us from the pressing concerns of the flesh so that we may maximally indulge our higher, rational, and creative faculties, those that distinguish us from purely animal beings" (2007, 122). However, it is precisely the lack of care (or *Sorge*, Martin Heidegger's term for the defining characteristic of the human) embodied by easily disposable commodities that "entail[s] a failure to be truly human" (122). Trash's quality of unclarity at the limit obliges us to consider it not simply as docile matter, but rather as an active force, an agent that disrupts subjectivity and identity, problematizes neat distinctions between inside and outside, public and private, life and death, human and nonhuman, or nature and culture, and thus stands as a constant reminder of the fragility of the systems that we produce in order to make meaning out of the world.

Given the ways that the notion of the Anthropocene is obliging us to reconsider the relationship between human activity and the natural world, trash's role as a complicating factor at the limit between nature and culture is crucial. While it does not do away with the importance of thinking about possible distinctions between nature and culture, trash makes us rethink the urgency of clarifying those distinctions. In other words, we might say that, although trash does not replace either nature or culture, it displaces both categories, pushing them slightly off to one side and compelling us to focus on what we typically think of as a valueless leftover. What is more, trash reveals a strange intermingling of nature and culture in that it can appear to belong to either the former or the latter (or some intermediate phase between the two) depending on how we look at it. Accumulations of trash evoke both natural, ahistorical processes (like decay) and cultural, historically specific processes of production rooted in human practices that, conceivably, can be traced to particular times and places (Pye 2010, 5). On the one hand, for instance, trash dumps are places of culture: they constitute vast repositories of human artifacts, and they are the site of human cultural practices like work, politics, and art. On the other hand, trash dumps are wild places where the forces of nature seem to be left to their own devices: the trash in a dump is decaying (we might say, "returning to nature"), and the dump itself is a breeding ground for all sorts of wild creatures like rats and vultures.

In this sense, trash and the places it accumulates and circulates are privileged sites that offer the possibility for us to move beyond modes of ecological thinking that pit nature against culture as antagonists in a struggle for survival; instead, they oblige us to grapple with issues of how to live in an environment that is always already an admixture of the two. Patricia Yaeger signals this shift in thinking when she writes the following: "If nature once represented the before (creating culture as a child, product, or second nature) and if detritus represented the after (that which was marginalized, repressed, or tossed away), these representations have lost their appeal. We are born into a detritus-strewn world, and the nature that buffets us is never culture's opposite. Instead, it is made by a wind machine—or compacted with refuse, ozone, and mercury: the molecular crush of already mingled matter" (2008, 323). For Yaeger, this shift underscores the emergence of what she calls rubbish ecology, "the act of saving and savoring debris" (329). She posits that a stance aligned with rubbish ecology is becoming more and more important in contemporary literary production and that it is a sign of the epistemological shift toward the material because of trash's ability to signal the failures of market logic and the limitations of Enlightenment paradigms of thought, as well as its capacity to suggest alternatives to universal commodification (335–37). In the end, Yaeger suggests that trash's ambiguous power underscores what is at stake in the way that we conceive of our relationship to the environments we inhabit: "In a world where nature is dominated, polluted, pocketed, eco-touristed, warming, melting, bleaching, dissipating, and fleeing toward the poles—detritus is both its curse and its alternative" (338). Yaeger also affirms the important place that literature occupies in imagining the promises and hazards that waste holds for us, an issue to which I turn below. First, however, I want to take measure of the specific waste challenges that face Latin America.

Latin American Trash Realities

While the problem of trash is global in scale, that does not mean that the way the problem is made manifest around the globe is even or equitable. To the contrary, some of the most pressing concerns surrounding trash are most immediately felt in Latin America and other locations throughout the Global South. Whether it be through the exportation of toxic medical and industrial refuse, used car batteries, scrap metal, defunct appliances, or electronic waste, countries from the North have long made it a practice to externalize environmental risk by sending all sorts of trash to countries across the South, where environmental regulations tend to be more lax.[3] This unjust redistribution of toxicity is, as Rob Nixon points out, both beneficial to wealthier nations—the turnover in excess goods creates an economic benefit while placating environmentalists who fear contamination "in their backyard"—and especially damning to poorer nations—their citizens and environment are disproportionately exposed to long-term harm, the results of which are invariably chalked up to their "backwardness" with regard to environmental practices (2011, 1–2). As such, the entrenched practice of countries in the Global North of using sites all over the Global South as trash dumps (with elites in the Global South following suit in marginalized areas of their own countries) is an important manifestation of what Nixon calls slow violence, "a violence that occurs gradually and out of sight, a violence of delayed destruction that is dispersed across time and space, an attritional violence that is typically not viewed as violence at all" (2). Following Nixon's line of thought, the trashing of places like Goiânia, Brazil—where, in 1987, recyclers found a container of radioactive cesium-137 that had been left behind by a medical facility moving to a new location, resulting in the death of four people and the contamination of hundreds more (*The Radiological Accident in Goiânia* 1988, 1–2)—is hard to see as the brutal violence that it really is. Rather, it is invisible because it is not spectacular, there is a spatial and temporal lag between the perpetrators and the victims, and its effects cannot be neatly contained in a moment of time but, instead, seep slowly and unpredictably into the future. While places across Latin America are not unique in their exposure to this and other forms of slow violence, taking up the study of trash in this region foregrounds the intersection of urgent matters of social and environmental justice that are relevant to Latin America's long history of marginalization (both the marginalization of Latin America as a whole vis-à-vis the "developed" world and the marginalization of numerous categories of people within Latin American societies) and its overdetermined status in the Western imaginary as both an ecological paradise and a site for the inevitable waste products that attend the West's march toward infinite progress.

Beyond the North-South dynamics of slow violence and the trashing of Latin America from the outside, the production and management of trash inside the region is what truly makes Latin America an ideal site for the study of trash. Since the onset of the neoliberal era, increasing urbanization and integration into a globalized free market that intensifies the gaps between rich and poor have profoundly affected consumer cultures across Latin America: while the region has been fully enmeshed in global circuits of consumption since the colonial period, its current consumers' ready "access to disposable consumer products, appliances, and packaged foods outpaces its otherwise high levels of economic poverty" (Nading 2012, 110). Furthermore, rapid urbanization and changes in consumption habits have not been attended by improvements in infrastructure that might deal with those changes, including the production of trash. South America, for instance, produces more than 120 million tons of trash every year, which represents about 16 percent of the world's solid waste, and when such a significant amount of trash is considered in light of the heavy debt loads carried by many of these countries, managing solid waste presents a major environmental challenge (Taylor 2012, 844). Often, when that challenge remains unaddressed by official power, it is solved informally: hence the prevalence of open dumps, illegal or clandestine dumps, and informal trash collection and recycling practices throughout Latin America.

Open dumps, for instance, are places where waste is collected (deposited, burned, or buried) without following necessary steps for mitigating possible ill effects for the environment or the human workers who process the waste. Thaddeus Chidi Nzeadibe and Ignatius Ani Madu estimate that as much as 30 to 50 percent of the trash produced in many urban areas across the Global South (including Latin America) is left uncontrolled by "official" trash collectors and ends up in open dumps (2012, 631). Mexico provides a salient example of illegal open dumps. Mexico City alone has some 1,200 of them, which, because of the extreme environmental health risks they pose, tend to be located in the city's most impoverished areas (Orlando 2012, 534). Across the nation, the process of getting trash to those precarious dump sites involves a patchwork of public service and private "enterprise," with a full 25 percent of trash pickup service being handled by businesses whose employees receive low wages and demand tips for continued service, which inevitably leads to spotty trash collection (534–35).

Even when trash is removed by municipal governments and taken to approved dumping sites, it still presents significant problems. Regarding Mexico once again, Angela Orlando notes that as of 2010, only about 11 percent of Mexico's roughly 100 officially controlled sites for waste disposal were landfills—as opposed to open dumps (534). Unfortunately, generally speaking, those landfills do not meet the environmental standards meant to prevent leachate and other toxins from seeping into the soil and groundwater. All told, a paltry 15 percent of Mexico's municipal solid waste receives adequate treatment (534). Brazil, one of the world's largest economies with an increasingly consumer-oriented middle class, is also feeling the weight of the garbage it produces. For Leonardo Freire de Mello and Rafael D'Almeida Martins, the pressing nature of the solid waste problem can be directly attributed to the twin factors of economic growth and inadequate urban planning (2012, 80). Besides the fact that a high percentage of Brazil's trash does not end up in sanitary landfills,[4] but rather in *lixões* (open dumps, many of which are located in wetlands on the outskirts of large urban areas), the current state of the country's landfill infrastructure is in danger of physical collapse. Given the rise in both the number of city dwellers and rates of consumption, Brazil's current landfill infrastructure is expected to be exhausted by the middle of this century (80).

While all this information about the generation of trash within different countries in the region is undoubtedly anecdotal and does not provide a systematically informed, detailed picture of the garbage landscape in the region, it suggests the complexities of the problem of trash in Latin America. Trash coming from both outside and inside the continent overwhelms the human and material infrastructures that are meant to corral it, and more often than not, the people and environments that suffer the most immediate (as well as the longest-lasting) consequences are already vulnerable due to the way that they have been exploited and marginalized by those who wield more political, social, and economic power than they do.

Latin American Trash Imaginaries

As an important part of social reality across Latin America, trash occupies the attention of writers and filmmakers who are attuned to the discursive power that it takes on as it flows through different spaces, colliding with and repelling bodies, inhabiting the ambiguous borderland between rigid conceptualizations of nature and culture. The entwined discursive and material practices that govern refuse open up a rich and timely field of inquiry, especially given the seemingly global profile of contemporary consumer cultures predicated upon the endless production and disposal of goods and the growing awareness of the role of human cultural practices—not the least of which relate to trash—in ecological crises of the past, present, and future. By paying attention to what seems superfluous and excessive, what is lacking in value and therefore unimportant, we are forced to rethink both our position in relation to other things and the constellations of material and discursive phenomena that situate our pasts, presents, and futures and imbue them with meaning. That work of rethinking is inextricably linked to a thorough examination of the dialectical interplay between the material and the discursive that trash evinces.

Literature, film, and other cultural texts play an essential part as grounds for rethinking the importance of trash in Latin America. They tell stories about trash without necessarily being indebted to a single overarching discursive mode (environmental, commercial, or political discourse, for instance). Instead, they make trash into narrative by appealing to multiple forms of discourse and recycling them by bending them to their own purposes while still maintaining a trace of dependence upon the power of those discourses for legitimation. By focusing on waste products (things that normally occupy only the periphery of our field of vision), the texts that I consider here bring to the fore the social and political structures of wasting and their relationship with aesthetics and narrative practice. The questions that I will address in this project revolve around what trash does when it appears in texts. What part does trash play in the construction of narrative plot? How is trash deployed rhetorically and to what ideological ends? What is the relationship between trash and aesthetics in Latin American literature? What kinds of portrayals of trash and people who work with trash gain purchase in these texts, and what is at stake in those portrayals? What do these trash narratives have to say about some of the most pressing issues facing contemporary Latin American societies, like violence, marginalization, neoliberal globalization, economic injustice, and environmental crisis? Does trash have anything to say about bridging the gap between aesthetics and ethics?

Texts that are attentive to the stories that trash has to tell manage to highlight the material ties that bind together issues that have long been important sites of critical reflection in Latin American cultural production: the uses and abuses of the environment, marginalization of the Other, and violence. By telling stories that show how these issues are simultaneously discursive and material, the texts that make up my archive constitute a series of complex aesthetic interventions that pose urgent questions regarding the nature of culture in contemporary Latin America and the aesthetic and ethical implications of the increasingly notable presence of trash in the region's cultural production. Whether we are talking about novels and documentary films that have dumps and landfills as major settings, short stories and *crónicas* (literary nonfiction) with main characters who are garbage pickers, or novels that portray writing as a process of digging through the trash and piecing together a story from the material found therein, it is clear that contemporary Latin American cultural production is full of trash.

While the trash that is present in the works I study throughout *Trash and Limits in Latin American Culture* is symptomatic of a myriad of historical, cultural, social, and economic factors that started taking shape at different points in different places during the twentieth century and intensified with the implementation of neoliberal socioeconomic policies across wide swaths of the region, the attention that these texts pay to trash is not exclusive to recent works. In fact, there are several significant works littered across the history of Latin American literature that, without necessarily presenting the same sensibility regarding trash as the texts I am working with here, certainly share with them an affinity for turning their narrative gaze to waste, its production, and its connection to culture. A paradigmatic example would be Esteban Echeverría's *El matadero* (written around 1838 and first published in 1871), with its lurid depiction of poor women battling dogs for scraps of innards thrown away after the butchers carve up beef cattle in the open-air abattoir in which the story takes place. Here, waste, the processes by which it is produced, and the space to which it is confined serve as the materialization of the barbarism against which Echeverría and a host of other liberal intellectuals would try to define Latin America's potential to be civilized. Along these lines, literary naturalism also provides several examples of texts that focus on the filthier aspects of the societies they depict, but two novels within this tendency are of particular relevance. One is Eugenio Cambaceres's *En la sangre* (1887). Notwithstanding the reactionary worldview it presents with regard to immigrants, Cambaceres's novel enacts social anxieties surrounding the threat of contamination posed by uncontained piles of trash: a child of Italian immigrants, Genaro (the protagonist) is born amid the filth and garbage of his family's tenement and manages to transmit the fetidness of that space to the native-born Buenos Aires bourgeoisie by the novel's end. The other naturalist novel that shows a proclivity for exploring the power that trash has is Aluísio Azevedo's *O cortiço* (1890), in which a poor but ruthlessly entrepreneurial Portuguese immigrant to Rio de Janeiro makes a fortune administering a large tenement house that he builds out of trash (discarded construction materials) and that in turn becomes a constant producer of material waste and wasted humans.

Not even novels that offer narratives for imagining national identities can resist the temptation to narrate spaces of trash. In Ignacio Manuel Altamirano's *El Zarco* (written in 1888 and first published in 1901), for instance, despite the narrator's preoccupation with punishing the outlaw *plateados* and establishing order, the narrator cannot help but linger in his description of Xochimancas, the decrepit hacienda where el Zarco and his gang lay low amid the jumbled mess of the things they have violently plundered and their own filth. In addition to the depiction of the outlaw band's hideout as a ruined space full of waste, the self-presentation of their leader is characterized as a display of waste. The silver (spoils of his plunder) that adorns el Zarco's clothing is "una ostentación insolente, cínica y sin gusto" (an insolent, cynical, tasteless ostentation) (1986, 46). Much like the trashy elements of "El matadero," *En la sangre,* and *O cortiço,* the waste on display in *El Zarco* attracts and fascinates the narrator, but, ultimately, it embodies the criminal, retrograde, barbaric elements that must be neutralized in order for civilization to win the day in Mexican (or Brazilian, or Argentine) society. So while trash is not necessarily central to these earlier works, it is certainly crucial in that it indexes anxieties related to social class, aesthetics, contagion, and nation formation. Indeed, paying heed to the trash in these texts serves to show that the contemporary preoccupation with trash in Latin American literary and cultural texts is not entirely new.

As the twentieth century rolled on, however, the political and economic projects of industrial modernization, followed by neoliberal reforms aimed at integrating the region into global flows of capital and consumer goods, led to the steady increase in the production of trash. This new material reality is reflected in many cultural texts that have deeply engaged with the social, political, and ecological stakes of waste over the past seventy-five years or so. The volume of works that make landfills and garbage dumps key settings is indicative of how the anecdotal or sporadic presence of trash in previous eras' literary texts has coalesced into a key element of cultural production. At the beginning of this period, novels like Bernardo Verbitsky's *Villa miseria también es América* (1957) and Enrique Congrains Martín's *No una sino muchas muertes* (1957), plus films like Luis Buñuel's *Los olvidados* (1950), center on urban spaces where trash accumulates as these works contemplate, respectively, the vicissitudes of recent arrivals in Buenos Aires who make a living by scavenging, the abject poverty of young people struggling to survive in Lima, and the misfortunes of members of a street gang in Mexico City, one of whom ends up dead in a garbage dump.

The image of the dump as a place to illicitly dispose of human remains with which Buñuel's classic film ends is reactivated in one of most significant works of Latin American literature of the twenty-first century: Roberto Bolaño's *2666* (2004), in which some of the many victims of femicide portrayed in the section "La parte de los crímenes" are found in a clandestine garbage dump called El Chile. If Buñuel's and Bolaño's dumps can be seen as bookends for the period that ranges from industrial modernization to neoliberalism, one of the core concerns of their works—the violence that extreme forms of capitalism inflict on individuals, communities, and the spaces they inhabit—is a through line in other portrayals of landfills in the twentieth and twenty-first centuries. While I will analyze many such portrayals in the pages that follow, others certainly deserve mention here. One of several provocative Brazilian landfill documentaries, Marcos Prado's *Estamira* (2004), challenges viewers with the indelible figure of a trash picker in Rio de Janeiro who feels more at home in the landfill than anywhere else. Prado's eerie, poetic collaboration with Estamira lays bare the heavy toll that neoliberalism takes on humans and the environment alike. Central American ecocritical novels like Nicaraguan author Gioconda Belli's *Waslala* (1996) use the dump to underscore the persistence of colonial relations in the contemporary world. Faguas, the fictionalized version of Nicaragua that is her novel's setting, is home to pristine forests that international agencies protect with lethal violence because those forests provide the developed world—overcome by pollution—with air fit for breathing. In a perverse new formulation of colonial economic structures, Faguas receives the developed world's trash as payment for the air it provides. The dump where that trash is stored and processed becomes the center of political resistance to oppressors from inside and outside of Faguas's borders. Finally, a pair of visual artists can help to round out this abbreviated tour of Latin American cultural dumps: Argentine Antonio Berni and Cuban Tomás Sánchez. Between the late 1950s and the 1970s, Berni produced a series of paintings portraying Juanito Laguna that incorporate waste materials into depictions of the daily life of this fictional young scavenger in an attempt to denounce the economic and environmental plight of Buenos Aires's urban poor and highlight the aesthetic potential of recycling (Heffes 2013, 226). Since the 1980s, Sánchez has been producing paintings of landfills in tropical settings, a genre that Francisco-J. Hernández Adrián calls "wastescapes" that "portray a kind of excoriation of material life that exhausts cities and megalopolises indirectly and insidiously," underscoring "notions of global expenditure, inadequate recycling, and environmental devastation" (2012, 18).

This small handful of stories from the dump shows us how significant trash is. As material problem and cultural artifact, it opens up an urgent, multifaceted conversation on materialism, matter, and wasting that is relevant to ecocriticism's primary concerns of human/nonhuman interactions, the representation of environmental issues, and the question of space. Scholars working in Latin American and Peninsular cultural studies have framed trash's import in a variety of productive ways that inform the approach I develop in *Trash and Limits in Latin American Culture*. Gisela Heffes's pioneering book *Políticas de la destrucción/Poéticas de la preservación*, for instance, signals the centrality of waste in tropes of environmental destruction, sustainability, and preservation that evoke the garbage dump, recycling, and utopian imaginaries in a wide array of contemporary Latin American cultural texts. Moving beyond Latin America to Spain and the United States/Mexico border region, Maite Zubiaurre's *Talking Trash: Cultural Uses of Waste* engages in a "strategy of pausing/looking down/musing" at "'small' trash and urban litter . . . against the background of the monumentality of garbage" (2019, 2, 203). My own consideration of waste in contemporary Latin American culture takes Zubiaurre's strategy to heart in excavating the types of environmental tropes that Heffes underlines by paying careful attention to how trash works within the fabric of literary and cinematic texts, how cultural "encounters with waste can be transformative," as Samuel Amago puts it (2021, viii). What is more, my readings, in the wake of Robert Stam's examination of Brazilian film, understand the ways Latin American culture "is figured . . . through the motif of garbage" (1999, 68). Whereas Stam sees the "redemption of detritus" as the through line in Brazilian films about trash whose "aesthetics share the jujitsu trait of turning strategic weakness into tactical strength" (59), I am more concerned with what Latin American trash narratives have to say about "human relations to the environment and our responsibility to the more-than-human world," as Odile Cisneros puts it in a more recent reflection on trash in Brazilian culture (2022, 208).[5]

A key contribution that my analysis makes to this conversation on trash is that the discards portrayed in contemporary Latin American culture are not inert; rather, they do things, they act, they provoke responses and reactions, and they make meaning. The insights of material ecocriticism, then, are important to bear in mind. The basic conceptual argument of material ecocriticism is that "the world's material phenomena are knots in a vast network of agencies, which can be 'read' and interpreted as forming narratives, stories . . . All matter, in other words, is a 'storied matter'" (Iovino and Oppermann 2014, 1). Reading trash—and other material objects—both *in* texts and *as* texts, then, underscores the fact that meaning and matter are not separate spheres. On the contrary, they merge together in such a way that all things (even bits of garbage) are "at once material and symbolic" (Iovino and Oppermann 2012, 457). Material ecocriticism, then, allows us to see how humans reside neither at the center of all things nor above the material world. Instead, "Human bodies and minds are fully ensconced in material environments, which shape us just as vividly as we shape them" (Sullivan 2012, 528). The eloquence of trash shows that contemporary Latin American culture is fully engaged in a critical examination of the types of material environments that we are currently shaping and that are shaping us. By paying attention to trash and the way that it is irrevocably tangled up in human cultural phenomena like violence, marginalization, cities, economics, environmental activism, and writing, the texts that I analyze here go beyond the denunciation of various types of violence and injustice. For they compel us to think about what it means to live with trash. Such cohabitation between humans and the waste materials that we produce is certainly not new, and it is not unique to Latin American societies; however, as the texts in my corpus show, Latin America is a particularly productive site for thinking about the parameters of human-trash relationships (and what those relationships have to say about human-human relationships), especially in the context of Latin America's rapid urbanization over the last century and the richness of its literary and cinematic cultures. In this sense, *Trash and Limits in Latin American Culture* takes a step toward thinking about how Latin American literary and cultural production can help us to imagine what it means for horizons—both aesthetic and real—to be increasingly littered with trash.

Chapter Summaries

Over the course of four chapters, *Trash and Limits in Latin American Culture* shows how trash both signals and interrogates a series of crucial theoretical limits: normative notions of the human, community, waste management, and environmental activism. While these four zones can be considered as separate case studies, they also take shape through lines and resonances, two of which I would like to signal at the outset. The first two chapters are joined together by the philosophical concept of the threshold, which grounds the notion of what trash is and what it materializes, and therefore allows me to contemplate waste's relationship to the liminal space between humans and animals (chapter 1) before moving on to an analysis of trash narratives that portray forms of human community that are both on the margins and suggestive of ways of being together that move beyond normative conceptualizations of community (chapter 2). Both of the final two chapters, on the other hand, draw on notions of how neoliberalism has affected ways of inhabiting space and engaging with the material world by considering work and the stories we tell about it (chapter 3) and frameworks for taking care of the environment (chapter 4). I should also add that, much like my use of the documentary *Cartoneros* at the beginning of this introduction, I open chapters 1, 3, and 4 by presenting and reflecting on pre-texts that provocatively display key elements of trash thresholds, trash works, and neoliberal environmentalism, respectively. While these critical vignettes postpone my arrival at the thrust of those chapters' arguments, my engagement with these brief bits of cultural ephemera (a children's book, an urban sketch, and a documentary short) matters because they gesture toward the widespread engagement with trash in Latin American cultural production that far exceeds the bounds of the corpus gathered in this book. At any rate, the following chapter summaries should hopefully serve to ameliorate the effect of my detours through these pre-texts.

Chapter 1 explores the way that human vulnerability to the violence of marginalizing economic regimes is represented as a function of people's proximity to trash and nonhuman animals by analyzing Julio Ramón Ribeyro's short story "Los gallinazos sin plumas" (Peru) and Jorge Furtado's short film "Ilha das Flores" (Brazil). In their portrayal of marginalized urban spaces (in Lima and Porto Alegre, respectively) and the people who inhabit them, Ribeyro and Furtado resort to an interesting play with tropes of animalization: the human subjects who are reduced to finding sustenance in the trash are rendered as not-quite-animals (vultures *without* feathers, people lower on the pecking order than pigs). The vulnerability of these characters is further underscored by the fact that they are the least powerful members of *machista* societies: two children in Ribeyro's story and (predominantly) women and children in Furtado's film. Ultimately, the trash and nonhuman animals with which the humans in "Los gallinazos sin plumas" and "Ilha das Flores" come into contact serve as a material manifestation of the threshold of undecidability that compels us to question what it means to be human. In other words, the trash in these works signals and calls into question normative notions of the limit between the human and the animal.

The vulnerability underlying "wasted lives" (to invoke Zygmunt Bauman's expression for the human bodies that modernity has rendered disposable) takes a different shape in chapter 2, where I examine Eduardo Coutinho's documentary film *Boca de Lixo* (Brazil), Luis Alberto Urrea's book *By the Lake of Sleeping Children* (Mexico), and Alicia Dujovne Ortiz's book *¿Quién mató a Diego Duarte?* (Argentina), three works of nonfiction that portray the lives of people who work in trash dumps. My reading of the film and the two crónicas proposes that trash is a material manifestation of a threshold that opens onto a form of collective life based not on preconceived notions of essentialized identity, but rather on what Italian philosopher Giorgio Agamben theorizes as "*inessential* commonality" in his work *The Coming Community*. The communities portrayed by Coutinho, Urrea, and Dujovne Ortiz emerge from the nexus of ecological, socioeconomic, and political catastrophes materialized in the garbage dump at the same time that they resist the forces that normalize those catastrophes.

In chapter 3, I examine the limitations of a specific kind of story about trash, trash spaces, and trash work that has gained prominence in literary fiction in Latin America since the 1990s. The novels (and one short story) by César Aira (Argentina), Horacio Castellanos Moya (El Salvador), Sergio Chejfec (Argentina), Fernando Contreras Castro (Costa Rica), Álvaro Enrigue (Mexico), and Andrés Neuman (Argentina) that I gather together are all stories in which male protagonists experience personal and professional crises that either stem from or put them into contact with trash and garbage dumps. These texts, which I call "trash works," can all be read as reflections of the social and environmental ills of the neoliberal era, but I also argue that they signal the shortcomings of the waste management paradigm, a form of dealing with trash that places enormous faith in our ability to neutralize the waste we produce. I also consider how the prominence of the work of these authors overshadows other kinds of stories about trash and trash work that do not allegorize crises of masculinity through garbage but rather portray work with waste as a form of care.

Chapter 4 continues the previous chapter's examination of trash work as a labor of care and maintenance, but the focus shifts away from self-contained portrayals of characters and moves toward cultural texts that depict social projects whose aim is to address the problem of waste and the precarious position of informal waste workers. I analyze Lucy Walker's documentary film *Waste Land* (Brazil) and the social media–based environmental campaign "Gallinazo Avisa" (Peru) as examples of the neoliberal approach to environmental activism: they frame the environmental and social problems that attend waste as matters of individual responsibility, and they generate a vague, unsustained sense of empathy and awareness among viewers. In this sense, these films and projects show that the limits of neoliberal environmental activism are a function of the inability to engage in efforts toward structural change. As a way of looking beyond the limits of that approach to environmentalism, I consider the work that Basurama, an urban environmental collective from Madrid that works with trash, has done in Latin America.

What my analysis of these novels, short stories, works of nonfiction, films, and environmental campaigns underscores is that, more than a problem to be solved, trash is a multivalent force that poses threats to humans and nonhumans alike, yes, but that is also an essential part of who we are. Across Latin America, writers and directors have produced work for decades that creatively and critically engages with the ways trash shapes our social and material environments. Serious engagement with their work is an urgent task for those of us who want to understand our place in the world and develop better ways of caring for it.

1

Excess and Lack

Trash and the Limits of the Human

In his polemical 1964 essay *Lima la horrible*, Sebastián Salazar Bondy, one of the most significant writers and intellectuals of mid-twentieth-century Peru, considers the weight of the colonial legacy in shaping the modern manifestation of Peru's capital city. For Salazar Bondy, Lima, which was at that time in the middle of intense transformations brought about by mass internal migration, was still in thrall to an idealized vision of the city's vice-regal past, a notion he calls "Arcadia Colonial" (Colonial Arcadia) (1964, 13). As Silvia Spitta notes, it is "the oligarchy's colonial fantasies" and "the survival of [Lima's] caste structure" that lead Salazar Bondy to call Lima horrible because this system of differentiation and hierarchization "effectively renders invisible the profound impoverishment of millions of people" (2007, 298). Some of these same notions of urban development, class hierarchies, and profound disregard for the plight of the urban poor can be found in a very different sort of book that Salazar Bondy published just a few years before *Lima la horrible*: the 1961 children's book *El Señor Gallinazo vuelve a Lima*.[1] In it, Salazar Bondy tells the story of Señor Gallinazo, an anthropomorphized vulture who returns to Lima after a long absence only to find that it has grown significantly since he was last there. One of the most disconcerting new features he finds is the proliferation of trash dumps abuzz with human beings, dogs, and pigs rooting around in the garbage. He decides to investigate one of these dumps and soon befriends a young boy named Bautista Huallpa, whose family makes a living scavenging recyclable materials. Upon overcoming his initial shock at encountering a talking vulture, Bautista explains the scavenging trade to Señor Gallinazo, noting that rich people throw away useful things that his family and other scavengers obtain in the dump. Señor Gallinazo wonders why Bautista's family does not simply ask rich families to give them the things they would throw away anyway in order to avoid having to work in the dump. The vulture offers to help Bautista to find and befriend some wealthy people, and they take flight, eventually spotting a young boy playing in the walled-in yard of a large house. But instead of recognition and solidarity, Bautista and his feathered friend are met with hostility and rejection. The rich little boy accuses them of being thieves, and soon his parents, their driver, and a police officer chase them off, with the latter even opening fire and grazing the vulture's leg with a bullet as he gains altitude with Bautista on his back. Shaken by what he has experienced, Señor Gallinazo arrives back at the dump with Bautista having learned that "las gentes están divididas en dos grupos que se ignoran" (people are divided into two groups that disregard each other) (2005, 33). Bautista invites Señor Gallinazo to join him and his friends in their games, adventures, and travails, and the vulture happily accepts.

In *El Señor Gallinazo vuelve a Lima*, Salazar Bondy may not approach questions surrounding urban expansion, capitalist modernization, classism, and marginalization with as much historical rigor and analytical depth as he does in a book like *Lima la horrible*, but this seemingly simple story offers a rich point of entry into the materials that I want to examine in the first two chapters of *Trash and Limits in Latin American Culture*. First, it views waste through an optic that allows us to see the relationship between the human, the animal, and trash in a way that is reminiscent of both "Los gallinazos sin plumas" and "Ilha das Flores," the two works I analyze in this chapter. Not only does Salazar Bondy's book feature an anthropomorphized scavenger animal, but also that animal, whose perspective grounds the story, perceives the way that the dump complicates neat distinctions between human and nonhuman animals. What the vulture first notices about the dump is how its inhabitants, "como seres de semejante condición, personas y chanchos, niños y perros, parecían disputarse o compartir el mismo lugar de vida y trabajo" (like beings of a similar station, people and pigs, children and dogs, seemed to be fighting over or sharing the same living and working space) (2005, 7). Even the dump's soundscape places people and animals on the same plane: "Oía el hozar de los cerdos, el ladrido de los canes, la bronca voz de los adultos y la risa cristalina de los pequeños" (He heard the rooting of the pigs, the bark of the dogs, the hoarse voices of the adults, and the crystalline laughter of the little ones) (8). After Bautista explains what all these creatures are doing in the dump, Señor Gallinazo points out what binds them together: "'Antes,' reflexionó en voz alta el ave, 'eso lo hacíamos nostros, los gallinazos, y por eso los limeños protegieron, mediante una ley, nuestra vida. Éramos los que manteníamos limpia la ciudad. Ahora todos los animales son gallinazos . . ."" ("Before," he reflected aloud, "we vultures would do that, and that's why the people of Lima protected our lives with a law. We were the ones who kept the city clean. Now all animals are vultures . . .") (16). One cannot help but read *animales* here as an all-encompassing term that applies to human and nonhuman animals alike. The way that Salazar Bondy suggests that having or not having something (money, this story suggests) is a key factor when it comes to normative definitions of what it means to be human is a thread that we will follow as we consider the way that the relationship between the human, the animal, and trash is staged in cultural texts.

Second, *El Señor Gallinazo vuelve a Lima* hints at possible forms of community and solidarity in and around the abject space of the dump. At first, Señor Gallinazo thinks the notion of shared humanity and human feeling will allow Bautista—and other members of the urban poor, by extension—to form mutually beneficial alliances with the upper class. But the rich do not see Bautista as a potential equal, opting instead to criminalize the boy scavenger and his vulture friend (a move that plays out in real life with deadly consequences in *¿Quién mató a Diego Duarte?*, as I show in chapter 2), perhaps because they are unable to admit the true connection between themselves and people like Bautista: that is, as Ronny Azuaje argues, "El basural y los 'asentamientos humanos' son . . . espacios que albergan y contienen la producción material y humana de la modernidad peruana durante la segunda mitad del siglo XX" (The dump and its "human settlements" are . . . spaces that shelter and contain the material and human means of producing Peru's modernity in the second half of the twentieth century) (2021). In the wake of his failure at fostering solidarity among humans, Señor Gallinazo abandons his attempts to generate recognition across the class divide based on shared humanity and instead joins Bautista and his friends in the dump, becoming their "maestro, protector y camarada de penas y alegrías" (teacher, protector, and comrade in sadness and joy) (Salazar Bondy 2005, 33). This form of inter-species solidarity in the dump serves to subvert the marginalization suffered by boys and vulture alike, and it "ilumina una zona del basural: la posibilidad de que se convierta en sitio de encuentro para los sujetos abyectos que lo transitan y, con ello, el surgimiento de iniciativas que le devuelvan la vida a la sociedad limeña desde sus márgenes más 'horrorosos'" (illuminates a zone of the dump: the possibility of it becoming a site both of encounter for the abject subjects that traverse it and of the emergence of initiatives that restore life to *limeña* society from its most "horrific" margins) (Azuaje 2021). Señor Gallinazo's recognition of the potential for community in and around the trash dump clearly resonates with the works of nonfiction that I examine in chapter 2. Before arriving at that point, however, I need to consider the way that trash highlights the ambiguous threshold zone between the human and the nonhuman.

Trash as Threshold

One of the central challenges with which Gisela Heffes grapples in her 2013 book *Políticas de la destrucción/Poéticas de la preservación* is that of developing a theoretical framework for interpreting what she calls "todo un fenómeno latinoamericano" (a full-blown Latin American phenomenon) of artistic, literary, and cinematic artifacts that engage with issues of ecological importance, especially ones dealing with trash and the sociocultural practices surrounding disposal and waste management (2013, 20). Throughout the book, she interrogates the limits of ecocritical paradigms of literary analysis (originating, in her telling, mainly in North American and British university settings and informed by and large by Anglophone literary traditions) in dealing with the specificity of Latin American cultural production, all the while hinting at the fact that a new and different interpretive apparatus is needed in order to account for the representation of trash in a relatively large and varied corpus of texts. For Heffes, this representational phenomenon in Latin America is the basis of "una nueva praxis de reflexión epistemológica" (a new praxis of epistemological reflection) (69). This new critical epistemological approach is one that combines "una ecocrítica y una biocrítica y que, en el contexto de las representaciones del medioambiente latinoamericanas, es la forma más apropiada para leer todo un fenómeno que excede al aparato teórico proveniente de la academia norteamericana e inglesa y que, tentativamente, voy a definir como una bioecocrítica" (ecocriticism and biocriticism and that, in the context of Latin American representations of the environment, is the most appropriate way of reading a full-blown phenomenon that exceeds the American and English theoretical framework, and which I will tentatively label as bioecocriticism) (329).

I think that Heffes's intuition about the limits of what we could call a Northern ecocritical discourse—rooted in pursuits like nature writing and wilderness preservation—when it comes to conceptualizing Southern environmental problems that are interwoven with the marginalization of the urban poor is an astute one. Even though she does not unpack the term *biocrítica*, I take it to be—at least in part—an allusion to a critical stance informed by biopolitics, since she adopts such a stance in her analysis of the trash dump as a figuration of what she calls "biopolítica global" (global biopolitics) (75–147). As such, the *bio* in what she calls *bioecocrítica* could be said to contain a veiled reference to biopolitics, and while I am not interested in adopting her idea of a "nueva episteme crítica" wholesale, I would like to take up her suggestion to look for the places where biopolitics and ecocriticism intersect in Latin American literary and cultural production.

Examining the terrain where ecocritical and biopolitical discourses meet offers the potential to further enhance the discussions surrounding materiality and material ecocriticism that I consider in the introduction. If biopolitics can be thought of as the materialization of knowledge, power, and action in and through the body—bodies of individuals and, by extension, the social body—then any examination of biopolitical discourse is at the same time a consideration of the ways the material world constrains and facilitates the exercise of power. In this sense, the foregrounding of materiality made evident by biopolitics also allows us to move beyond some of the debates surrounding organicist versus constructivist views of nature and culture that characterize what Lawrence Buell identifies as the first and second waves of ecocriticism (2005, 21–22). Instead, establishing a dialogue between ecocritical and biopolitical thinking is part of an overarching trend developing within ecocritical circles, which "explores all facets of human experience from an environmental viewpoint" (Adamson and Slovic 2009, 7).

The facet of human experience that concerns me here is the relationship between people and trash and how that relationship is portrayed in a number of Latin American cultural texts. Whether or not it is people who make a living by working with trash, live in and around garbage dumps, or are treated like refuse, the texts I consider throughout this book—especially in this chapter and the next—all contend with what it means to be human in an era in which the trash we make seems to occupy a central role in our interaction with each other and with the environments we inhabit. In other words, these texts help us to discern a discourse on the human in which human subjectivity is neither the center of all things nor a totally outmoded and irrelevant construct, but rather an essential component in mediating the way that the material world constitutes meaning, much in the same way that Arjun Appadurai argues in a thought-provoking and timely intervention into the emerging field of critical inquiry known as new materialism. In his essay, he underscores the role that human subjectivity has to play in mediating the relationships among things. Appadurai points out that the decentering of humans from the field of agency carried out by critics like

Jane Bennett, Donna Haraway, and Bruno Latour is a welcome development in that it dethrones the "classic humanist view of the convergence of actor, self, person, subject, and agent" and reveals to us that "there are more forms of social life on earth than we have grown used to imagining" (2015, 222). However, he finds that the egalitarian distribution of agency across all "actants" (Latour's well-known term for human and nonhuman entities that converge in networks of activity and that can be thought of as bearers of agency) discounts the role that humans play in mediating materiality through embodied practice. As such, he proposes an analytical shift from actants to what he calls *mediants*, especially "*the ones that are primarily defined by their human dividuality,*" which allows them to "play a vital role in mediating the force of other mediants and actants, both human and nonhuman (and frequently combinations of the two)" (228). This modulated view that emphasizes human *dividuality* over its individuality (the enmeshment of humans in more-than-human environments) "allows us to foreground the socialities that emerge through specific materialities ... without ignoring other actants" (228).

Focusing on humans as both part of a material network and mediators in that network is key to understanding the socialities that emerge through the material convergence of people and trash. It is through the lens of biopolitics that the contours of those socialities come into sharper focus. More specifically, my aim here is to consider how the connections between people and trash are represented in a number of texts in light of Giorgio Agamben's concept of the threshold.

Ever since Michel Foucault's initial reflections on biopower in the 1970s, thinkers attracted to the notion of biopolitics have developed a multitude of divergent insights regarding what the French philosopher identified as modernity's "explosion of numerous and diverse techniques for achieving the subjugations of bodies and the control of populations" (1990, 140).[2] Among those developments with regard to the materialization of power in and through the body, Giorgio Agamben's concept of the threshold as it relates to the logic of exclusion or exception is of particular interest because, as we will see, it sheds light on the way people are rendered as trash and the way the line between the human and nonhuman is blurred.

For Agamben, the threshold is a key textual and conceptual device that signals the potentiality of a limit, whether positive or negative (McLoughlin 2011, 189). In *The Coming Community*, Agamben clearly identifies the basic logic of linkage inherent to the concept of the threshold (in this case referring to the notion of "the outside" of something): "The outside is not another space that resides beyond a determinate space, but rather, it is the passage, the exteriority that gives it access" (1993, 67). In this sense, the threshold, which marks the limit between two things, is not "another thing with respect to the limit; it is, so to speak, the experience of the limit itself" (68). He furthers his conceptualization of the threshold in *Homo Sacer*, where he examines the limit zone between political life and biological life or *bare life*, as he calls it.[3] This zone is the domain of sovereign power, a threshold whose logic "is not one of opposition, but of abandonment, in which the outside is included through its exclusion. This means that the threshold is a space where inside and outside enter into a zone of indistinction" (McLoughlin 2011, 191).

Trash is a material manifestation of the threshold. The logic underlying the latter is strikingly similar to systems that we use in our attempts to distinguish between useful and useless material objects, or rather, things worth keeping and things that are trash. The words Agamben uses to name the actions that constitute the threshold—abandonment and exclusion—resonate with the gesture that turns a thing into trash: disposal. What is more, the threshold underscores the fundamental connection between things that seem to be disconnected because they are opposed to one another but are in fact intimately related to one another via the act of exclusion itself.[4] In other words, the concept of the threshold serves to remind us that things do not fall into one category or another because of their inherent qualities; rather, the categories in which they are included (or from which they are excluded) are a function of the ceaselessly updated mechanism of exclusion. In the same vein, the production of trash is an effect of dynamic, open-ended, always-emerging mechanisms of classification (Hawkins 2005, 2–3). Finally, as McLoughlin notes, for Agamben the threshold is a zone of indistinction, a space in which the difference between things (inside and outside or political life and bare life, for example) is impossible to identify (2011, 191). Indeterminacy is a key characteristic of trash as well. On a material level, processes like putrefaction and corrosion can make it hard to tell what a discarded object is or once was, a difficulty that is compounded by garbage dumps, which group together discards into a "mountain of indistinguishable stuff that is in its own way affirmed by a resolute dismissal" (Scanlan 2005, 14). Like the abject, which occupies an indeterminate threshold between subject and object (Kristeva 1982, 3), trash is the material manifestation of the indistinction of the threshold, the in-between that signals the experience of the limit itself. As John Scanlan puts it, "Between something and nothing; between whole and part; between the body as source of unique being and the universal matter of the garbaged self. This stateless condition of being one thing and then another (or even being at any time *neither one thing nor another*) symbolizes garbage" (2005, 53).

The stateless condition of indistinction that trash exhibits also provides an opening for the consideration of the limits that confront capitalist modes of production and consumption. The bodily regimentation, marginalization, and violence that are part and parcel of capitalist techniques of control—what might otherwise be called biopolitical impulses—are indexed in a number of Latin American cultural texts that bring into focus the way that contemporary regimes of waste management lay bare the limits of normative discourses on the human. By examining texts and films that focus on two types of thresholds or limit zones—between humans and animals and the Self and the Other—and the essential role that trash plays in revealing them, I argue in both this chapter and the next that detritus is the material basis for negotiations between what are supposed to be opposing categories. In other words, the connections between human beings and trash that are present in the texts I analyze function in two important ways: first, they call into question the neatness of a series of binary distinctions; second, they show that what is not thought to pertain to the human as such (animality, pure biological carnality, radical alterity) should, rather, be considered very much part of the human experience.

In considering what trash has to tell us about the limits of the human, I turn to two relatively brief texts from Peru and Brazil: Julio Ramón Ribeyro's short story "Los gallinazos sin plumas" (1955) and Jorge Furtado's short film "Ilha das Flores" (1989). Both texts articulate damning indictments of the violence that is symptomatic of capitalist regimentation of human and nonhuman bodies by bringing trash to center stage in their meditation on what it means to be human.

The Human/Animal Threshold, the Anthropological Machine, and Trash

At the heart of both Julio Ramón Ribeyro's "Los gallinazos sin plumas" and Jorge Furtado's "Ilha das Flores" lies the question of what it means to be human in the context of the experience of living with trash not only as a part of one's surroundings, but also as the material from which one draws physical sustenance. As is the case in Salazar Bondy's *El Señor Gallinazo vuelve a Lima*, the connection between (de)humanization and trash taken up in both works is further complicated by the notable presence of scavenger animals—vultures and pigs—that are strongly associated with garbage. This complex knot of trash people and trash animals moving around together in the trash foregrounds the status of undecidability that attains for all three categories: the human, the animal, and trash. Where exactly is the dividing line between people and animals that scavenge the garbage in order to survive? And does a piece of trash used for food regain its status as a useful object (that is, as something that is not trash)?

These questions highlight the problematic nature of ignoring the murky thresholds that serve to link opposing categories. With respect to the human/animal distinction, there is certainly a great deal more at stake in drawing a dividing line than simply being able to make precise identifications, since that division almost always sets up a hierarchy as well, one in which the human occupies a position of supposed superiority to the animal. Also, as Cary Wolfe has noted, this system of classification that presupposes human superiority to animals helps to mobilize "violence against human others" that "has often operated by means of a double movement that animalizes them for the purposes of domination, oppression, or even genocide—a maneuver that is effective because we take for granted the prior assumption that violence against the animal is ethically permissible" (2009, 567). Such a scenario of animalization of humans that leads to seemingly justifiable violence is certainly one upon which "Los gallinazos sin plumas" and "Ilha das Flores" meditate. But before turning to an examination of how that scenario plays out in both works, I must address the question of how it is that humans and animals can enter the threshold of indistinction that links them together.

In *The Open: Man and Animal*, Agamben makes note of the fact that language has been a key element in the definition of what is human: "In identifying himself with language, the speaking man places his own muteness outside himself, as already and not yet human" (2004, 34–35). He calls this distinction on the basis of language into question by noting that the category "human" is a construction upon which the production of language is based; therefore, the supposed causal relationship between language and personhood (that is, the ability to use language is what gives rise to the distinction between animals and people) supposes the category "human" a priori. Hence, what is at work in this distinction is what Agamben calls the *anthropological machine*, a mechanism that can either exclude beings from or include them in the category "human." He elaborates by saying: "Indeed, precisely because the human is already presupposed every time, the machine actually produces a kind of state of exception, a zone of indeterminacy in which the outside is nothing but the exclusion of an inside and the inside is in turn only the inclusion of an outside . . . . Like every space of exception, this zone is, in truth, perfectly empty, and the truly human being who should occur there is only the place of a ceaselessly updated decision in which the caesurae and their articulation are always dislocated and displaced anew. What would thus be obtained, however, is neither an animal life nor a human life, but only a life that is separated and excluded from itself—only a *bare life*" (37–38).

Being relegated to a zone that is not quite human and not quite animal seems to be the fate of the characters in the works I examine in this chapter. This zone, this threshold between the human and the animal comes into being in the very act of disposal: not only the disposal or the trashing of the humans that inhabit it, but also the disposal of material waste, the production of trash itself. I now turn to "Los gallinazos sin plumas" in order to see the anthropological machine at work.

On Vultures and Pigs: What Is Lacking in "Los gallinazos sin plumas"

While his name is often invoked as a marginalized figure vis-à-vis the literary superstars of the Boom, the Peruvian writer Julio Ramón Ribeyro is consistently recognized as a master of the short story, and one of his most famous stories is "Los gallinazos sin plumas."[5] Published in the 1955 collection of the same name, the seven brief fragments of "Los gallinazos sin plumas" tell the story of Efraín and Enrique, two young brothers who live in a squalid shanty on the outskirts of an unnamed city that we are quite safe in assuming is Lima.[6] The story opens with a personified description of the city just before dawn that is quite suggestive in light of the concept of the threshold that I am advancing. Not only is the time of the day with which the story begins—"las seis de la mañana" (six in the morning) (1994, 21)—a threshold between the night that has passed and the day that is about to begin, but Ribeyro's description of the city itself and the people who traverse it at this hour is also evocative of an in-between state: "Una fina niebla disuelve el perfil de los objetos y crea como una atmósfera encantada. Las personas que recorren la ciudad a esta hora parece que están hechas de otra sustancia, que pertenecen a un orden de vida fantasmal" (A fine mist dissolves the profile of objects and creates an enchanted atmosphere. The people crossing the city at this hour seem to be made of some other substance, to belong to a ghostly class of life) (21). In this sense, from its very outset the story intimates that it will operate within the parameters of the experience of the limit that is the threshold, the contours of which only come into sharper focus as the plot unravels.

After ticking off a list of the people who traverse the city at this hour—drunks, trash collectors, police officers, workers, and the like, all "secreciones del alba" (secretions of the dawn) as Ribeyro refers to them further on (27)—the narrator narrows his focus to one group in particular: the *gallinazos sin plumas* (vultures without feathers), young children who scavenge the city's trash for food and other items. Efraín and Enrique are two such scavengers, and as the narrator puts it, "Ellos no son los únicos. En otros corralones, en otros suburbios alguien ha dado la voz de alarma y muchos se han levantado. Unos portan latas, otros cajas de cartón, a veces sólo basta un periódico viejo. Sin conocerse forman una especie de organización clandestina que tiene repartida toda la ciudad. Los hay que merodean por los edificios públicos, otros han elegido los parques o los muladares. Hasta los perros han adquirido sus hábitos, sus itinerarios, sabiamente aleccionados por la miseria" (They are not the only ones. In other tenements, in other slums, someone has raised the alarm and many have arisen. Some carry cans, others cardboard boxes, sometimes an old newspaper suffices. Without knowing each other, they form a sort of clandestine organization that divvies up the city. There are ones who prowl around public buildings, and others prefer parks and trash heaps. Even the dogs have acquired their habits and itineraries, wisely schooled by squalor) (21–22). Ribeyro portrays a sort of shadow network of children;[7] they are scattered across the city rummaging through the garbage, which certainly places Ribeyro's story within a discourse that is critical of the social and economic inequalities that attended the uneven process of modernization in Peru's capital in the middle of the last century, as several critics have correctly argued.[8] Nevertheless, after the story's first fragment, Ribeyro leaves behind this sociologically inflected bird's eye view of scavengers in Lima to focus on the plight of Efraín and Enrique. The brothers live with their grandfather, don Santos, an intimidating and abusive man in his sixties whose wooden leg prohibits him from joining his grandchildren as they dig through the trash cans of the upper class in search of food for themselves and, more importantly, for Pascual, a pig that lives in their hovel with them and that Santos wants to fatten and sell for slaughter.

As time passes, Pascual's appetite grows and he is no longer sated by the amount of food that Efraín and Enrique can gather from the trash on the streets, so Santos sends them to a *muladar*, a garbage dump near the city's seaside cliffs. The dump's abundance of rotten and rotting food is enough to placate Pascual, but soon enough this precarious arrangement falls apart when Efraín cuts his foot in the muladar. The wound becomes seriously infected, and his foot swells so much that he can no longer walk. For a while, Enrique is able to shoulder the burden of retrieving food for the pig from the dump (he even finds a companion, a stray dog that he takes home and names Pedro), but he also falls ill and can no longer make the trek to the dump. As the days go by, Pascual becomes crazed with hunger, while Santos's obsession with finding food for the pig and his rage against Efraín and Enrique grow to a boiling point. When Santos starts beating Efraín in a fit of rage, Enrique intervenes and tells his grandfather that he will go to look for food in the dump. Upon returning, he discovers that Santos has fed the dog to the pig, so he angrily attacks his grandfather with a stick. Santos slips on his wooden leg and falls into the pigsty, and Enrique sees an opportunity to escape. He lifts a feeble Efraín from his bed, and as the brothers flee the shanty, they hear "el rumor de una batalla" (the sound of a battle) coming from the pigsty (29). We can only imagine that Santos will share Pedro the dog's fate of being devoured by Pascual.

It should be quite obvious that trash plays a key role in Ribeyro's story. It is what compels Efraín and Enrique (along with the multitude of other gallinazos sin plumas alluded to in the story) to leave their house and move about the city day after day, it provides them and their pig with sustenance, and it is the material through which some very interesting socialities emerge: Efraín and Enrique's relationship with each other and with other scavenger animals; the psychologically and physically abusive family environment in which the brothers live; and the threat of violence (and its actualization) that runs across a complex web of relationships, including ones between humans (Santos and his grandsons), ones between humans and animals (Santos and Pascual), and ones between animals (Pascual and Pedro). However, for all its centrality in the story, very little critical attention has been paid to the trash in "Los gallinazos sin plumas" beyond recognizing its presence and attributing to it a role in dramatizing the squalor in which the characters portrayed in the story live, as if it were some sort of social realist window dressing that acts as a shorthand way of signifying the many problems of urbanization in mid-twentieth-century Lima.[9] A closer look at trash in the story, however, can be found in Tania Pérez-Cano's 2013 dissertation, in which she dedicates a chapter to an ecocritical analysis of Ribeyro's story alongside Rubem Fonseca's "Intestino grosso" and José María Merino's *El lugar sin culpa*. Regarding the presence of trash in the Peruvian author's text, she writes, "[E]n 'Los gallinazos sin plumas' Ribeyro construye una eco-narrativa urbana de la carencia y del fracaso, donde la basura y los desperdicios se convierten en la alegoría de la vida moderna" (In "Los gallinazos sin plumas" Ribeyro constructs an urban econarrative of scarcity and failure in which trash and discards become an allegory of modern life) (2013, 67). She fleshes out that declaration by arguing that the trash in the story is an allegorical signifier of a degraded present that somehow expresses nostalgia for a premodern (or premodernized) Lima (64–70). However, the idea that Ribeyro uses trash to erect a Manichaean opposition between a present that is viewed negatively and a past that is viewed positively is simply not borne out in the text for two main reasons. First, there are no references to a cityscape that predates the one portrayed in the relatively circumscribed timeframe of the story's diegesis, which seems to span several weeks at most. It seems to me that references to a premodernized Lima devoid of trash—or at least without as much trash—would be necessary in order to construct the type of nostalgic gaze toward the past that Pérez-Cano posits.[10] Second, Pérez-Cano's attribution of a different value to the past (good, pristine) and the present (bad, degraded) presupposes a purely negative value for trash, which, once again, is not borne out in the story. While it is clear that, on balance, the connection between the characters and garbage in the story is part of a scenario of violence, degradation, and dehumanization, I would argue that this is not due to some noxious quality that is inherent to trash, but rather it arises out of the use to which trash is put in the story.

The primary use for trash in "Los gallinazos sin plumas" is the pig-feeding operation, which, as Peter Elmore astutely argues, allows for the story to be read as a parable of the primitive accumulation of capital in which Santos instrumentalizes his grandsons, the pig, and the garbage that the former gather for the latter in a sort of proto-capitalist enterprise of exploitation (2002, 40). In this sense, trash can be seen as signifier of degradation, especially since it constitutes the material parameters of the operation by which humans and nonhumans are instrumentalized in the text. However, there is also a moment toward the beginning of the story that hints at the possibility that trash may lend itself to less exploitative uses. The narrator describes the way that Efraín and Enrique go about their work sifting through the trash cans in the streets:

> Los cubos de basura están alineados delante de las puertas. Hay que vaciarlos íntegramente y luego comenzar la exploración. Un cubo de basura es siempre una caja de sorpresas. Se encuentran latas de sar-

dinas, zapatos viejos, pedazos de pan, pericotes muertos, algodones inmundos. A ellos sólo les interesa [*sic*] los restos de comida. En el fondo del chiquero, Pascual recibe cualquier cosa y tiene predilección por las verduras ligeramente descompuestas. La pequeña lata de cada uno se va llenando de tomates podridos, pedazos de sebo, extrañas salsas que no figuran en ningún manual de cocina. No es raro, sin embargo, hacer un hallazgo valioso. Un día Efraín encontró unos tirantes con los que fabricó una honda. Otra vez una pera casi buena que devoró en el acto. Enrique, en cambio, tiene suerte para las cajitas de remedios, los pomos brillantes, las escobillas de dientes usadas y otras cosas semejantes que colecciona con avidez.

The trash cans are lined up in front of the doors. They have to be dumped out completely for the exploration to begin. A trash can is always a box of surprises. You can find cans of sardines, old shoes, chunks of bread, dead rats, filthy bits of cotton. They are only interested in food scraps. In the back of the pigsty, Pascual accepts everything, but he has a taste for slightly rotten vegetables. Each boy's small can fills with rotten tomatoes, bits of fat, strange sauces that don't appear in any cookbook. It's not uncommon, however, to make a valuable find. One day Efraín found some suspenders he used to make a slingshot. Another time an almost-good pear that he scarfed down. Enrique, on the other hand, has good luck finding medicine boxes, shiny jars, used toothbrushes, and other such things that he avidly collects. (Ribeyro 1994, 22)

What interests me about this passage is the way that it captures the surprises that trash has to offer. There is an obvious tension between the stated aim of the brothers' daily outings—the narrator declares categorically that they are only interested in finding food that has been thrown away—and what the boys actually look for when they dig through the trash. Despite the fact that their work produces results that are meant to satisfy Santos's demands, the passage makes it clear that Efraín and Enrique are actually much more interested in other things that can be found in the trash. The slingshot that Efraín fashions from a pair of suspenders, while indicative of a certain level of violence that typically accompanies play, signifies his desire to incorporate waste into play instead of work. Enrique's collection of objects related to personal care seems to be left open to many possible interpretations. The avidness with which he seeks out such items could indicate that he aspires to be part of the social class that uses (and throws away) disposable consumer goods; at the same time, however, his desire to accumulate may indicate an affinity for the objects as such. At any rate, his practice of accumulation is certainly opposed to that of don Santos, who wishes to leverage the things gathered under his command into profit.

What I want to emphasize by pointing out the tension made apparent in the text between what the boys are supposed to focus on as they dig through the trash and the additional things that catch their eye is the way the tension introduces a note of ambiguity regarding what trash means in the story. While the overall tone of the story is one of foreboding, and the degradation and putridity that we rightly associate with trash is an essential element in the disquiet the text produces, the narrator's observations about the *hallazgos valiosos* that Efraín and Enrique make as they scavenge for slop hint at the ludic and affective possibilities people can find in the trash. This is definitely a small glimmer of possibility, but it is enough to reinforce the fundamental ambiguity of trash, an ambiguity that has everything to do with what people do with it.

This suggestion of the fundamentally ambiguous nature of trash is by no means the only note of ambiguity present in the text. In fact, the story's most important facet is the ambiguity with which it portrays the distinction between the human and the animal. As is clear from even a cursory reading, Ribeyro's story places humans and animals in very close contact: Efraín and Enrique dig through the trash alongside vultures and dogs; the boys and their grandfather more or less share living quarters with a pig; and everyone in the story, whether human or animal, eats the same slop scavenged from the garbage. The portrayal of people and animals living cheek by jowl in desperate, squalid conditions certainly responds to Ribeyro's desire to produce a mordant critique of the social costs of capitalist modernization in mid-twentieth-century Peru, but these elements are not simply window dressing for a social critique. Rather, the question of what it means to be human in the conditions portrayed in the text is one that is present throughout the story and that is complicated by the crossover way Ribeyro describes both humans and nonhumans in terms of each other. In other words, while Ribeyro resorts to metaphor as the primary device for confronting the human and the nonhuman, his metaphorics do not give the impression of seamless substitution (one thing standing for another), but rather they seem to operate based on a logic of incompleteness (one thing is not quite another thing). Instead of comparing the human and nonhuman characters in the story in order simply to make the point that economic modernization in mid-century Lima reduced people to the status of animals and was therefore bad, Ribeyro subtly deploys metaphor (and the related device of simile) in a way that draws attention to the threshold between the human and the nonhuman and emphasizes the slippery, undecidable nature of the distinction between the two. And while "Los gallinazos sin plumas" certainly exhibits a discourse that is suspicious of capitalism and critical of its effects, the story is not so much a full-throated denunciation of modernization as it is a meditation on a limit case of capitalist society's inexorable need to turn things—whether they be consumer goods, people, or animals—into trash.

The most obvious and significant of these metaphors that serve to heighten the undecidability of the threshold between vehicle and tenor is the one put forth in the story's title and invoked throughout the text: los gallinazos sin plumas. Efraín and Enrique (not to mention the legion of unnamed scavengers described at the beginning of the story) are compared to the vultures that seek sustenance in Lima's cliff-side trash dumps to the point that they seem at times to be the birds' equivalents. Toward the story's end, for instance, the narrative voice, focalized on Enrique, declares, "En el muladar se sintió un gallinazo más entre los gallinazos" (In the dump he felt like a vulture among vultures) (Ribeyro 1994, 27). Elsewhere, the narrator further develops the idea that the boys and the vultures share a common ground: "Desde entonces, los miércoles y los domingos, Efraín y Enrique hacían el trote hasta el muladar. Pronto formaron parte de la extraña fauna de esos lugares y los gallinazos, acostumbrados a su presencia, laboraban a su lado, graznando, aleteando, escarbando con sus picos amarillos, como ayudándolos a descubrir la pista de la preciosa suciedad" (Since then, on Wednesdays and Sundays, Efraín and Enrique made the trip to the dump. They soon became part of the strange fauna of the place, and the vultures, used to their presence, worked by their side, screaming, beating their wings, digging with their beaks, as if helping them discover the clue to the precious filth) (23). In spite of the solidarity evinced here between the boys and the vultures, at other times, Ribeyro emphasizes the fundamental strangeness that divides the two species, as in his initial description of the dump:

> Visto desde el malecón, el muladar formaba una especie de acantilado oscuro y humeante, donde los gallinazos y los perros se desplazaban como hormigas. Desde lejos los muchachos arrojaron piedras para espantar a sus enemigos. Un perro se retiró aullando. Cuando estuvieron cerca sintieron un olor nauseabundo que penetró hasta sus pulmones. Los pies se les hundían en un alto de plumas, de ex-

crementos, de materias descompuestas o quemadas. Enterrando las manos comenzaron la exploración. A veces, bajo un periódico amarillento, descubrían una carroña devorada a medias. En los acantilados próximos los gallinazos espiaban impacientes y algunos se acercaban saltando de piedra en piedra, como si quisieran acorralarlos.

Seen from the pier, the dump was a kind of dark, steaming cliffside, where vultures and dogs moved around like ants. From afar, the boys threw rocks to scare away their enemies. A dog made a howling retreat. When they got closer, a sickening odor penetrated their lungs. Their feet sunk into a mess of feathers, excrement, rotting and burnt material. They dug their hands in and started exploring. Sometimes, beneath a yellowed newspaper, they would find some half-eaten carrion. From the nearby cliffs, the vultures spied them impatiently, some jumping from rock to rock to get closer, as if trying to corner them. (23)

The stark contrast between these two passages highlights the crossover dynamic that underlies the human/nonhuman comparison invoked in the story's title. In the first passage, the vultures befriend the boys, help them, and almost seem to consider them members of their own species; in the second, there is palpable animosity between humans and animals, and the difference between the two is underscored when the narrator identifies the vultures in the dump (as well as the dogs) as the boys' enemies. Nor does the trash abandoned in the dump escape the divergent perspectives that these two passages present. In the first, the waste that boys and vultures work in common to gather is precious: its description suggests something akin to treasure in that it is extracted through digging and scraping the surface of the dump according to a clue (*pista*) that must be discovered. The second passage, on the other hand, emphasizes the revolting and foreboding characteristics of garbage: noxious smells, excrement, rot, decomposition, and the danger of sinking into the filth.

That these two passages appear a few lines apart from one another is, I think, significant. The juxtaposition of seemingly contradictory perspectives on the way that people, animals, and trash interact in a given space undermines the simplistic idea that Ribeyro's story employs animalization and personification in a mechanistic way in order to show that extreme poverty makes people behave like animals, as some critics have argued. For Dick Gerdes, for instance, "El proceso de transformación metafórica y personificación invierten los valores básicos entre el ser humano y los animales, creando así una ironía mordaz" (The process of metaphorical transformation and personification inverts the basic value of the human being and animals, thus creating a biting irony) (1979, 53). The thrust of Gerdes's argument is that this inversion of the human and the animal gives the story universal import because it elevates "una anécdota un poco trillada" (a bit of a worn-out premise) to the level of true art by injecting irony into the equation (52). However, the irony that he sees in Ribeyro's deployment of metaphors of animalization and personification depends on a reading that assumes a hierarchical relationship between humans and animals in which the latter are inherently inferior to the former. While such a reading is certainly understandable given the general hegemony of the view that animals are inferior to humans, if we approach the text through a different ideological framework—one in which alterity is not assigned superior or inferior value—the story opens itself up to a rich reflection on the ways humans and nonhumans are both connected to and alienated from one another. Such a reading allows us to return to the story's key metaphor, opening it up to a more complex interpretation than simply saying that Efraín and Enrique are like vultures because they scavenge for food. Ultimately, instead of resorting to metaphor to suggest an equivalence between children and vultures for the story's didactic or denunciatory purposes, Ribeyro uses the phrase "gallinazos sin plumas" to signal the slippage between the categories he is comparing, the impossibility that they can be one and the same. In other words, Ribeyro's metaphor revolves around what is lacking in order for the comparison to be seamless. Because of their connection to trash, Efraín and Enrique are vultures that lack some quality that would make them fully human; however, they also lack the feathers that would make them fully vultures. Instead, they are something else entirely, featherless vultures that occupy the threshold between the human and the nonhuman, a threshold whose material constitution is trash.

Efraín and Enrique are not the only characters in the story caught up in the overlap between the human and the nonhuman. Their grandfather, don Santos, is cast in a light that calls his humanity into question as well. Some pointed lexical choices on Ribeyro's part serve to hint at his animality. For instance, before day breaks at the beginning of the story, we read, "A esta hora el viejo don Santos se pone la pierna de palo y sentándose en el colchón comienza a *berrear*" (At that time, old don Santos puts on his wooden leg and, sitting on the mattress, starts *bellowing*) (1994, 21, emphasis mine). Toward the story's end, his bellowing becomes a roar: "Cuando el cielo comenzó a desteñirse sobre las lomas abrió la boca, mantuvo su oscura oquedad vuelta hacia sus nietos y lanzó un *rugido*" (When the sky began to fade above the hills, he opened his mouth, concentrated the darkened cavity toward his grandsons, and let loose a *roar*) (27; emphasis mine). The narrator's subtle use of animal noises to describe the sounds that Santos makes (especially when hurling abuse at his grandsons and threatening them with violence if they do not produce ever larger amounts of garbage for the pig and themselves to eat) suggests what Enrique begins to sense about his grandfather: "Solamente Enrique sentía crecer en su corazón un miedo extraño y al mirar los ojos del abuelo creía desconocerlos, como si ellos hubieran perdido su expresión humana" (Only Enrique felt a strange fear growing in his heart and upon looking at his grandfather's eyes he thought he didn't recognize them, as if they had lost their human expression) (26–27). So in the end, the eminently human *don* Santos (the narrator insists on this gentlemanly title throughout the story), who is engaged in the quintessentially human activity of trying to make money, is not only animalized through the narrator's devices; he also fails at doing what a human being should do: instead of eating Pascual the pig, the pig eats him.

Finally, we come to Pascual the pig, the story's most ominous figure with regard to the entanglement of trash, people, and animals. Above and beyond Ribeyro's story itself, pigs' connection to garbage and people is fundamental: alongside human beings, they have developed into a sort of rudimentary trash disposal system because biology has given them a taste for the slop that people throw out (Soper 1995, 87). In this sense, pigs not only mediate the relationship between humans and trash by acting as agents of disposal; they also turn that relationship in on itself, intensifying the intimacy between people and what they throw away because the ultimate purpose of raising pigs is to eat them, a practice of consumption that inevitably bears the taint of garbage. What is more, pigs like Pascual are domestic animals who almost seem to be part of the family. In Pascual's case, his status as quasi-family member is underscored by the fact that he inhabits the same domestic space as Santos, Efraín, and Enrique; that they all eat the same (garbage) food; and that he has a name like the other family members. Pascual's name in itself seems to heighten his uncertain position on the border of the human and nonhuman. As Kate Soper notes, "Prior to this transformation [that is, the slaughtering of the pig], the pig, as a member of the family who was yet to end up on its table, was an object of more confused emotions: a creature whose revolting habits both gained it a certain indulgence as a wayward child and justified its eventual slaughter. Indeed, it has been said that the vilification of the pig can be attributed to the need to assuage the guilt of killing and eating such a commensal associate" (1995, 88).

By virtue of the overtones of Pascual's name and its invocation of the paschal sacrifice, he seems destined to serve an expiatory role in the sacrificial economy that Soper describes. However, by eating don Santos at the end of the story, Pascual turns that economy on its head by exacting the violence that he was destined to suffer. That violence, while seeming to spring forth from some reserve of pure animality, may in fact be more complex. Before the story's gory denouement, as all the characters experience increased anxiety due to the lack of feed for Pascual, the narrator says, "Enrique había oído decir que los cerdos, cuando tenían hambre, se volvían locos como los hombres" (Enrique had heard that when pigs went hungry, they'd go crazy like men) (Ribeyro 1994, 27). This line, whose function in the story seems to be that of heightening the tension by suggesting that a breaking point is being approached, offers some unsettling insight when projected onto Santos and Pascual's final confrontation. If starving pigs go crazy like men, that is, if a pig's behavior can be confused with a man's, then perhaps Pascual's act of violence at the story's end is not simply animal, but also human. Or perhaps we could say that it is neither and both at the same time. My point is not that Pascual somehow *turns into* a person or that the human characters turn into animals, but rather, that in the unstable, trash-filled milieu that they inhabit, the status of their actions is unclear. They form a dense knot of material and social interactions that constitute the uncertain threshold of the human and nonhuman. "Los gallinazos sin plumas" turns our gaze toward that threshold and suggests that even though Efraín and Enrique seem to escape its immediate consequences at the very end of the story, it is likely that they are simply trading a small-scale version of it for a much larger one: the city itself, which, "despierta y viva, abría ante ellos su gigantesca mandíbula" (awake and alive, opened before them its gigantic jaws) just like Pascual in the pigsty (1994, 29).

Brains, Thumbs, Money, and Freedom: Defining the Human in "Ilha das Flores"

While Ribeyro's main tactic for drawing attention to the indeterminate threshold between humans and nonhumans is the subtle use of ambiguity in the tropes of animalization and humanization that he deploys throughout "Los gallinazos sin plumas," Brazilian director Jorge Furtado employs much less subtle techniques to achieve similar ends in his short film "Ilha das Flores."[11] I say less subtle not to mean less complex or lacking in sophistication; rather, whereas the ambiguous metaphors of "Los gallinazos sin plumas" seem to suggest the threshold qualities of trash in an offhand, naturalized manner, "Ilha das Flores" explicitly confronts anthropocentric systems of order and classification through a caustic brand of satire that suggests that the act of disposal is a notion that binds together people, animals, and objects.

The basic plot of Furtado's film is quite simple: it tells the fictional story of a tomato grown in the city of Porto Alegre in southern Brazil.[12] The tomato is cultivated by Senhor Suzuki, who sells it, along with many other tomatoes, to a supermarket. Then Dona Anete, a door-to-door perfume saleswoman, buys the tomato to make some sauce to go with the pork she is making for her family. She deems the tomato, which has bruised and rotten spots, inadequate for her sauce, so she throws it away. Now part of a heaping truckload of trash, the tomato heads to a garbage dump called Ilha das Flores. There, men who own bits of land for raising pigs separate the organic waste to feed to the pigs, and whatever the pigs do not care to eat is left in a pen to be picked over by the human inhabitants of Ilha das Flores, who are mostly women and children. Due to the large number of people vying for the pigs' leftovers, the landowners have devised a strict system that allows group after group of ten people to enter the pen and scavenge for five minutes at a time until the garbage is gone. The tomato that the film follows is passed over by the pigs and made available to the human population of Ilha das Flores.

This plot summary of "Ilha das Flores" should make the thematic import of trash to the film quite evident. However, trash is not simply one of the film's central themes; its importance is also suggested by the form of the film itself. In this sense, Furtado employs two essential formal elements that merit attention: the film's visual style and narrative style. Both of these elements—sight and sound—exhibit two features in turn that are reminiscent of human practices related to garbage: recycling and sorting.

When I say that the narrative and visual style of "Ilha das Flores" is reminiscent of the recycling of waste, I mean that both elements of the film exhibit a tendency to reuse fragments (spoken lines or shots) that the viewer has already heard and seen earlier in the film. Toward the beginning of the film, the narrator (whose voice is the only one we hear throughout "Ilha das Flores") offers a definition of the term *ser humano* that focuses on two specific physical characteristics common to all human beings: "o telencéfalo altamente desenvolvido e o polegar opositor" (the highly developed cerebrum and the opposable thumb) (Furtado 1989). This phrase (or some slight variation of it) is repeated about a dozen times during the remaining twelve or so minutes of the film in a variety of different contexts, often with a very comedic effect. Other textual elements that are recycled throughout the script include references to specific types of humans (*japoneses, católicos, judeus*) or nonhumans (*baleias, galinhas, porcos*), along with elements in the chain of economic exchange described in the film (*tomate, a troca, dinheiro, flores, perfume,* and so on). All of these words and phrases are spoken early in the film only to be reused time and again. And the images that appear onscreen when these phrases are uttered follow a similar procedure. That is, virtually every time the narrator mentions whales (about five times in the film), the same rudimentary animated image of a whale appears onscreen. The same is true for certain shots of the film's main characters (the tomato, Senhor Suzuki, and Dona Anete), the model human brain shown when the narrator makes mention of a "telencéfalo," a striking photo of a dead pig, and so on.

The effect that this barrage of recycled phrasing and imagery has is disconcerting because it suggests that the discursive and visual material on display in the film, while seemingly ordered in a very tidy, logical way, is immune to order and control; instead, it simply continues to accumulate. This brings me to the second garbage practice evoked by the form of "Ilha das Flores": sorting. Sorting, the practice of picking through an unorganized mass of objects and imposing a certain order on them, is a common way of dealing with trash (as is evinced in Furtado's film by the workers who sort garbage into organic and inorganic categories in order to find food for their bosses' pigs), but this imposition of order cannot be conceived of in isolation, especially where trash is concerned. On the contrary, order is always engaged in a dialectical relationship with disorder. The very act of ordering or sorting things not only depends on the prior existence of disorder, but it also produces disorder and waste because the multifaceted nature of things resists easy categorization, and classification itself depends on including certain things while excluding others.[13] This dialectical interplay between sorting and throwing out, order and disorder, undergirds the relationship between the narrative and visual elements of "Ilha das Flores." On the one hand, the general aim of the narrator's fast-paced, meticulously repetitive telling of the story of Senhor Suzuki's tomato is to impose sense or order on the chaotic, aleatory networks of exchange and transaction occurring among humans, animals, and objects. An example of this general narrative impulse toward the categorization of things and ideas comes early in the film, when the narrator explains the utility of having a highly developed cerebrum and opposable thumbs: "O telencéfalo altamente desenvolvido permite aos seres humanos armazenar informações, relacioná-las, processá-las e entendê-las. O polegar opositor permite aos seres humanos o movimento de pinça dos dedos o que, por sua vez, permite a manipulação de precisão. O telencéfalo altamente desenvolvido, combinado com a capacidade de fazer o movimento de pinça com os dedos, deu ao ser humano a possibilidade de realizar um sem número de melhoramentos em seu planeta, entre eles, cultivar tomates" (The highly developed cerebrum allows humans to store information, compare it, process it, and understand it. The opposable thumb allows humans to have a gripping movement, which in turn allows precise manipulation. The highly developed cerebrum, combined with the hand's gripping movement, gave humans the possibility of making infinite improvements to their planet, including growing tomatoes) (Furtado 1989).

Not only is the discourse here highly structured and clearly ordered (that is, it reads like the end result of a meticulous process of sorting through possible defining traits of humanness and their benefits to humankind and the planet), but also it celebrates the very concept of imposing order, both on an intellectual and on a material plane. However, the film's visual elements end up calling that celebratory tone into question by suggesting that the ordered discourse of the narrative only barely covers up an underlying foundation of disorder and waste. While the narrator utters the passage quoted above, the screen shows a series of images: an animated cutaway of a woman's head with a fast sequence of random images popping up in the space occupied by the brain, several close-up shots of human hands doing things that require the use of an opposable thumb (writing, using tweezers, applying makeup), then a sequence of cutout animation with images from antiquity (Adam and Eve in the Garden of Eden, the Tower of Babel, Egyptian pyramids, the Acropolis, and other images) that pile on top of one another until filling the frame and then falling out of it. All of this leads to a video image of mushroom cloud from a nuclear explosion, which comes onscreen just as the narrator is saying that humans have made innumerable improvements to the planet by coordinating the faculties bestowed upon them by their brains and opposable thumbs. So while the film's visual elements at first seem simply to be illustrating the narrative discourse, they actually undermine that discourse through both the frenetic, uncontrollable accumulation of images on the verge of disorder and the explicit invocation of the threat of total disorder: nuclear annihilation.

Another particularly salient example of the narrative-visual dialectic that Furtado employs so expertly in this film comes when the narrator explains the benefits afforded to humanity by money, namely, that the intermediary quality of money solves the problems occasioned by trying to exchange goods directly for one another. The narrator says, "A partir do século três Antes de Cristo, qualquer ação ou objeto produzido pelos seres humanos, fruto da conjugação do telencéfalo altamente desenvolvido com o polegar opositor, assim como todas as coisas vivas ou não vivas sobre ou sob a terra, tomates, galinhas e baleias, podem ser trocadas por dinheiro" (Since the third century BC, any action or object produced by humans as the result of the combination of the highly developed cerebrum and opposable thumb, as well as all living and nonliving things above and below the earth, tomatoes, hens, and whales, can be exchanged for money) (Furtado 1989). Once again, the images onscreen seem to play the ambiguous role of both illustrating and critiquing the narrative discourse. While the narrator speaks, we see another sequence of cutout animation. First, there is a series of paintings: one from ancient Egypt of a man carrying a tray, Vermeer's *Lady Standing at a Virginal*, Raphael's *Portrait of a Cardinal*, Goya's *La maja desnuda*, and a painting of a Roman market scene. The cutout animation comes in the form of late-twentieth-century consumer goods popping up on top of these classic works of art: a bottle of Coke on the Egyptian man's tray; stereo equipment for Vermeer's lady; sunglasses and binoculars for the Cardinal; and a bathing suit, teddy bear, and bottle of whiskey for the *maja*. Then, the images of the *maja* and the Roman market scene are completely overwhelmed by cutouts of what look to be text and images from newspaper and magazine advertisements. So, the order that, according to the narrator's claims, arises from the use of money only brings disorder in the form of the ever-accelerating rate of production and accumulation of consumer goods. Furthermore, all of the cutout images that pile up in the paintings in this sequence—Coke and whiskey bottles, speakers, swimsuits, and, especially, newspaper ads—are destined to become trash once they fall out of style, expire, or become useless. Furtado's choice of using cutout animation here and elsewhere in the film is particularly effective at suggesting the incipient trashiness of things, because of the way that the stop motion makes the cutouts appear and vanish in the blink of an eye, filling frame after frame with jumbled, messy images.

Now that we have seen the way that trash and concepts related to waste management suffuse "Ilha das Flores" thematically and formally, making trash an essential part of both the film's vocabulary and its grammar, so to speak, we will consider how Furtado's film engages with the idea of trash as the material manifestation of the human/nonhuman threshold. Whereas Ribeyro resorts to the foregrounding of ambiguity in his use of metaphor in "Los gallinazos sin plumas" in order to call into question the distinction between people and animals whose lives are connected by trash, Furtado relies on the arrangement of the formal techniques discussed above into a tripartite structure that leads from the seemingly innocuous activity of growing tomatoes to a scenario in which people and pigs compete for discarded food. Taken together, the film's three sections—which cover the questions of humanness, money, and trash—ultimately cloud the highly logical explanation of what it means to be human that the narrator so confidently proclaims.

From the outset, "Ilha das Flores" shows a concern for defining the human, and this question is the central one with which Furtado grapples. One of the ways this concern is demonstrated is the narrator's aforementioned obsession with providing a clear, logical definition of the term "ser humano" and applying that definition in a consistent manner throughout the film. Shortly after the title sequence, a handheld camera moves through a field of tomato plants and approaches a man. All the while, the narrator says, "Caminhamos neste momento numa plantação de tomates e podemos ver à frente, em pé, um ser humano, no caso, um japonês" (Now we are walking through a tomato field and in front of us we see, on foot, a human being, in this case, a Japanese man), and soon thereafter, the narrator formulates his definition of the term "human" by saying, "Os seres humanos são animais mamíferos, bípedes, que se distinguem dos outros mamíferos, como a baleia, ou bípedes, como a galinha, principalmente por duas características: o telencéfalo altamente desenvolvido e o polegar opositor" (Human beings are bipedal mammals that are distinguished from other mammals, like whales, and bipeds, like hens, by two main characteristics: the highly developed cerebrum and the opposable thumb) (Furtado 1989). This straightforward definition sets up a clear "inside" (bipedal mammals with big brains and opposable thumbs) whose very existence depends on pushing other beings to the "outside" (whales, hens, and so on), which is reminiscent of the way that Agamben describes the functioning of the anthropological machine. What is more, this inside/outside dynamic is further complicated by the narrative perspective taken by the film, which is established just before the scene in the tomato field, during the title sequence. As the soundtrack plays the first few bars of Antônio Carlos Gomes's opera *Il Guarany* and the intertitles proclaiming the film's nonfiction status give way to a black screen, a small globe appears in the center of the screen and the camera slowly zooms in as the Earth completes a rotation. The film's title appears, encircling the globe, and as the camera continues to zoom in, white smoke rises to fill the frame. Then we cut to the shot with the handheld camera moving through the tomato field, at the beginning of which the smoke from the title sequence continues to rise through the frame, which links the two shots, suggesting that the movement forward of the handheld camera is a continuation of the camera's zoom toward the globe. Then the narrator declares, "Estamos em Belém Novo, município de Porto Alegre, estado do Rio Grande do Sul, no extremo sul do Brasil, mais precisamente na latitude trinta graus, doze minutos e trinta segundos Sul e longitude cinquenta e um graus, onze minutos e vinte e três segundos Oeste" (We are in Belém Novo, municipality of Porto Alegre, state of Rio Grande do Sul, at the southern end of Brazil, or more precisely, at thirty degrees, twelve minutes, and thirty seconds South latitude, fifty-one degrees, eleven minutes, and twenty-three seconds West longitude) (Furtado 1989). This sequence clearly establishes the narrative perspective of the film as one that curiously inhabits the *outside* of the inside/outside binary posited in the narrator's definition of the term "ser humano." It is as if both narrator and viewer, linked by the unstated subject of the film's first spoken line—*nós*—are onlookers coming from outside the perspective of humanity, a perspective that is underscored by the camera that seems to travel to Senhor Suzuki's tomato field from outer space. But we, the viewers and the narrator, are in fact human beings, and this outsider perspective is part of Furtado's parodic appropriation of the conventions of wildlife documentaries, which would in turn put us in the position of humans making observations about nonhuman others. In this sense, Furtado's play with narrative perspective produces a logical dead end in which the human and its other occupy such unstable positions that is hard to determine which category is which.

This pernicious undermining of a solid, unassailable definition of the human is also exhibited during two moments in the film that focus on specific subsets of human beings: Japanese people and Jews. In the first case, after the narrator identifies Senhor Suzuki, the man in the tomato field, as a human being, he specifies that he is Japanese and says, "Os japoneses se distinguem dos demais seres humanos pelo formato dos olhos, por seus cabelos pretos e por seus nomes característicos" (The Japanese are distinguished from other human beings by the shape of their eyes, their black hair, and their characteristic names), while the following images appear on-screen: the eye of a Japanese person in extreme close-up, black hair (again in extreme close-up), a photo ID of a Japanese person, and a close-up of two Japanese men (one in profile and one facing the camera) with a jump cut to a shot of the same two men after switching stances (Furtado 1989). This sequence is subtly disquieting for a couple of reasons. First, there is the insistence upon making a clear delimitation between one type of human and another based on "objective" racial characteristics whose objectivity is bolstered by the extreme close-ups. Second, the two shots of Japanese men with which the sequence ends are strongly evocative of mug shots, not only due the men's position in front of the camera, but also because of the drab gray clothes with numbers on the shirts the men are wearing and the wall with horizontal lines on it that is behind them. The biopolitical overtones evident in these shots suggest not only that the definition of the human is a matter of dispute, but also that the dispute has to do with exerting power and control over certain types of bodies.

This biopolitical edge becomes much more evident in one of the narrator's asides. While talking about the invention of money, which he attributes to King Gyges of Lydia during the seventh century BC, the "antes de Cristo" forces the following narrative detour: "Cristo era um judeu. Os judeus possuem o telencéfalo altamente desenvolvido e o polegar opositor. São, por tanto, seres humanos" (Christ was a Jew. Jews possess a highly developed cerebrum and opposable thumbs. They are, therefore, human beings) (Furtado 1989). But the images onscreen contradict this straightforward claim: there is film footage of two emaciated men facing the camera, followed by footage of an emaciated corpse being thrown into a mass grave, then two shots of naked bodies jumbled together in a mass grave. The visual presentation of human beings literally being rendered garbage and thrown away during the Holocaust squarely calls into question any attempt to ground a definition of the human in clear, biological terms. On the contrary, it indicates that any definition of the human is the result of a "ceaselessly updated decision in which the caesurae and their rearticulation are always dislocated and displaced anew" (Agamben 2004, 38).

The film's second and third sections—which focus on money and trash, respectively—interject into the discussion of what counts as human further considerations regarding the value (or lack thereof) of things. Just before the narrator enters into his discussion of the superiority of the money economy to the exchange economy, he notes that Senhor Suzuki spends his time cultivating tomatoes. He then says, "A utilidade principal do tomate é a alimentação dos seres humanos" (The primary function of the tomato is as food for human beings) (Furtado 1989). Curiously, though, this basic function is never quite realized in the case of the specific tomato on which the film focuses; instead, it ends up being thrown in the trash, passed over by the pigs of Ilha das Flores, and made available for human consumption (with the question of whether or not someone picks it up to eat it being left open). Before the tomato makes its way into the waste stream, it participates in a series of economic exchanges (between Senhor Suzuki and the supermarket, then between Dona Anete and the supermarket) that are linked to still other economic exchanges (between Dona Anete and the perfume makers from whom she buys wholesale, then between Dona Anete and the clients who buy perfume from her). In this sense, the tomato seems to be both more and less than a tomato: it is more than a tomato in that it functions as a point of coalescence for a significant amount of economic and social activity, and it is less than a tomato in that it fails to meet its obligation to provide sustenance to either people or animals.

Seen in the light of the tomato's journey from field to trash dump, the sequence that I analyze above in which famous works of art are overlaid with consumer goods and advertisements presents a suggestive connection between money and the production of trash. As the images are increasingly overwhelmed by stuff, the narrator declares that "A qualquer ação ou objeto produzido pelos seres humanos, fruto da conjugação do telencéfalo altamente desenvolvido com o polegar opositor, assim como todas as coisas vivas ou não vivas sobre ou sob a terra, tomates, galinhas e baleias, podem ser trocadas por dinheiro" (Any action or object produced by human beings as a result of the combination of a highly developed cerebrum and opposable thumbs, as well as all living and nonliving things above or below the earth, tomatoes, hens, and whales, can be exchanged for money) (Furtado 1989). In other words, money is the thing that facilitates making disparate objects into equivalent ones, the idea that performs the magic trick of turning perfume into tomatoes. It is the lubricant of the engine of production and consumption, but as both the accumulation of cutouts that drown out image after image and the tomato's trajectory toward the trash dump suggest, that engine is also one of disposal, and the magic by which money makes one thing into another hides the fact that all of those things are left to rot in the trash.

This brings us to the film's final section, which foregrounds not only trash itself, but also the way trash, animals, and people are positioned relative to one another. The dump is where all of these elements, the film's main concerns, come together. As the narrator puts it, "O tomate, plantado pelo Senhor Suzuki, trocado por dinheiro com o supermercado, trocado pelo dinheiro que Dona Anete trocou por perfumes extraídos das flores, recusado para o molho do porco, jogado no lixo e recusado pelos porcos como alimento está agora disponível para os seres humanos da Ilha das Flores" (The tomato, planted by Senhor Suzuki, exchanged for money with the supermarket, exchanged for the money that Dona Anete exchanged for perfumes extracted from flowers, rejected as part of the sauce for the pork, thrown in the trash and rejected by pigs as food is now available to the human beings of Ilha das Flores) (Furtado 1989).[14]

But the film is not only interested in tracking the journey of a tomato through the waste stream. It is also concerned with shedding light on what is at the heart of the idea of the human as it relates to both trash and animals. In this sense, the narrator's precise definition of these terms as they relate to the dump at Ilha das Flores is instructive. Regarding trash, he says, "Lixo é todo aquilo produzido pelos seres humanos numa conjugação dos esforços do telencéfalo altamente desenvolvido com o polegar opositor, e que segundo o julgamento de determinado ser humano, não tem condições de virar molho" (Trash is everything produced by human beings as a result of the combined efforts of the highly developed cerebrum and opposable thumbs that, according to a given human being's judgment, is not fit to be turned into sauce) (Furtado 1989). This comically simplistic definition serves to underscore not only the link between production and disposal, but also the capricious nature of deciding what things to discard. The narrator talks about pigs, the specific kind of animal found in Ilha das Flores, in the following terms: "O porco é um mamífero, como os seres humanos e as baleias, porém quadrúpede. Serve de alimento aos japoneses, aos católicos e aos demais seres humanos, com exeção dos judeus . . . . [O] porco não tem nem mesmo um polegar, que dirá opositor. O porco tem, entanto, um dono. O dono do porco é um ser humano com telencéfalo altamente desenvolvido, polegar opositor e dinheiro" (The pig is a mammal, like human beings and whales, but it is a quadruped. It serves as food for the Japanese, Catholics, and other human beings, with the exception of Jews. . . . The pig has no thumbs, not to mention opposable ones. The pig does have, however, an owner. The owner of a pig is a human being with a highly developed cerebrum, opposable thumbs, and money) (Furtado 1989). This additional trait—money—ascribed to the owners of the pigs is important to keep in mind when considering the humans (largely women and children) who inhabit the dump at Ilha das Flores and about whom the narrator says, "Mulheres e crianças são seres humanos com telencéfalo altamente desenvolvido, polegar opositor e nenhum dinheiro. Elas não tem dono, e o que é pior, são muitas" (Women and children are human beings with a highly developed cerebrum, opposable thumbs, and no money. They have no owner, and, what is worse is that they are numerous) (Furtado 1989).

The lack at the heart of each of these definitions—trash lacks characteristics that make for a good sauce, pigs lack thumbs, and the women and children of Ilha das Flores lack both money and owners—is of fundamental importance, and it certainly resonates with the lack that is central to the metaphors of "Los gallinazos sin plumas." This is precisely where Ribeyro's story and Furtado's film find common ground. Just as Efraín and Enrique's connection to trash constitutes them as featherless vultures situated on the interstices of the human and the nonhuman, the women and children who scrounge garbage left over by pigs in "Ilha das Flores" are both less than human and less than pigs. As the narrator points out, they have no money, which seems to be a disavowed but fundamental trait of the other humans portrayed in the film. The fact that they lack an owner to provide them with food, ironically enough, makes them less than pigs. This irony is highlighted by the words of the narrator as the film comes to an end, which are spoken over images of dozens of people combing through mountains of trash in an enormous landfill: "O ser humano se diferencia dos outros animais pelo telencéfalo altamente desenvolvido, pelo polegar opositor e por ser livre. Livre é o estado daquele que tem liberdade. Liberdade é uma palavra que o sonho humano alimenta, que não há ninguém que explique e ninguém que não entenda" (The human being is differentiated from other animals by virtue of its highly developed cerebrum, its opposable thumbs, and by being free. Free is the state of that which has freedom. Freedom is a word that is fed by human dreams, a word that no one can explain but that no one fails to understand) (Furtado 1989).[15] Certainly, the freedom of the people we see onscreen scavenging in the landfill is being called into question. While they are, in a sense, free (that is, they have no owners to constrain them like the pigs), that freedom is ultimately illusory. Just like Efraín and Enrique, who seem to make their escape from squalor only to find themselves in a city whose monstrous jaws are poised to clamp down on them, the people who live and work in the trash in "Ilha das Flores" are not free because the threshold that they inhabit between the human and the nonhuman has no place for the exercising of freedom as it is understood in the context of modern liberal subjectivity. The rights and options that such a subjectivity encompasses are instead buffeted by both the material and discursive weight of the trash that travels the arc bending between Senhor Suzuki's tomato field and the pestilent pigsties of Ilha das Flores. In the end, the women and children portrayed in Furtado's film and the brothers from Ribeyro's story inhabit a zone of exclusion: exclusion from normative concepts of both the human and the animal. And the only freedom they can exercise in that zone is to choose which bits of trash to pick up and eat.

2

In and Out of the Dump

On the Limits of Community

The trash threshold that I examined in the preceding chapter—which signals and calls into question the limit between the human and the animal—is shot through with violence and exclusion. It exemplifies the destructive nature of power as it is unevenly distributed through economic, social, and material networks. More specifically, by attending to how Ribeyro and Furtado deploy literary language and cinematic techniques, we see the role that trash plays in cultural representations of what Giorgio Agamben calls the anthropological machine, a mechanism that polices the boundary between the human and the animal by relying on the logic of the exception and the production of bare life. But do the threshold and trash, its material manifestation, offer the possibility of something other than violence and exclusion, something akin to the community and solidarity that Salazar Bondy's Señor Gallinazo finds in the dump with Bautista Haullpa and his friends? In her discussion of *Homo Sacer*, Ewa Plonowska Ziarek notes a difference in the mode of operation between sovereign power and transformative power that underscores the limitations of Agamben's theorization of biopolitics: "The excess of sovereign power manifests itself as a suspension of the law, as the exclusion of bare life, as a state of exception that either confirms the norm, or, in extreme cases, collapses the distinction between the exception and the norm. The mode of operation of the transformative power, however, is not the decision on the exception but the negation of existing exclusions from the political followed by the unpredictable and open-ended process of creating new forms of collective life—a process that resembles in certain respects more an aesthetic experiment 'without truth' . . . than an instrumental action" (2012, 204). In this sense, the destructive nature of sovereign violence and the creative potential of transformative power are both forms of excess that operate outside of the constituted order although they are linked to it; they differ, however, in that the question of excess with regard to the former is one of location (*Where* is sovereign power located?), while that of the latter is one of praxis (*How* can the excess produced by biopolitical regimes work to transform the constituted order?). Ziarek is right to point out that the type of theorization Agamben undertakes in books like *Homo Sacer* and *State of Exception* is apparently not concerned with transformative practice. The reason that he "does not consider the practice of liberation in greater depth is that his ontology of potentiality is developed to undermine sovereign will and not to transform bare life into a site of contestation and political possibility" (204). Can this type of transformation take place? Does bare life as it manifests itself in the threshold zone of garbage offer the possibility of creating new forms of collective life?

I think that we can find at least the beginning of an answer to these questions in another of Agamben's books: *The Coming Community*. There, Agamben explores the possibility of thinking about community in a way that refuses criteria of belonging based on preconceived notions of identity or essence. Reflecting on Baruch Spinoza's conceptualization of the common, Agamben says, "All bodies ... have it in common to express the divine attribute of extension .... And yet what is common cannot in any case constitute the essence of the single case .... Decisive here is the idea of an *inessential* commonality, a solidarity that in no way concerns an essence. *Taking-place, the communication of singularities in the attribute of extension, does not unite them in essence, but scatters them in existence*" (1993, 18–19). Key to understanding this concept of a community of scattered existence instead of bound essence is the enigmatic opening sentence of the book: "The coming being is whatever being" (1). Michael Hardt, the book's translator, glosses his translation of the Italian *qualunque* as "whatever," noting that the term presents a difficulty because it can be rendered as both "particular" and "general" depending on the context; he affirms, however, that for Agamben, "'whatever' (*qualunque* or *quelconque*) refers precisely to that which is neither particular nor general, neither individual nor generic" (107). As Jenny Edkins affirms, "Whatever being is being *such as it is*, with all its properties. In other words ... it is immaterial whether whatever being is human or inhuman, politically qualified or excluded" (2007, 73). So here we find ourselves once again on the threshold, a state defined as neither one thing nor the other, a space that is not beyond another space, but rather a passage and "the experience of the limit itself" (Agamben 1993, 68). As I have argued so far in this book, the indeterminate space of the threshold and those who occupy it find their materialization in trash as the "wasted lives" of the people (and animals) whose bodies are caught up in waste flows.[1] Trash is a substance that always finds itself in flux, neither completely worthless nor valuable, neither fully disintegrated nor whole. It is material with no essence, for it is always defined in terms of its relationships to other things. In order to further develop this book's reflections on the ties that bind together human beings and the trash we produce, I would like to consider how three works of nonfiction open themselves up to a reading that is grounded in Agamben's reflections on community: Argentine writer Alicia Dujovne Ortiz's book ¿*Quién mató a Diego Duarte? Crónicas de la basura* (2010), Brazilian director Eduardo Coutinho's documentary film *Boca de Lixo* (1993), and Mexican American writer Luis Alberto Urrea's book *By the Lake of Sleeping Children* (1996). What I am proposing is not an exhaustive reading of these works, but rather a concentrated look at how they offer suggestive connections with Agamben's theorization of a transformative power that, as Ziarek indicates, exceeds the constituted order, which is to say that it is defined in terms of excess, just like trash. These excessive representations ultimately point beyond not only the normative notions of belonging that Agamben criticizes, but also the idea of the human as something that transcends and outlasts material processes like the ones that attend waste. What these three works of nonfiction have to show us is that the communities they portray do not exist in spite of trash, but because of it. This is a sobering message, but perhaps it affords some hope given the way trash increasingly defines human habitation of this planet.

Dujovne Ortiz's book tells the story of the author's investigation of the case of Diego Duarte, a fifteen-year-old boy who disappeared while scavenging recyclables from trash in a CEAMSE (Coordinación Ecológica Área Metropolitana Sociedad del Estado, the state-owned enterprise that manages Buenos Aires's solid waste) landfill in the Buenos Aires suburb José León Suárez in 2004.[2] When police patrolling the area saw him, they ordered a sanitation worker operating a bulldozer to unload hundreds of pounds of compacted trash on the spot where the boy was hiding. Duarte's body has never been found, and no one has faced charges for his death. Dujovne Ortiz, whose initial thought was to write a book about cartoneros in Buenos Aires and only happened upon Diego's story when it was mentioned to her by different trash workers and activists in the city, develops a particularly close relationship with Diego's older sister Alicia, who faces seemingly insurmountable odds in her attempts to find justice for her brother in a context in which police regularly exercise violence against marginalized *cirujas* and cartoneros with impunity to the extent that, as Dujovne Ortiz puts it, "más allá del Buen Ayre, los derechos humanos quedan en suspenso" (beyond the Buen Ayre Highway, human rights are suspended) (2010, 183).[3]

Coutinho's film is a documentary about *catadores* in the Itaoca garbage dump in the municipality of São Gonçalo, about forty kilometers from Rio de Janeiro.[4] As he and his film crew interview people who work and live in and around the dump, a relationship of trust and mutual understanding seems to develop, an arc that Coutinho elegantly summarizes with a brief montage right after the film's title sequence. At first, the catadores shy away from the camera: we see a series of several people turning their faces away or covering them up, shooing the camera away with their arms, and even trying to escape the camera's gaze by running away from it; however, the last person in this sequence stares into the camera with her face covered, hesitates for a moment while glancing at something out of frame, then removes the rag covering her face and smiles into the camera. The rest of the film could be seen as an unpacking of that montage. Coutinho and his crew interview several catadores, asking them open-ended questions about how they manage their lives and what it is like to work in this place. The workers speak at length about their lives, what they do in the dump, and their relationships with one another, and the camera captures the domestic and social lives that unfold amid mountains of trash with no voiceover narration and only the slightest bit of contextualization.[5] The film ends with a sequence in which the catadores watch videotaped footage of themselves in the dump.

Urrea's book chronicles the writer's time spent working with communities in and around Tijuana throughout the 1980s and early 1990s, a moment in which the NAFTA-era conceptualization of the United States–Mexico border was taking shape.[6] In broad terms, the view of the border that emerges in this moment (and that Urrea aims to capture) is undergirded by a central paradox. On the one hand, it is a conceptualization of the border as a space of unlimited freedom from economic and environmental regulatory restraints; on the other, it becomes an increasingly regimented, militarized space designed to curtail human freedom through the harsh regulation of the movement of racialized bodies (bodies that move in pursuit of various forms of freedom that do not seem to be covered by the "free" in "free trade," like freedom from violence, oppression, and poverty).[7] The book is a series of loosely related vignettes, many of which center on a community of trash pickers in a dump in Tijuana and recount their interactions with each other and with outsiders like Urrea, aid organizations, and the state. Urrea approaches this space and community from an equally paradoxical position that highlights the intersection of a number of thresholds. As a Mexican American, his approach to writing about the border and the community of people from Tijuana he portrays constantly negotiates the difference between being Mexican and being American, speaking Spanish and speaking English, observing a community and its space from a distance and immersing himself in that community and its space. He writes from an unstable position that is simultaneously apart from his object of representation and a part of it. In this sense, *By the Lake of Sleeping Children* is both a meditation on many different instantiations of the threshold and a text that comes into being at the point where those thresholds converge.

Dujovne Ortiz, Coutinho, and Urrea portray communities of people who, due to a complex web of social and economic factors, find themselves depending on the waste of consumer societies for their livelihood and sustenance and who, because of this dependence on trash, are marginalized to the point of near invisibility, much like the community that Señor Gallinazo encounters in Salazar Bondy's tale. But the stories they tell are not satisfied with simply turning our gaze toward the margins. Dujovne Ortiz, Coutinho, and Urrea are also concerned with the part that they themselves have to play in the representations they produce. In this sense, all three manage to portray not only the socialities that emerge within marginalized groups of people who work in and with garbage, but also those that develop between themselves and the trash workers. To my mind, this explicit foregrounding of the way that these members of a privileged class (economically privileged, without a doubt, but more important, epistemologically privileged) are embedded in the socialities of their supposed objects of representation is a fundamental element in the stance they take with regard to the radical alterity of the people they portray in their texts. In other words, they grapple with the difficult task of how to be together with people who are radically different.

Trash Thresholds

The threshold is a key conceptual element in Agamben's thinking, and it serves as a point of inflection for his theorization of the possibility of transformative power through community. There is no denying the fact that Agamben anchors this concept in spatial terms. The terminology he invokes in his reflection on the threshold is rooted in physical space: *outside, door, space, passage, house* (1993, 68). In this sense, I think it is appropriate to imagine the threshold in terms of space. In a way that is similar to the way in which I have contended that the idea of the threshold can be manifested materially in garbage, we can think of the landfill—the predominant setting in all three of these works—as a spatial translation of Agamben's concept of the threshold. The question, then, is how Dujovne Ortiz, Coutinho, and Urrea approach this setting.

In the case of *¿Quién mató a Diego Duarte?*, there are a few key passages that give the sense that the trash that dominates the book's setting is not defined by "a determinate concept or some actual property ... but *only by means of this bordering*" (67). Upon reading a conference presentation on solid waste management given by Alexandre Roig, a researcher with CONICET, Dujovne Ortiz offers the following reflection: "Paradojas, paradojas.... Basura-mierda, basura-tesoro, basura-cadáver: es como para preguntarse si cada cual no fantasea con su propio desecho, si no entabla una relación personal con lo que se sacude de encima, lleno de sentimientos ambiguos: ¿darle vuelta la cara, horrorizado, o volverse a mirarlo con una suerte de nostalgia?" (Paradoxes, paradoxes.... Trash-shit, trash-treasure, trash-cadaver: it's enough to make you wonder whether we all fantasize about our own waste, whether we establish a personal relationship with what we get rid of, full of ambiguous feelings: Do we turn away with horror, or look back at it with some kind of nostalgia?) (2010, 109–10). Toward the beginning of the book, she wonders at the way trash slips between determinacy and indeterminacy: when items that have been deemed no longer useful are thrown "en la bolsa mezclándolas entre sí," they become "lo desechable ... una masa indiscernible [y] desdeñable" (in the bag all mixed together [they become] disposable ... an indiscernible [and] detestable mass), but they are at the same time concrete, particular items, "fragmentos de algo que ya había servido, que podía volver a servir y que no se llamaba desperdicios sino botella, caja de zapatos, envase de yogur" (fragments of something that had been useful, that could be become useful once more and that wasn't called waste but rather bottle, shoebox, yogurt container) (13–14).

This ambiguous, borderline material is, quite literally, the foundation of the community of trash workers in José León Suárez with which she comes into contact. This is true not only in the sense that the livelihoods of Lalo, Lorena, Raúl, Alicia, and the other *suarenses* she meets in the process of writing her book depend on trash, but also, as Dujovne Ortiz reminds the reader time and again, because "José León Suárez fue construido sobre un basural" (José León Suárez was built on a garbage dump) (20). In an interview with Lorena, a woman who runs a recycling center in the CEAMSE facility, she learns that the low-lying part of the Río Reconquista watershed, where most of the garbage workers live, served historically as trash dump, and, despite inhabitants' best efforts to cover the dump with soil, the periodic floods to which the area is prone tend to unearth buried trash all around people's homes (65–73). As Dujovne Ortiz quips after traversing the rough, uneven ground of a neighborhood in José León Suárez with some difficulty, "rellenar un basural con tierra no asegura el pulido, la lisura, el acabado final" (filling in a dump with soil doesn't guarantee a polished, smooth, finished surface) (75). Taken as a whole, these passages underscore the way that Dujovne Ortiz characterizes the trash that imbues the setting of her book: it is not simply expelled material, but rather a site of ambiguity, unstable identity, and undecidability.

Boca de Lixo also highlights the threshold quality of the trash that serves as the film's setting, principally through the way that the Itaoca garbage dump is shot. As David William Foster has noted, the importance of trash in *Boca de Lixo* "is reinforced by the production decision to make use of expensive photographic resources to capture it in high-definition color. There is here none of the distancing effect of traditional black and white and often grainy documentary filmmaking, a distancing effect commonly driven by the fact that the viewers are presumed not to be sharing the social subjectivity of what is being documented" (2009, 160). This full-color depiction of the dump is put to good use from the very beginning of the documentary. The first shot is a close-up of trash, but it is not taken by a stationary camera that would allow us to take in and process what we are seeing; instead, this opening shot has been edited in such a way that it begins with the camera already in motion. So before the viewer has the chance to digest the first frame, the camera has moved on to another piece of the garbage patchwork. Coutinho returns to this type of shot a few more times during the documentary, and the effect is always the same: it is jarring and disorienting. Despite the fact that we have realized that we are looking at trash, the vertiginous movements of the camera do not allow us to identify any particular item, which reinforces the impression that trash is an amorphous, generalized substance.

On the other hand, there are moments during the film when the movement of the camera is slower as it records various pieces of trash in the landfill. These sequences are much more contemplative and static, and they lack the frenetic quality of the shots described above. During these moments, the camera lingers on certain items, inviting us to contemplate them in their particularity. We see, for instance, an assortment of shoes, a rotten chicken swarming with flies, a squished globe, and used syringes. These two ways of filming the trash in the dump are best understood in dialogue with each other, for, taken together, they assert that trash—and by extension the setting of the landfill—does not hold predetermined definitional properties. It is not a general, amorphous mass or collection of particular things with their own inherent identity; rather, it seems to be neither of those things and both of them at the same time.

While the threshold quality of trash and the places it accumulates is certainly felt in ¿*Quién mató a Diego Duarte?* and *Boca de Lixo, By the Lake of Sleeping Children* offers a more sustained, aesthetically complex sense of trash thresholds both in and out of the dump. Throughout the text, Urrea continually highlights the tension between Tijuana's supposed location on a series of cultural, geographical, economic, and temporal peripheries and its centrality in his own life and the lives of the people he portrays in his book, in addition to, most importantly, its centrality as a key space for understanding the way the world works under the sway of neoliberalism. These tensions and contradictions are neatly translated into temporal terms, as in when Urrea declares, "It is still 1896 in Tijuana. And it is also 2025" (1996, 6). This kind of hyperbolic impossibility—a moment simply cannot pertain to both the nineteenth and the twenty-first centuries—gives expression to an unsettling truth: the present, which is the threshold between the past and future, contains both within it. Such a notion sheds light on Urrea's observations from what he calls the "*basura* fault line," another instantiation of the threshold (41). A passage describing the evolution of the *dompe* reads:

> Once a gaping Grand Canyon, it gradually filled with the endless glacier of trash until it rose, rose, swelling like a filling belly. The canyon filled and formed a flat plain, and the plain began to grow in bulldozed ramps, layers, sections, battlements. New American Garbology affected the basic Mexican nature of the place. From a disorderly sprawl of *basura* to a kind of Tower of Babel of refuse.
>
> Still, the poor Mexicans, transformed now by NAFTA into a kind of squadron of human tractors, made their way through the dump, lifting, sifting, bagging, hauling, carting, plucking, cutting, recycling. The original *dompe* rules, a set of ordinances that sprang up organically from the people who have to work in the garbage, prevailed. (40–41)

The dump is a liminal space of encounter for a number of opposing notions: the hollow canyon meets the swollen mountain of garbage, horizontality entwines with verticality, neoliberal technology confronts working human bodies that use age-old techniques, Spanish and English and the waste that they name blend into a discursive Tower of Babel and a material tower of trash. The conjunction of space and time that Urrea depicts is an attempt to capture the impossible: the liminal quality of both the border environment in general and the trash dump to which he constantly returns throughout the book and that is the space of encounter with the families, social workers, municipal employees, missionaries, and others who come and go in his episodic narrative involves a constant churn of attachments that form, dissolve, and form again.

By paying attention to the particular material qualities that trash possesses, Dujovne Ortiz, Coutinho, and Urrea develop formal strategies that highlight trash's limit qualities. Whether it be Dujovne Ortiz's meditations on the nature of trash that swerve away from the main thrust of her narrative (a murder investigation), Coutinho's contrasting modes of presenting trash onscreen that destabilize a univocal perspective on what waste signifies, or Urrea's wandering, episodic prose that maps trash's threshold quality onto a host of other experiences (the passage of time, living on the border, environmental degradation), all three take care to present the material reality of the communities they portray as contingent and in flux.

Communities beyond Identity

The next salient feature of the communities portrayed in these stories that linger in and around the dump is their irreducibility to fixed identities based on a binary of inclusion versus exclusion. As Agamben puts it, the community of whatever beings "is mediated not by any condition of belonging (being red, being Italian, being Communist) nor by the simple absence of conditions... but by belonging itself" (1993, 85). This is, in other words, "the idea of community that is based on the notion of belonging without identity. This is a community of singularities, fragments" (Devadas and Mummery 2007). Agamben's idea of belonging without identity means that community is not a previously constituted social arrangement in which people passively participate, but rather it is constantly elaborated through activity: "As an activity, community calls for the opening up of other possible and potential networks of relations, of living and being with others. In that sense, as activity, community can be conceived as process, a battle or struggle to establish linkages, connections and relations even though the very impossibility of categorisation, of communities, continues to haunt the activity of community" (Devadas and Mummery 2007).

The idea of "community without community" (to use Vijay Devadas and Jane Mummery's turn of phrase) is one in which categories of identity matter less than contingent couplings, and the work of figuring out how to be together, how to make community, is the stuff of community itself. In this section, I would like to analyze the way this perspective on community comes to the fore in *¿Quién mató a Diego Duarte?* and *Boca de Lixo*. This is not to say that such a perspective is lacking in Urrea's book; it is simply more diffuse, and my wager is that dwelling on it would not provide a great deal of critical insight beyond what a closer look at Dujovne Ortiz's and Coutinho's works afford.[8]

For her part, Dujovne Ortiz fashions a discourse that chips away at the notion of preestablished, reified forms of community in favor of exploring solidarity among more contingent groupings of people. From the outset of her book, she foregrounds the strangeness of her establishing ties with the cartoneros and cirujas. Reflecting on an initial meeting with the core group of suarenses who would lead her down the path of investigating Diego Duarte's disappearance, she says, "Después me confesaron que todos se habían preguntado lo mismo: '¿Y esta mina de dónde sale?'. El interrogante se comprende, no tengo aspecto de militante setentista ni de ONG alemana ni de evangelista carismática ni de hermanita del Sagrado Corazón de nadie ni de señora bien. En el peor de los casos, lo inclasificable suscita desconfianza, y en el mejor, perplejidad" (Later they confessed that they had all asked themselves the same thing: "What's this lady's angle?" An understandable question, since I don't have the look of an activist from the seventies, or somebody from a German NGO, or an evangelical church member, or a Sister of the Sacred Heart of whoever, or a rich lady. In the worst case, the unclassifiable arouses mistrust, and in the best case, bewilderment) (2010, 12).

This "no tener aspecto de"—or as she puts it elsewhere in the book, "no dar el perfil de"—is very suggestive in terms of the way that it recognizes traditional forms of community that engage with the poor and marginalized (religious or political organizations, NGOs, good-hearted wealthy people), while dismissing them as the foundation for the relationship that Dujovne Ortiz hopes to establish with the people she meets from José León Suárez. Instead, that relationship is one that arises out of contingency and a desire to establish linkages across the divide of traditional class identities. In this sense, Dujovne Ortiz's own reflection on her initial idea of the project that would eventually turn into *¿Quién mató a Diego Duarte?* is enlightening. In her telling, the idea dates back to the 1990s, when she first happened to see cartoneros collecting trash in the streets of Buenos Aires. She tells of her desire to talk to them and ask them about their lives; however, this initial encounter was frustrated: "Al menos por el momento, con ellos mismos parecía imposible detenerse a echar un parrafito: mi timidez inmigratoria—ese convencimiento de ser sapo de otro pozo en todo sitio y país—y su concentración en la tarea nos volvían mutuamente inabordables. Por pudor, por respeto, por cobardía, imité su actitud y miré hacia otro lado. Puesto que ellos empujaban sus carros y revolvían en la basura sin levantar la vista, como si anduvieran por adentro de un túnel que los volviera inexistentes a ojos de los demás, deduje que no querían ser mirados. El tabique invisible entre 'ellos' y 'nosotros'—su mera presencia en la calle nos oponía—estaba hecho de párpados" (For the time being at least, it seemed impossible to stop and exchange a few words with them: my immigrant's timidity—that conviction of being a fish out of water in any place or country—and their focus on their work made us mutually unapproachable. Out of shyness, out of respect, out of cowardice, I imitated their behavior and looked away. Since they were pushing their carts and digging through the trash without looking up, as if walking through a tunnel that made them cease to exist in the eyes of others, I supposed they didn't want to be looked at. The invisible partition between "them" and "us"—their mere presence in the street resisted us—was made of eyelids) (13). Despite this initial failure at establishing a dialogue, the question of what connected her to the people who handled her garbage remained with Dujovne Ortiz and eventually compelled her to step through that "tabique hecho de párpados" (partition made of eyelids) and connect with a cartonero she saw on the street. This conversation and the ones that followed it over the span of almost ten years eventually led to the meeting with members of different cartonero cooperatives with which the book opens (14–16). It was only through the series of people she met and the connections that they formed that she even found out about Diego Duarte, as she mentions various times in the book (11, 34).

In addition to the way Dujovne Ortiz highlights the contingency that grounds her interactions with the community of trash workers in José León Suárez, she captures several moments of the process of making community that Devadas and Mummery identify as central to Agamben's thinking, two of which I will mention here. The first comes when she is spending the afternoon in the home of Alicia, Diego's sister. The two are about to drink *yerba mate*, and Dujovne Ortiz writes, "Sólo cuando [Alicia] me ceba el mate me doy cuenta cabal: estamos encima de la basura y cerca del [Río] Reconquista mezclado con el juguito de CEAMSE que contamina la napa. Pero si hay algo sagrado, es que el agua del mate no debe hervir. Me entrego" (Only when [Alicia] steeps the *mate* for me do I realize it: we're on top of trash and close to the Reconquista [River], mixed with the juices from CEAMSE that contaminate the groundwater. But if anything is sacred, it's that water for *mate* must not reach the boiling point. I give in) (79). What is interesting about this moment is the way that it manages to blur the lines between a traditional sense of community and one based on contingency and the act of being together. On the one hand, the two women seem to be affirming the idea of belonging to an imagined community that employs strict ritualistic practices (steeping yerba mate in water that has been heated to a temperature short of the boiling point, for instance) to define the core of national identity. However, the scene also stages the way in which this sacred ritual of *argentinidad* is effectively trashed by the specific circumstances of this instantiation. When Dujovne Ortiz realizes that the unboiled water used to steep the tea she is about to drink is contaminated by the trash that surrounds the home in which she is sitting, the *cebada de mate* becomes less linked to Argentine identity and is instead reconfigured as an encounter between two women who are engaged in the work of forging a connection grounded in the circumstances in which they find themselves.

The other instance of the process of making community that I will briefly mention here appears toward the end of the book. Lalo, a third-generation ciruja and one of Dujovne Ortiz's first friends in José León Suárez, invites her to participate in a literary workshop that inmates at the San Martín Prison in the Buenos Aires suburb want to get off the ground. Dujovne Ortiz dedicates an entire chapter to retelling her visits to the prison and her interactions with the more than ninety inmates participating in the workshop. They tell her their stories, share their poetry, and collectively make cartonera books with the works they have written. Dujovne Ortiz includes fragments of several inmates' poems (along with the full name of each author) in her own book and comments on the literary community that these men have cobbled together. This community's ethos is best summed up by Mosquito, one of the writers, whom Dujovne Ortiz quotes talking about the reasoning behind the workshop's name, *la flor del loto*: "'Todo esto es barro y basura. Suárez siempre fue un basural, acá tiraron a los fusilados del '56, acá la gente come las sobras de los demás. La cárcel también está hecha sobre la basura, y nuestras vidas son igual, basura. Pero como la flor del loto crece en el barro . . . por eso digo'" (All this is muck and trash. Suárez was always a trash dump, the ones who were executed in '56 got thrown away here, here people eat everyone else's scraps. The jail's also built on the trash, and our lives are the same thing, trash. But just like the lotus flower that grows in the muck . . . that's what I mean) (2010, 158). Once again, this focus on the intersection of contingent belonging (exemplified by the haphazard intersection of the life trajectories of people who occupy space together in a prison), on the active forging of connections (in this case, ones that arise from artistic expression), and on trash (in both metaphoric and literal terms) provides an evocative reflection on the stance toward community evident in the pages of Dujovne Ortiz's book.

Boca de Lixo exhibits a similar perspective regarding community as arising from a shared effort to be together instead of static, reified notions of identity. First, the documentary shows the way that the people who work in the dump, much like the trash that seems to end up there without rhyme or reason, arrive at that destination as a result of the vagaries of life and not as a result of some overarching manifestation of teleology. On the one hand, there is a man who explains that his time working in the landfill is highly sporadic and contingent upon other employment opportunities, so he may be absent from the dump for weeks or months at a time; on the other hand, there are people who have lived and worked in the dump since they were children. There are even Jurema and Flávio, a couple who met working in the dump and are happily raising their family of seven children on the living they make scavenging. Overall, Coutinho's documentary transmits the sense that the catadores find dignity in the activities that bring them together and that help them provide a life for themselves, their families, and their loved ones. Woven into the interviews that structure the film is footage of these people engaged in the everyday activities that link people to one another. Along with the work of scavenging and sorting trash, we see people preparing and eating food in groups, men and women in conversation, a man and a boy playing soccer, and an adolescent girl singing *sertaneja* music along with the radio, all in the middle of a landfill. These are activities that do not ever seem to begin or end, nor do they respond to a purpose other than to find a way of making community in the midst of mountains of detritus. When Coutinho asks Enock, an older catador, whether trash has a role to play in the rhythm of life, he responds, "Faz parte da vida. É o final do serviço o lixo. É ali o final e é dali que começa . . . . O final do serviço é que é a limpeza da casa e se joga fora o que desprezou, reciclou, findou ali mas ele continua ali. E dali sai para continuar e continuar mais longe ainda" (It's part of life. It's the end of usefulness, trash is. It's the end and it's where it starts . . . . The end of usefulness is when the house gets cleaned and you throw out what got ignored, recycled, finished, but it continues there. And from there it goes on to continue and continue even further) (Coutinho 1993). The rootless, continuous movement of trash that Enock describes is also mapped onto life and sociality, and Coutinho's camera manages to capture both the beauty and difficulty of that movement.

What is more, Coutinho conceives of his own connection to this community of catadores as one that "is mediated . . . by belonging itself" (Agamben 1993, 85). In a presentation he gave on alterity and documentary filmmaking, Coutinho made the following remarks about his work on *Boca de Lixo*, among other films: "Tento ser digno da confiança que essa comunidade depositou em mim, quer dizer, eu me sinto responsável diante dessa comunidade e não diante da classe camponesa, da classe dos favelados, etc. É evidente que me sinto responsável por aquela favela, por aquelas pessoas do lixo que filmei. Obviamente se é uma imagem decente que eu transmito deles, suponho que vou ser fiel também a uma relação com os favelados em geral, com as pessoas do lixo em geral, etc., mas o importante são aquelas pessoas que têm nome; não é uma confiança de classe desencarnada, é encarnada em pessoas que foram gentis comigo" (I try to be worthy of the trust that that community put in me, that is, I feel a responsibility toward that community, not to the peasant class, the *favela* class, etc. Clearly, I feel a responsibility toward that favela, toward the people in the garbage dump I filmed. Obviously, if the image of them that I transmit is a decent one, I suppose I'm being faithful to a commitment to people from favelas in general, to people in garbage dumps in general, etc., but what's important are the people who have names; it's not a disembodied kind of trust, it's embodied in people who have been kind to me) (1997, 170). What Coutinho is talking about here is a clear distillation of Agamben's thinking: a community that is not based on preconceived general identity categories arises from relationships that find embodiment in expressions of solidarity among people who happen to find themselves together. Such an ethos is evident in all three of these works of nonfiction.

Representing the Unrepresentable

The final aspect that links the communities of trash workers in Buenos Aires, São Gonçalo, and Tijuana is that they are "without either representation or possible description"; in other words, they are examples of "an absolutely unrepresentable community" (Agamben 1993, 24–25). Perhaps it seems strange, and even paradoxical, to analyze these works of nonfiction, which are quite obviously representations of real communities, within the framework of Agamben's thought if, for him, community-without-identity is "absolutely unrepresentable." But just as paradox cuts both ways (it can be either a seemingly sound proposition that leads to a self-contradiction or a seemingly self-contradictory proposition that is actually well founded), I would argue that it is possible to talk about the representation of this "unrepresentable" form of community. In order to do so, I should be clear about what I mean by "representation." *¿Quién mató a Diego Duarte?*, *Boca de Lixo*, and *By the Lake of Sleeping Children* are unavoidably descriptions or representations in that they portray communities of people who work with trash in and around Buenos Aires, São Gonçalo, and Tijuana, as well as the relationships between those communities and the authors and director who portray them. It is precisely in the way that Dujovne Ortiz, Coutinho, and Urrea handle the latter dynamic—their own involvement in the representational process—that they manage to problematize the assumption that the communities they attempt to represent in their works are transparent objects of representation. In other words, if we take "representation" to mean not only the portrayal of, but also the act of standing up for or speaking for the cartoneros, cirujas, catadores, and pickers in these texts, then we can see that all three creators deploy formal techniques that point up the ultimate impossibility of representing the communities with which they engage.

From the outset of *By the Lake of Sleeping Children*, Urrea posits his own split identity (as a Mexican, as an American, as a Mexican American) and his childhood in Tijuana and San Diego as occurring in liminal zones or thresholds between different cultural, affective, and geographic categories. For him, the border is a barbed-wire fence that neatly bisects his heart (1996, 4), a phenomenon that simultaneously gathers him into and excludes him from multiple political and social categories, while it serves as the basis for the voice he cultivates in his writing. His authorial subjectivity is grounded in an in-between space that never allows the reader to forget that the representation of the Other that they are reading about is articulated from unstable, shifting grounds. The formal techniques evident in his description of the dump that I analyze above (the accumulation of antitheses and a narrative perspective that allow for the contemplation of distended time periods and environmental transformations) generate and sustain Urrea's complex approach toward the ethical, political, economic, and ecological injustices experienced by the community that he engages with. These stakes always seem to lead back to the dump, that ultimate threshold space that exists precariously between past and future, nature and culture, life and death. In an especially horrific sequence, Urrea recounts how recent flooding had unearthed the remains of a number of children who had been buried next to the dump, creating a lake of sorts (this is the "lake of sleeping children" that gives the book its title). Such a scene is hard to stomach, but Urrea forces the reader to confront it and consider their own part in bringing it about when he says, "Swim in this lake for a minute.... Jump in—you own it: it's Lake NAFTA" (46).

A subsequent vignette in which he tells a story about the dump, opens with "Imagine this" (49), a command that invites us as readers to activate our imaginations; at the end of the episode, he concludes with the rhetorical question, "Can you imagine such a scene?" (51), as a way of underscoring the generalized inability to imagine, understand, or identify with what has been told. This command and this question ("Imagine this . . ."; "Can you imagine such a scene?") are key rhetorical elements for framing all of the book's scenes of the dump and its role in the life, economy, and nature of the border. In this sense, by simultaneously commanding us to enact our imaginative faculties and calling them into question, Urrea signals the representational limits of the scenes he narrates, his ability to narrate them, and our ability to perceive them. It is an invocation of an unrepresentable community. By the same token, however, it is only through attempting to tell the story (and listen to it) that we can glimpse the thresholds that bind us.

With regard to *¿Quién mató a Diego Duarte?*, Dujovne Ortiz frustrates the facile, unreflecting brand of representation in which a book about marginalized populations who scavenge trash in landfills could easily engage. This is particularly evident in the way that she writes about Alicia González, Diego's sister, who is the person with whom Dujovne Ortiz develops the closest relationship in the process of investigating Diego's disappearance and writing her book. A moderately attentive reader would quickly realize that they share the same first name, and since Alicia González ends up being a central character in Alicia Dujovne Ortiz's book, it certainly would not be too outlandish to imagine the author using this coincidence as a way to bolster her authority to represent Alicia González (and, by extension, her story and those that have a stake in it) textually. In other words, although it is obvious that they are two different people, the fact that they share a name could serve as a subtle suggestion that Alicia the author is in a position *to stand for* or *speak for* Alicia the character. At times, it seems like Dujovne Ortiz does just that, but she ultimately undermines this gesture in order to highlight her fundamental inability to reduce Alicia and the other suarenses she writes about to a textual representation.

A clear example of this feigned gesture toward transparent representation comes when Dujovne Ortiz accepts an invitation from Alicia to attend a neighborhood *asado* to celebrate May Day. Dujovne Ortiz notes that in Costa Esperanza, where Alicia lives, "[h]ace más calor que en Buenos Aires" (it's hotter than in Buenos Aires) and that the sweater and boots she is wearing were a foolish choice (2010, 75). Alicia lends her a T-shirt and sandals so she will be more comfortable, and Dujovne Ortiz's narrative voice takes stock of Alicia's house: "La casa se compone del dormitorio de Alicia, *donde me visto de ella*, y de una cocina" (The house is made up of Alicia's bedroom, *where I dress up as her*, and a kitchen) (75–76; emphasis mine). After dressing as Alicia, Dujovne Ortiz notices a paper pinned to the wall:

> Pinchados con dos chinches, un par de versos:
> *Que brille el entendimiento,*
> *la justicia y la razón.*
> *Que las pague el que las hizo,*
> *también quien lo permitió.*
> La firma, Francisco Urondo, me hace dar un respingo.
> "¡Paco!" exclamo. "Éramos amigos, bueno, lo conocía, lo mataron,
>   ¿de dónde sacaste ese poema?"
> "No sé, lo vi por ahí y me gustó."
>
> (Pinned up with two tacks, a couple lines of poetry:
> *May understanding shine forth,*
> *and justice and reason.*
> *May he who made them pay for it,*
> *as well as he who allowed it.*
> The author's name, Francisco Urondo, made me jump.
> "Paco!" I exclaim. "We were friends, well, I knew him, he was killed.
>   Where did you get that poem?"
> "I don't know. I saw it somewhere and liked it.") (76)

Here we see two moments in which it could be said that Dujovne Ortiz is trying to emphasize that the similarities between the two Alicias are more than mere coincidence: she does not simply wear Alicia's clothes, *she dresses up as Alicia*; also, the poem on the wall seems to be presented as an uncanny connection between the two. However, this gesture is undercut in several ways. Despite the apparent connection that Francisco Urondo's poem establishes between the two, their exchange regarding the text underscores an irreducible difference: for Alicia Dujovne, the poem is linked to its author and her friendship with him. Alicia González, on the other hand, pays no heed to the authorial position from which the poem is uttered; rather, its importance lies in the fact that she happened to find it somewhere, and she liked it. The suggestion that the similarities between the two women authorize Dujovne Ortiz to speak for González erodes further when Alicia and Alicia go to the asado. Dujovne Ortiz is overtaken by "una timidez paralizante" (a paralyzing shyness) (77) and begins to feel acutely that, despite wearing Alicia's T-shirt, she is very different from Diego's sister, who takes charge of organizing a bingo to raise funds for the cooperative she runs with verve and joy: "se goza su papel, ejerce la monarquía con bondad" (she enjoys her role, she practices monarchy with kindness) (79). Finally, any lingering notion that Dujovne Ortiz is leveraging coincidences between her and Alicia González like the ones mentioned above is done away with completely when she is reading through some files associated with Diego's case: "Víctima o denunciante: Duarte Diego Miguel, González Carmen Alicia—la condición especular me anonada: yo me llamo al revés, Alicia Carmen" (Victim or accuser: Duarte Diego Miguel, González Carmen Alicia—the mirror image stuns me: I have the same name, only the other way around, Alicia Carmen) (116). This astonishing specularity is, ultimately, just an *espejismo*, a mirage that troubles Dujovne Ortiz's ability to represent Alicia, Diego's case, and the community with which she connects, because from this point on, the book focuses on trying to figure out what happened to Diego that night in the CEAMSE facility, which proves to be as impossible to reduce to narrative prose as it is to find the body of a boy who was thrown out with the trash.

If Dujovne Ortiz resorts to foregrounding the false specularity at play in her work, in *Boca de Lixo*, Coutinho and his film crew use their presence and the presence of their filming equipment to call into question their ability to represent the community of catadores in Itaoca in a cinematic translation of Urrea's simultaneous invocation of and provocation against the powers of representation. Throughout the documentary, the presence of the film crew is felt in that they are both seen and heard, whether it be Coutinho's voice coming from out of frame to ask questions of the scavengers, a boom microphone dipping into view, or footage of members of the crew following people around and trying to film them as they pick through the trash. Regarding the metafilmic impact of such moments in *Boca de Lixo*, Foster argues that

> what is important is that, in order for the spectator to see Coutinho's assistants doing their best to jockey themselves into an advantageous position to report the operations of the dump, it is necessary to have yet another crew filming the first crew . . . . Such a practice has a double effect. On the one hand, it affords the viewers the impression that . . . they stand in direct relationship to the scene itself, as though they were standing next to the director himself rather than watching a projection screen. Yet paradoxically, it is as though the foregrounded crew were there to remind viewers that what they are seeing is, if not a staged reality, a reality mediated by the presence of the film crew, which vies with the scavengers for access to a front-row position with the object of attention of both groups, the garbage that has just been dumped out before them. (2009, 159)

So, the intermittent presence of the film crew onscreen serves to foreground the act of representation that is taking place, which in turn causes the viewer to reflect on the fact that, despite Coutinho's best efforts, he is unable to represent the actual lived reality of the socialities that emerge from the threshold zone of the landfill.

This foregrounding of the representational process that serves to question that very process is on display in a different form at the end of the film. One of the last scenes we see is of the catadores gathered around television monitors in the landfill viewing segments of the film that we have just seen. They see themselves portrayed onscreen in the very setting that they occupy as viewers. Both Coutinho himself (1997, 170) and Foster (2009, 164) emphasize the ethical dimensions of this gesture: allowing the catadores to see the way that the camera has captured them amounts to involving them in the process of documenting their lives. While I agree that there is a strong ethical element in this gesture of returning the image to the subjects of the documentary, I would like to move beyond that recognition and argue that this gesture also contains a commentary on the limits of representation. As the scavengers watch the footage, shots of their faces gazing into the monitors are crosscut with shots of the monitors displaying faces of catadores looking directly into the camera. This editing choice creates a vertiginous *mise en abîme* of spectating, of consuming filmic representation in which we as the viewers might end up questioning who is viewing whom. To my mind, this moment of hyperreflexivity simultaneously succeeds and fails. That is to say, it succeeds at signaling Coutinho's failure, his inability to truly represent the community that is the subject of his documentary.

In the end, all three works exhibit the same brand of successful failure. Dujovne Ortiz, Coutinho, and Urrea turn their attention toward the threshold zone of the landfill and the lives of those who inhabit it in an attempt to portray them not as social outcasts or pathetic victims, but rather as people who struggle to make community. But these artists also foreground their own contingent entanglements with these communities, signaling the representational limits of their art forms vis-à-vis the socialities that emerge from the dump. Those limits, I think, are a point of entry for reflection on what it means to be human in the context of a world irrevocably marked by the trash that we produce, reflection that is of a piece with the consideration of how trash's threshold quality draws our attention to the limit between the human and the animal undertaken in this book's first chapter.

In that chapter, I suggested that looking for the points where ecocriticism and biopolitics intersect is a crucial part of highlighting the importance of materiality in the way that we think about our interactions with the environment. After seeing those points of contact in the works that I have discussed in this chapter, I would add that this type of analysis also serves as a call to reflect on how to include radical difference as a part of the way we think about what it means to be human. Serenella Iovino has argued that an ecocritical humanism would be an ethical vision of culture that explores the "wilderness zones" that are traditionally held to be *opposed to* the human as elements that are really *part of* human experience (2010, 54–55). Trash, a substance that we so often send away from ourselves with little or no thought, is, in this sense, an integral part of humanity in the broadest, most multiple of senses: it emerges as part of the animality that is within and outside of us, and as part of communities we inhabit with each other and with the more-than-human world.

3

Trash Works

On the Limits of Waste Management

Shortly before his death in 1959, the great Mexican writer Alfonso Reyes wrote a brief text about municipal waste collection called "La basura."[1] In three short paragraphs that amount to a single printed page, Reyes sketches a vignette that captures the moment when the garbage truck passes by on a city street, and the trash collectors gather the cans lining the edge of the pavement, dumping their contents into the back of the truck before moving along to continue their route. This is an unremarkable moment if ever there was one, but Reyes's keen eye and prodigious prose transform it into a sensuous event that offers a glimpse of the inner workings of the universe itself. More than mere municipal employees, "[l]os Caballeros de la Basura, escoba en ristre, desfilan al son de una campanilla, como el Viático en España, acompañando ese monumento, ese carro alegórico, donde van juntando los desperdicios de la ciudad" (the Knights of the Trash, brooms at the ready, march to the tinkling of a bell, like the *viaticum* in Spain, alongside that monument, that allegorical float where they gather together the city's waste) (1970, 162). For Reyes, the garbage truck is an object lesson on display for the city's inhabitants, and the bell that announces its presence rings out with the same urgency and sacred authority as the bell that would accompany a priest marching through the streets of a Spanish city on his way to administer the sacrament of the last rites. In other words, waste management is a matter of life and death, as well as a meeting point of the profane and the sacred. The "muchedumbre famularia—mujeres con aire de códice azteca" (crowd of servants—women with something of an Aztec codex about them) dutifully participate in this daily ritual, "acarreando su tributo en cestas y botes" (carrying their tribute in baskets and cans) (162). Together, the *Caballeros de la Basura* and the *muchedumbre famularia* wield their brooms and baskets in a battle against litter in the streets and in domestic spaces, respectively.

But the martial image of the Knights of the Trash working together with an "afán del aseo" (zeal for tidiness) gives way to a more intriguing articulation of acceptance and celebration of the messy materiality of trash (162). The narrator of this vignette takes notice of one trash collector in particular, who stops his work for a moment with a look of ecstatic epiphany dawning across his face: "Lo ha entendido todo, o de repente se han apoderado de él los ángeles y, sin que él lo sepa, sin que nadie se percate más que yo, abre la boca irresponsable como el mascarón de la fuente, y se le sale por la boca, a chorro continuo, algo como un poema de Lucrecio sobre la naturaleza de las cosas, de las cosas hechas con la basura, con el desperdicio y el polvo de sí mismas" (He has understood everything, or the angels have suddenly seized control of him, and, without him knowing, without anyone realizing but me, he opens his irresponsible mouth like the mascaron of a fountain, and from it bursts forth an unbroken stream, something like a poem of Lucretius on the nature of things, things made with trash, with their very own waste and dust) (162). The epiphany of the trash collector (or perhaps the epiphany that the authorial persona projects onto him) is that the world is constantly done and undone by and because of trash. For making this fundamental truth manifest, the trash collectors deserve our attention and respect, for as Reyes tersely puts it at the end of "La basura," when the trash truck rolls by, "[d]ebiéramos arrodillarnos todos" (we should all bend the knee) (162).

In this brief glimpse of city life, Reyes transforms the banal, repetitive phenomenon of trash collection into a ritual full of meaning by infusing the scene with the trappings of ceremony and literary discourse. The nods to Roman Catholic and Aztec traditions, along with both Latin and Greek literature (in addition to mentioning Lucretius, Reyes compares the flow of garbage to Penelope's weaving) elevate trash to a level of timeless, universal import. At the core of this trash rhapsody is a deep appreciation for the work connected to trash and the workers who undertake it. This vignette portrays waste management as a harbinger of plenitude, balance, and epiphany, a key to realizing the vital materiality buzzing all around us.[2] It is a dazzling, charming sketch of linguistic craft and seemingly effortless erudition (both hallmarks of Reyes's vast body of work) that proves the power that literary language has to open up moments of experience and infuse them with new meaning.

I begin this chapter by reflecting on Reyes's portrayal of waste management because it so elegantly evokes several of the issues that will be considered in the following pages. On the one hand, Reyes's vision of a world that is constantly made and unmade by and through waste is a recognition of the importance of trash as evidence of the materiality that links us all together, humans and nonhumans alike, in a mesh, to use Timothy Morton's terminology for the "nontotalizable, open-ended concatenation of interrelations that blur and confound boundaries at practically any level: between species, between the living and the non-living, between organism and environment" (2010, 275–76). On the other hand, his focus on labor is key. Above and beyond any agency that trash may exhibit or its role as an actant that exerts concrete effects, trash's thing-power is often mobilized in concert with human beings who come into contact with it, move it around, and do things with it (Bennett 2010, viii–ix). Not only does Reyes pay homage to the garbage collector; he also tacitly acknowledges the gendered division of labor that attends many standard waste management practices: in his accounting, women gather trash in the domestic sphere and take it to the curb, but it is the *caballeros*—both gentlemen and trash men, but always *men*—who take things from there, handling waste in the streets and shepherding it along to wherever it will end up. The gender dynamics of how trash work is portrayed in literature is a thread that I follow here, particularly in terms of how working with waste as a means of subsistence is mobilized in literary fiction as a way of exploring masculine subjectivity in the neoliberal era.

And what of the remarkably positive light in which Reyes casts his scene of garbage collection? Not only does he contemplate the basic transcorporeal nature of existence by paying heed to trash, the "polvo de la Creación" (dust of Creation);[3] but also he portrays the trash/human interface as a moment of exuberance and joy: "Hay un alboroto, un rumor de charla desordenada y hasta un aire carnavalesco. Todos, parece, están alegres; tal vez por la hora matinal, fresca y prometedora; tal vez por el afán del aseo, que comunica a los ánimos el contento de la virtud" (There is a racket, the sound of disorderly conversation and even a carnivalesque atmosphere. Everyone, it seems, is happy; maybe it is the early-morning hour, fresh and full of promise; maybe it is the zeal for tidiness, which conveys the contentment of virtue to the spirit) (1970, 162). This ecstatic recognition of trash as a signal of interconnectedness raises the question of how to conceive of what it means to come into contact with waste as a condition of employment and a means of survival. Does working with trash lead to epiphanies and the singing of Lucretian odes to materiality, as is does for the anonymous trash man in "La basura"? Or does that simply amount to a projection by the authorial subject who announces his presence in the vignette, as I speculate above? How an author depicts the effects of trash work on the trash worker matters because it marks a potential limit with regard to the kind of ethical world that a text imagines. Does the depiction of human contact with trash open the individual to a sense of his place in the world as part of an interconnected, material relationality, what Rosi Braidotti calls "the critical posthuman subject" (2013, 49)? Or does it reinforce "the cultural logic of universal Humanism," which is predicated upon rigid forms of binary logic and exclusion, anthropocentrism, and the mastery of nature (15)? I admit that Braidotti's concerns—as well as the broader notion of posthumanism altogether—may sit uncomfortably with Reyes's worldview in general and with the strain of his thinking in particular that is evident in "La basura." My point is not to turn Reyes into a posthumanist. Rather, my aim is to point out the curious way that trash and trash work provide an opening for seeing some of the concerns of posthumanism within the eminently humanist writing of a figure like Alfonso Reyes. His vignette, which indexes the social reality of statist modernization, still manages to prefigure some of the key questions raised in texts written under the sway of neoliberalism. While "La basura" sees waste management through decidedly more rose-colored glasses than more recent treatments of the topic (as will be evident in what follows), it inspires the key questions that I ask of those texts: How do novels and short stories portray the connection between trash and work? Who is portrayed doing trash work and what kinds of effects are wrought upon them, the spaces they inhabit, and the ways they make sense of the world? How do the stories about waste and work that authors choose to tell engage with or foreclose the possibility of embracing human vulnerability and taking responsibility for our relationships with the waste we produce?

These are the questions that will guide my exploration of several works of Latin American fiction from the 1990s and 2000s, a moment with remarkable political and aesthetic differences from that of Reyes, but that nonetheless provides a context in which several authors engage with elements that were already comprehended as important by the great Mexican writer in 1959. There are a number of works from this period that share some of the same basic characteristics: they are written by men and feature male protagonists whose contact with trash and waste management is a central element of both their own character development and the overall plot. What I am calling their "contact" with trash manifests itself in different ways: either they are waste workers from the outset of the story, or, through personal setbacks like downsizing, chronic unemployment, or domestic troubles (or some combination of these), they end up surrounding themselves with trash by scavenging and hoarding. This is a corpus of what I call *trash works*, a label that activates two meanings of the word "work" simultaneously: labor and aesthetic object. In other words, these are texts that are about trash work or waste management and they are works (of fiction) about trash. There are many such trash works, and here I focus on six texts from across the region. From Argentina, there are novels by César Aira (*La villa*, 2001) (*Shantytown*, 2013; translated by Chris Andrews), Sergio Chejfec (*El aire*, 1992) (*The Air*), and Andrés Neuman (*Bariloche*, 1999); from Central America, novels by Honduran-Salvadoran writer Horacio Castellanos Moya (*Baile con serpientes*, 1996) (*Dance with Snakes*, 2009; translated by Lee Paula Springer) and Costa Rican writer Fernando Contreras Castro (*Única mirando al mar*, 1993) (*Única Looking at the Sea*, 2017; translated by Elaine S. Brooks);[4] and from Mexico, a short story by Álvaro Enrigue ("Ultraje," from the collection *Hipotermia*, 2005) ("Outrage," from the collection *Hypothermia*, 2013; translated by Brendan Riley).[5]

All of these texts engage with a number of the crises that attend neoliberalism, ranging from economic instability and job insecurity to the affective and subjective ennui brought about by the so-called end of history, not to mention the environmental problems that arise from the inevitable outcome of ever-increasing rates of consumption: the production of trash and the question of what to do with it.[6] These two issues—waste and the work that is undertaken to deal with it—prove to be important elements in the representation and consideration of the experience of neoliberalism in the societies portrayed in these trash works, so in the next section, I delve into the texts themselves to see how they stage the encounter between trash and work.

Trash Works

In one way or another, the six texts I have proposed as trash works echo the basic features of Reyes's vignette "La basura": all of them focus on an individual's experience of the intersection of labor and trash, and they allow us, as readers, to consider what is at stake in that intersection and to imagine what the experience of close contact with garbage might mean for that individual. In order to tease out these elements, it will be most useful for me to proceed not by considering each trash work in isolation, but instead by analyzing a series of thematic concerns that shift in pertinence and intensity depending on the text in question. In other words, while the texts to be analyzed in this chapter share common ground, close attention needs to be paid to the differences in the way that they stage the encounter between trash and work and the implications that arise from those differences. As such, my analysis focuses on specific elements of one work at times, while on other occasions, I read multiple works in dialogue with each other on a particular question. What is more, certain works fade to the background or come to the fore in different moments of what follows, sometimes because of thematic relevance, and sometimes to avoid redundant analyses.

In concrete terms, my presentation of these trash works takes shape between the concepts of "management" and "care," two approaches to dealing with material waste that I glean from Chilean sociologist Sebastián Ureta's work on copper mines (and that I delve into in greater detail below). Broadly speaking, management frames waste as an apolitical problem to which technological fixes can be applied until it is ultimately resolved, while approaching waste from the perspective of care entails a clear recognition of human beings' profoundly vulnerable position in relation to the waste we produce and the world we inhabit in general. All six of the texts I consider in this chapter evince certain elements of the waste management framework, while at the same time signaling its limits through the way trash enacts ruptures in neoliberal rationality's brand of spatial and temporal dynamics. And two of the texts in particular—*La villa* and *Única mirando al mar*—offer glimpses of a different way of living and working with trash, an ethics of care that helps us to see beyond the limits of the mode of storytelling that predominates in these trash works.

In order to initiate my consideration of the part trash plays in these works and how work is folded into their plots, it will be useful for me to give a relatively detailed plot summary of each of the texts. This will allow me to show how these works relate to one another, while providing the added benefit of grounding the reader in the specifics of each story and giving clear reference points for the subsequent thematic analysis of the works that I sketch out. The six works I describe in detail below can be grouped into three categories in terms of the characteristics of their protagonists and the way they find themselves interacting with trash. *Bariloche* and "Ultraje" feature men who, at the beginning of their stories, are employed as municipal garbage men (that is, they are "formal" waste workers). *El aire* and *Baile con serpientes* have protagonists who are unemployed and end up inhabiting what we could call spaces of trash (while they are not waste workers strictly speaking, their relationship with trash stems from their lack of employment). The main characters in *La villa* and *Única mirando al mar* develop relationships with and, to one degree or another, work with scavengers, whether it be in city streets or a landfill (in other words, they are "informal" waste workers).[7]

Bariloche, Neuman's novel, tells the story of Demetrio Rota, a municipal garbage collector in Buenos Aires who picks up trash with his partner el Negro along the same route day after day.[8] He is increasingly disillusioned with his job, and his somewhat unorthodox actions while on the clock (piecing together fruit rinds or broken dolls he extracts from garbage bags and buying breakfast for a homeless man and giving him rides in the garbage truck, for instance) unnerve el Negro, causing him to worry about his workmate's mental and emotional well-being. When he is not working, Rota spends his time engaged in one of two pursuits: obsessively putting together jigsaw puzzles, all of which portray scenes of Nahuel Huapi Lake and the wooded areas surrounding the city of Bariloche (Rota's home town), and carrying on a rocky affair with el Negro's wife Verónica behind his partner's back. As the novel's fragmented narrative progresses, we piece together the connection between Rota's obsession with puzzles and his first sexual experience, which occurred by the shores of the lake, as well as the trauma brought about by his family's move from Bariloche to the Argentine capital after his father lost his job at a sawmill. The discrepancy between the idealized space represented by the jigsaw puzzles and the spaces that Rota inhabits in Buenos Aires triggers a deterioration in his mental state, and, at the novel's end, Rota quits his job and walks into the landfill, sinking into the waste of Buenos Aires.

The other portrayal of a municipal waste worker that we will examine here is that of Drake Horowitz, the protagonist of Enrigue's "Ultraje."[9] Unlike Neuman's Rota, Horowitz is not from Latin America: he was born and raised in Baltimore, Maryland, where he works as a trash collector.[10] However, much like Rota, Horowitz also suffers from both professional dissatisfaction and romantic troubles. On the professional front, he resents both the tedium of his work in waste management and the constraints the job places on his personal freedom. In order to cope with his professional discontent, he scavenges items that spark his interest from the curbside trash of the upper-class neighborhoods along his route (things like books, magazines, and video game consoles), often to the delight of his partner Verrazano and the chagrin of their superior, the unnamed *conductor* of the truck they work in day after day. Horowitz's desire for freedom is evoked by the narrator through a nautical simile comparing the highway to the high seas that opens the story and recurs with slight variations both partway through the text and at the end. The simile is a reflection of Horowitz's frame of mind, and he tries to bring the comparison to life through relatively minor gestures like riding down the highway hanging off the back of the truck (instead of sitting in the cab) and flying the Jolly Roger from the truck's antenna; however, his superior, citing company policy, refuses these requests, although he does allow Horowitz and Verrazano to name the truck and affix a sign to the rear end of the vessel with the name *Outrageous Fortune*, and he indulges Horowitz's insistence on employing a nautical lexicon (the truck is a ship, the sign goes on the stern, the doors are hatches, and so on). Horowitz's quirky approach to dealing with his job takes a serious, violent turn when his wife leaves him, absconding with the couple's young son and leaving behind bits of waste in their apartment that confirm that she was having an affair. This represents a breaking point for Horowitz, who takes a gun to work with the vague idea of tracking down his wife and killing her. However, when his boss laughs at the situation Horowitz's wife left him in, Horowitz attacks him and, with Verrazano opting to join him in this act of mutiny, leaves him tied up by the side of the road. Then, like two pirates roaming the sea in search of plunder, Horowitz and Verrazano drive around aimlessly, sowing "degradación y barbarie" (Enrigue 2005) ("barbarous depravity and cruelty") (Riley 2013, 77), as the narrator puts it. As their time and luck run out, knowing that they will soon be in police custody, Verrazano opts to turn himself in, but Horowitz seems to envision only one conclusion to his own story: that it should end in the briny deep. So he asks Verrazano to drive him to an abandoned marina where his father used to take him fishing, and our last glimpse of Horowitz has him riding on the back of the truck (hanging off the stern of the ship) en route to the sea.

Next, we have two novels featuring unemployed middle-class men, who, in one way or another, are compelled to follow the trajectory that trash takes as it circulates around the cities they inhabit. In Chejfec's novel, *El aire*, the protagonist is a man named Barroso, who returns home from work early one day because of a fire in his office building that effectively leaves him without a job.[11] This change in his daily routine allows him to be in his apartment the very moment when Benavente, his wife, slides a letter under the door telling him that she is leaving him. These two virtually simultaneous crises seem to almost freeze time for Barroso, or at least open it up in a way that makes it impossible for him to fill it with any sort of meaningful activity. The plot itself is rather thin: over the course of what seems to be several days, Barroso observes the ever-increasing amount of detritus that fills his apartment, and he wanders the streets of a Buenos Aires where glass has become money, and people dig through the trash to find bottles to pay for the things they want to buy. His meanderings frequently take him to ruined, abandoned pockets of the city that are strewn with litter, and his observations (which are captured by an extradiegetic narrator closely focalized through Barroso's subjectivity) revolve around questions of space and how it is quantified, as well as processes of material deterioration, such as the following meditation that follows on the heels of his attempts to tidy up some of the trash and muck in his apartment: "Según Barroso, el deterioro de los objetos tenía como objeto prefigurar el propio. Benavente, pensó, podía opinar distinto: que el deterioro de los objetos acompaña el propio. Para Barroso era previo no sólo por lo más obvio, por consistir en aquello percibido en primera instancia, sino porque su ruina ofrecía a los sentimientos la imagen aproximada y propia de la decadencia, similar a un espejo: aquello que antes había existido como una noción, repentinamente ahora y para siempre, al confrontarse con ellos, los sentimientos, pasaba a ser también una experiencia" (According to Barroso, the purpose of the deterioration of objects was to prefigure one's own deterioration. Benavente, he thought, might see it differently: the deterioration of objects accompanies one's own deterioration. For Barroso, one preceded the other not only for the most obvious reason that it had to do with what is perceived in the first instance, but also because an object's ruin offered the feelings an approximate and appropriate image of decadence, much like a mirror: what had existed previously as a notion, now suddenly and permanently, upon confronting them, the feelings, also became an experience) (Chejfec 1992, 31). The ontological hairsplitting evident in this passage is typical of the novel. Ultimately, however, it matters little whether it is Barroso who is right about the sequential, specular nature of the relationship between deteriorating things and people, or Benavente's idea that is true (as Barroso imagines it) that all people and things accompany each other in the process of decay. By the novel's end, what is important and unavoidable is the simple fact of material deterioration: the result of Barroso's feeble attempts to follow or track down his wife, his aimless wandering, and his efforts to deal with different kinds of waste (food scraps, old newspapers, glass bottles) ends with him alone in his bed, about to die.

In a departure from Chejfec's elliptical, ruminative prose, Castellanos Moya's *Baile con serpientes* is fast-paced and plot-driven.[12] The novel is divided into four parts. In the first and last parts, a young man named Eduardo Sosa tells his story: he is a recent university graduate with a degree in sociology, but he cannot find work and is forced to live with his sister and her husband in a cramped apartment. Listless and unoccupied, Eduardo spends most of his time at home, and one day, while looking out the window, he notices an old, beat-up yellow Chevrolet parked on the street outside his building. While the neighbors are scandalized by the presence of this hunk of junk, Eduardo is oddly fascinated by it and makes several halting attempts to befriend its owner and occupant: a man named Jacinto Bustillo, who is characterized as homeless, drunk, and filthy. Eduardo finally manages to strike up a conversation with Jacinto and subsequently accompanies him one day as he traverses the city scavenging trash cans and dump sites.[13] Eduardo learns that Jacinto, a former accountant, lost his job and family as the result of an office romance gone wrong and began to live out of the yellow Chevrolet that he fills with the junk that he finds on the street. At the end of the day, in an unexpected outburst of violence, Eduardo kills Jacinto, returns to the street where his car is parked, and decides to start living in it. He soon discovers four talking snakes living among the scavenged items in Jacinto's car, and he immediately develops a strange, magnetic connection with the serpents, which precipitates an odd transformation in Eduardo: somehow he becomes Jacinto, the erstwhile scavenger. As he puts it, "yo era el nuevo don Jacinto ... sintiéndome don Jacinto, pensando que la navaja cacha color hueso que portaba en mi bolsillo había sido una especie de escalpelo gracias al cual había abierto tremenda hendidura para penetrar al mundo en el que quería vivir" (Castellanos Moya 2012, 25) ("I was the new Don Jacinto ... feeling as if I were Don Jacinto, as if the pocket knife with the bone-colored handle were a kind of scalpel I'd used to make an enormous incision that allowed me to penetrate the world in which I wanted to live") (Springer 2009, 22–23). Following this moment of transformation, Eduardo/Jacinto and the snakes drive around San Salvador and, in a few short days, unleash a brutal and strange wave of violence that leaves dozens of people dead and mires the whole country in chaos. At the close of the novel, following an all-out assault by the police that reduces the yellow Chevrolet and the snakes to ash in a junkyard, Eduardo/Jacinto escapes, turns back into Eduardo, and returns to his sister's apartment unscathed. Bracketed between the first and last parts of the novel (which are narrated by Eduardo/Jacinto) are two chapters that narrate the attempts of the police and the press to investigate and make sense of the chaos and the destruction that Eduardo/Jacinto and his snakes have caused. Unsurprisingly, their attempts to uncover the truth of the case are ineffective.

The last two trash works that I would like to introduce have protagonists who combine certain characteristics evident in the previous two groupings: like *Bariloche* and "Ultraje," they feature people who engage in the work of municipal waste management in a way that is perhaps clearer than the protagonists of *El aire* and *Baile con serpientes*, but, like the main characters of the latter texts, they come into contact with trash work by way of unemployment and downsizing. Fernando Contreras Castro's *Única mirando al mar* gives us access to the story of a community of *buzos*, or garbage pickers, in the Río Azul landfill in San José, Costa Rica, through the perspective of Momboñombo Moñagallo, a former library security guard who was fired from the job he had held for twenty-six years after filing a complaint about an illegal scheme in which the library sold books by the ton to a private manufacturer of toilet paper.[14] Finding himself unemployed and alone, he throws himself into the back of a garbage truck in an act of what he calls "identicidio" (identicide) (1994, 24)—including shedding his given name and taking the comically difficult moniker he goes by throughout the novel—that eventually leads him to the Río Azul landfill and the community of scavengers that make a life there.[15] He is quickly taken under the wing of Única Oconitrillo, a former teacher who had been forced out of her own job in her early forties and who has a penchant for rescuing those who have been abandoned: years earlier, she had found a small child in the dump, started calling him El Bacán, and raised him. Over the course of the novel, these three become something of a family unit. As Momboñombo becomes more integrated into the community in the dump, he goes to some lengths to organize the buzos as they attempt to navigate a municipal waste workers' strike that cuts off their daily supply of material to scavenge; also, they face the closure of the dump due to the environmental threat it poses and its unwelcome presence in the surrounding community. The process for closing down the dump and finding an appropriate site for a new one constitutes something of a parallel plot with respect to the experiences of Momboñombo, Única, and the other buzos, and it hints at the corruption, ineptitude, and shortsightedness of all the parties involved in the management of municipal solid waste. Momboñombo's efforts at organizing take a tragic turn: after the police use a water cannon on the buzos during their march on the presidential palace to demand government assistance, El Bacán falls ill and eventually dies. Unable to cope with this loss, Única falls into a catatonic state, and Momboñombo decides to take her to Puntarenas, on the Pacific coast, so that she can be near the ocean. The novel ends with Momboñombo trying to eke out a living for the two of them by combing through the trash on the beach and selling things he scavenges to tourists.

Finally, in *La villa*, Aira presents us with Maxi, a young bodybuilder who lives in the Flores neighborhood of Buenos Aires close to a *villa miseria* or shantytown.[16] Maxi has abandoned his secondary education in the middle of his exams and has no interest in finding work, so he spends his days lifting weights and wandering around his neighborhood. One day, without ever knowing why, he starts putting his enormous muscles to use by helping the cirujas or cartoneros who roam his neighborhood at twilight with the heavy carts in which they collect trash and recyclable materials that they find in the street. Little by little, Maxi becomes a fixture in the cartoneros' work life, and his cart pulling takes him closer and closer to the shantytown where they live, a space that he finds increasingly fascinating. While all of this is occurring, Cabezas, a police inspector who suspects that the villa is the epicenter for the trafficking of an illegal drug called *proxidina*, becomes interested in Maxi's presence in the villa and his connection to the cartoneros. As a result of a frenzied chain of events that is very characteristic of Aira's slapdash approach to plot, Maxi, his sister, and one of his sister's friends get caught up in a police investigation that sets the stage for a reflection on police, judicial corruption, and the media-driven spectacularization of marginalized spaces like the villa miseria, where the inhabitants end up saving Maxi from the malicious designs of Inspector Cabezas.

The stories that these trash works tell about the people who work with waste can and should be read in light of the effects of the subordination of all spheres of life to the primacy of neoliberal rationality. Neoliberalism, as Wendy Brown puts it, "is best understood not simply as economic policy, but as a governing rationality that disseminates market values and metrics to every sphere of life and construes the human itself as a *homo oeconomicus*. Neoliberalism thus does not merely privatize—turn over to the market for individual production and consumption—what was formerly publicly supported and valued. Rather, it formulates everything, everywhere, in terms of capital investment and appreciation, including and especially humans themselves" (2015, 176). Neoliberal rationality's focus on the the individual—who is rational, self-sufficient, and autonomous—calls for individuals to be valued based on their ability to satisfy their own needs and desires through the marketplace as producers and consumers who have an equal opportunity to gain access to that marketplace; the ability (or inability) of individuals to do this is solely their responsibility, and any positive or negative consequences they experience simply amount to what they deserve for their actions (2009, 42). So according to this way of thinking, the fact that characters like Horowitz and Rota are unhappy in their dead-end jobs has a simple solution: they should try harder to get better ones. The situation of characters like Única, Momboñombo, Barroso, and Eduardo, while sad, is not an indictment of larger social systems or structures. Simply put, they have no one to blame but themselves for their troubles. Clearly, however, the point of these texts is not to offer cautionary tales of the pitfalls to avoid in order to be the best *homo oeconomicus* you can be. Instead, what they do is signal the violence and noxiousness of neoliberal rationality by calling into question the freedom that the free market affords the characters whose stories they tell. By focusing not on work in general, but on work with trash, what becomes apparent for almost all of these characters is that the freedom offered by the neoliberal paradigm that structures their lives—the freedom to dig through the trash—leaves them exposed to violence, danger, and death: *homo oeconomicus* meets *homo sacer*.

The work in these trash works serves to foreground a number of the outcomes of the implementation of neoliberal rationality: feelings of estrangement, the inadequacy of community as a form of protection from economic misfortune, and labor as a daily struggle for survival. In this sense, an argument can be made for reading the trash in these texts in primarily allegorical terms. In other words, the trash as such is not so important; it merely functions as part of an allegory of the harm neoliberalism has wrought across Latin America. In one way or another, all of these stories' protagonists are unable to deal with the ways that neoliberal rationality has captured and colonized all forms of social life, transforming them into a series of market strategies. They are stuck doing waste work as a result of the disintegration of local industries that spurs internal migration (Demetrio Rota in *Bariloche*), because they made the wrong professional moves (Jacinto Bustillo in *Baile con serpientes* and Momboñombo Moñagallo in *Única mirando al mar*), because their jobs disappeared into thin air (Barroso in *El aire*), or because there is simply no other option (Drake Horowitz in "Ultraje"). Alternatively, they end up following trash around because they have studied things like sociology, which makes them unattractive to the market (Eduardo in *Baile con serpientes*), or they lack the skills to compete on the market altogether (Maxi in *La villa*). In this sense, trash would simply be a stand-in for the extreme nature of neoliberal capitalism, on account of both its viscerally unattractive material qualities and the way that scavenging neatly expresses capitalism's drive to extract value from absolutely everything.

Such a "symptomatic" reading of this group of texts is by no means misguided; in fact, it strikes me as generative, especially if we recognize the masculinist nature of these works: they are written by men and feature male protagonists.[17] By this logic, what the trash in these works *really* is amounts to a way of contemplating the personal and professional crisis of masculinity in the neoliberal era. It is a symbol of how neoliberalism lays men low, unmooring them from their traditional roles and, in some cases, rendering them incapable as romantic or familial partners. Despite the insights that this interpretive framework could provide, paying short shrift to trash as such and the role it plays in these stories is shortsighted and reveals the limitations of a purely allegorical reading like the one that I have just sketched out. In these texts, as is the case for all the works I analyze in this book, trash *does* things; we could say that it *works*, to add a third meaning to the the expression "trash works."[18] Further, it creates effects and affects. In the case of the trash works that I have gathered together in this chapter, one of the things trash does is provoke affective responses in the characters who come into contact with it. As the plot summaries above indicate, these responses are typically negative and spell disaster to a greater or lesser extent. But in a couple of cases, the trash that the protagonists work with opens them up to new forms of community that are collective and relational, forms of community that evince "an enlarged sense of inter-connection between self and others, including the non-human or 'earth' others" that characterize a "posthuman ethics for a non-unitary subject" (Braidotti 2013, 49). In other words, paying attention to trash and its effects in these works allows us to see just how well their characters (and the narratives as a whole) cope with the posthuman condition. As theorists like Alaimo and Bennett contend, the human experience in the world is marked by transcorporeal flows of vibrant matter. Whether we recognize it or not, our condition is, as Braidotti would have it, posthuman. Put simply, my contention is that Latin American trash works, as I am defining them here, tend not to recognize fully the posthuman condition. To explore this idea, Sebastián Ureta's critique of waste management proves especially useful.

The editors of *Waste Management*, the academic journal devoted to this paradigm for dealing with solid waste, define waste management as "the generation, prevention, characterization, monitoring, treatment, handling, reuse and ultimate residual disposition of solid wastes" (Ureta 2016, 1533). It is meant to be an all-encompassing material practice that, as Ureta notes, sidesteps political concerns and presents itself as a series of technical solutions for addressing the production of waste that just keep getting better and better (1533). It is a quintessentially neoliberal outlook on the human relationship with materiality. For Ureta, the idea that waste can be managed in this sense is a fantasy, and he proposes the alternative of care as an approach for living and dealing with waste, an approach that I return to toward the end of this chapter. Management is a fantasy because it presupposes that the problem of waste can be solved through technical solutions that are usually presented as "utterly apolitical" (1533). This sort of depoliticization is dangerous because how waste is handled, who handles it, and where it goes is nothing if not political. But beyond the disavowal of waste's political valences and the concomitant erasure of the political struggles of those who come into closest contact with waste is an issue that clearly relates to the posthuman condition: "At the very center of the concept of management is the notion that the problems faced in WM [Waste Management] are ultimately 'soluble' once and for all, if the right tools are applied. . . . In most cases the solution is based on different materializations of the 'ultimate sink' principle . . . or the notion that the solution for the issue is to lock wastes in ever more sophisticated containers, in the hope that they will remain there forever" (1533). The "ultimate sink" may appear to be a comforting idea that allows us to confidently assume that the waste we produce is under control, that once we throw things out, matters like pollution, contamination, noxious smells, and the like are of no concern. The problem, though, is that no such perfect container for trash exists. "Waste in sinks is alive; it leaks and permeates barriers, transforming into different entities in the process: leachate, polluted water, toxins, etc." (1534).

The spatial and temporal elements central to Ureta's critique of waste management are noteworthy. Managing waste means keeping it in a certain place (preferably one that is *away*) for a certain amount of time (preferably *forever*). Both the spatial and temporal underpinnings of the philosophy of waste management raise fairly obvious questions. Away from whom should waste be kept? How can current forms of technology, which are constantly changing, make reliable promises about containing waste over the course of an uncertain future? The thorniness implied by answering these kinds of questions makes it easy to see the problems with waste management's self-presentation as a set of apolitical technical solutions that will always be at least a few steps ahead of the problems trash presents. To put it simply, it is an ethos based on the unquestioned assumption that we (human beings) are the masters of our environments, that we can control the spaces we inhabit and bend time to our will so that it conforms to our notions of progress. Trash, with all its unruliness and vibrancy, gives the lie to this kind of thinking. Latin American trash works allow us to explore the limits of mastery under which notions like waste management operate. All of the texts considered in this chapter present work with waste that adheres to a waste management paradigm, and, in doing so, they all reveal the shortcomings of that framework for dealing with the trash we produce. In some instances, as I have alluded to already, they show glimpses of another orientation toward trash, one that Ureta categorizes under the notion of care (and that resonates with the experience of Reyes's anonymous trash man in "La basura"). Before focusing on what those glimpses have to show us, however, I would like to consider how these trash works engage with the production of space in ways that question the assumptions of waste management and the neoliberal rationality that underpins it.

Trash and Space

In *The Production of Space*, Henri Lefebvre posits that space does not exist a priori; that is, it is not a preexisting dimension into which social actors step, but rather, space becomes constituted as the subject inhabits it, and, therefore, space itself is an ongoing manifestation of a process of signification in which the subjective experience of space is one and the same with the production thereof (1991, 17). This leads Lefebvre to theorize that the production of space is a dialectical process that occurs in the tensions and flows that arise among three spatial vertices: spatial practices (how space is perceived by those who inhabit it), representations of space (how space is conceived by the technicians that design and execute allocations of space), and representational spaces (how the inhabitants of a space appropriate and modify it by means of engaging with it on an imaginative-symbolic level) (33–39). These three elements—space as it is perceived, conceived, and lived—"should be interconnected, so that the 'subject,' the individual member of a given social group, may move from one to another without confusion—so much is a logical necessity. Whether they constitute a coherent whole is another matter. They probably do so only in favourable circumstances, when a common language, a consensus, and a code can be established" (40).

The common language, consensus, and code that Latin American trash works engage with is provided by neoliberal reason (Lefebvre uses the term *neocapitalism*), which attempts to produce space that privileges consumerism without the pesky obstructions of the waste that consumption always entails and the social and political issues that attach themselves to it. By this logic, the coherent production of space would depend on the smooth, frictionless removal of solid waste to secure containers, that is, spaces outside of or disconnected from consumers' experience of urban space. Simply put, this is the philosophy of waste management. At times, our trash works portray something that would seem to reflect just such a coherent, rational approach to waste removal. The smooth, almost unnoticeable flow of trash throughout the city is especially evident in *Bariloche* and *La villa*. In Neuman's novel, for example, Rota and el Negro go out every morning to pick up trash in the section of Buenos Aires that lies west of Puerto Madero, traveling through a zone delimited by Avenida Independencia, Paseo Colón, and 9 de Julio (1999, 15). The novel even details how they stop for breakfast every day at the same bar on Calle Bolívar (17).[19]

Aira's novel exhibits a similar concern with establishing the route traveled by the anonymous cirujas: "Venían de las populosas villas miseria del Bajo de Flores, y volvían a ellas con su botín" (2001, 13) ("They came from the crowded shantytowns in Lower Flores, to which they returned with their booty") (Andrews 2013, 7). In fact, Aira dedicates several pages to a detailed description of their daily trajectory as they walk through the streets, filling their homemade carts with materials they pick from other people's garbage: they leave the shantytown at sunset and head toward Plaza Flores, and from there they follow Avenida Rivadavia; then they travel the length of both Directorio and Bonorino before arriving back at the villa with their cargo (2001, 13–17; 2013, 7–11).

Besides the fact that Aira and Neuman describe the circulation of trash as a fluid movement among diverse pockets of urban space, both novels also emphasize the apparent invisibility of this material flow. In *Bariloche*, we are reminded time and again that Rota and el Negro do their job in the wee hours of the morning when the streets are empty and no one is there to notice them. Aira's narrator gives us a more explicit reflection on the naturalization of the phenomenon of garbage pickers: "La profesión de cartonero o ciruja se había venido instalando en la sociedad durante los últimos diez o quince años. A esta altura, ya no llamaba la atención. Se habían hecho invisibles, porque se movían con discreción, casi furtivos, de noche (y sólo durante un rato), y sobre todo porque se abrigaban en un pliegue de la vida que en general la gente prefiere no ver" (2001, 13) ("Cardboard collecting or scavenging had gradually established itself as an occupation over the previous ten or fifteen years. It was no longer a novelty. The collectors had become invisible because they operated discreetly, almost furtively, at night [and only for a while], but above all because they took refuge in a social recess that most people prefer to ignore") (2013, 7). By underscoring the efficiency with which trash travels through the city (whether it is collected by people hired by the city or not) and the banality of its circulation, Aira's and Neuman's novels manage to represent how waste management regimes participate in the production of coherent, cohesive urban spaces. To return to Lefebvre's terminology, waste management seems to help to strike a balance between the conceived space of city planners and the lived space of the city's residents. This gives us an image of the city as a rational system, a body or organism whose smooth operation depends on efficiently moving around or altogether eliminating trash.

Alas, that image of a city swept clean almost surreptitiously so that consumers can move about unobstructed is a mirage. As waste and workers come together and flow through the streets in these works, the neatly managed containment of trash that we see at the beginning of Aira's and Neuman's novels begins to break down. Opting to sidestep the detailed itineraries of trash collection at the beginnings of *La villa* and *Bariloche*, Enrigue and Contreras Castro suggest the difficulty of containing trash by resorting to maritime metaphors to open their texts. "Ultraje," Enrigue's story, begins by portraying the highway, a key piece of urban infrastructure, in terms of the open sea: "Una autopista puede ser como el mar. El sol ardiendo en la cara, la brisa que limpia las tuberías del sistema respiratorio, las manos aferradas a los barrotes en la cubierta de acero, el olor a podrido subiendo desde la sentina" (2005) ("A highway can be like the high seas. The sun burning on your face, the fresh cleansing breeze in your lungs, your hands tightly gripping the rails along the steel deck, the rotten stench rising from the bilge") (Riley 2013, 66). This figurative liquefying of the roadway that allows for the quick and easy transfer of trash from people's driveways to a landfill that is presumably out of sight and out of mind opens the door to the possibility of that trash exceeding its container, escaping, floating away. Indeed, the last sensory description in the story's opening passage seems to portend precisely such an eventuality. The source of the rotten smell emanating from the "ship's" bilge is obvious, as is the practical solution for dealing with it: it will inevitably be pumped out into the sea that is actually a highway but that, in any event, is not the secure ultimate sink that waste management professionals designed for it.

While "Ultraje" does not foreground this type of waste leakage and its potential impact on the urban environment, it does showcase how the encounter between waste worker and waste can destabilize waste management's notion of containment and the broader production of space under neoliberal rationality. The very idea of christening the garbage truck occurs to Horowitz and Verrazano only after seeing a *National Geographic* photo spread on trucks with catchy names painted on them in Latin America. Where did they get the magazine? Unsurprisingly, from the trash:

> La idea de bautizar al camión vino de una foto del National Geographic rescatada de una bolsa negra de polietileno. Todo llegaba así al bajel, como siguiendo el patrón de una marea secreta. Al cargar con la bolsa, el gordo Verrazano sintió el lastre del material impreso. La sopesó un momento, cargándola de arriba abajo tomada con el puño, los ojos entrecerrados y apretados los labios. Luego la depositó en el suelo, se puso en cuclillas y le dijo a su compañero mientras palpaba el contenido: Estos hijos de puta creen que pueden engañar a un hombre que ha recogido basura por quince años. Su olfato experto ponderaba los olores emanados del interior tras cada apretón: Son revistas—siguió—, recientes, en buen estado; perfectamente reciclables. No echó el paquete a la compresora. Ya en el camino de regreso a la planta abrió el bulto y vio que contenía catálogos y ejemplares del National Geographic. Nada de pornografía. (Enrigue 2005)

> (The idea of christening the truck came from a photo in a *National Geographic* they fished out of a black plastic garbage bag. All sorts of things drifted to their ship in that way, as if following the course of a secret tide. Hefting the trash bag, fat Verrazano noticed the dead ballast of printed material inside. He weighed it a moment, raising and lowering the bag clenched in his fist, eyes narrowed, lips drawn tight. Then he dropped it to the ground and squatted down, prodding and squeezing the contents: Those sons of bitches think they can fool a man who's been collecting trash for fifteen years! he said to his coworkers. After every squeeze his expert nose pondered the smells emanating from the bag: They're magazines, he continued, recent issues, good condition, perfectly recyclable. He didn't throw the bag into the trash compactor. Later, as they were heading back to the plant, he opened the sack and saw that it contained shopping catalogs and issues of *National Geographic*. Nary a hint of pornography.) (Riley 2013, 66–67)

A couple of elements from this anecdote are worth noting. First, Verrazano's embodied experience as a sanitation worker, from his tactile expertise to his fine-tuned sense of smell, guides his encounter with trash, enabling him to find objects that he thinks are worth diverting from the waste stream, regardless of any rules or regulations his employers may have in place. Second, the "patrón de una marea secreta" that is invoked as an explanation for how this specific bag of trash—figured as ballast—ended up in Horowitz's truck serves the purpose of keeping the story's nautical motifs in the front of readers' minds and thereby maintains focus on trash's leakiness, its tendency to exceed the boundaries placed on it. A bit further along in the story, Horowitz finds a trash bag full of books that he and Verrazano toss out of the truck's windows as it makes its way along their route. What both of these incidents suggest is that in spite of the goals of waste management, the encounter between waste workers and waste is shot through with contingency. Ultimately, this is a significant impediment to the regime's aim of neutralizing waste in an ultimate sink.

Contreras Castro uses maritime imagery to similar effect in *Única mirando al mar*. The novel opens with a description of the Río Azul dump at sunrise that is replete with such imagery: there is a "flota de zopilotes" (fleet of vultures) hovering over a "mar sin devenir" (aimless sea) that is surrounded by shacks built on "las playas reventadas del mar de los peces de aluminio reciclable" (the wiped out beaches of the sea of fish of recyclable aluminum) (1994, 11). And who inhabits those precariously built dwellings? Why, buzos, or divers, of course. This is the local term used for trash pickers, akin to the cartoneros, cirujas, and catadores we have seen in other works discussed in this book. Contreras Castro goes all in on the figurative valence of the term, casting the arm motions made by buzos while scavenging as "brazadas" (strokes) that allow them to gain access to "las profundidades de su mar muerto" (the depths of their dead sea) (11). Admittedly, all of this is a bit on the nose, but what the novel lacks in subtlety it makes up for in its consideration of the limits of waste management as a means of dealing with the 800 tons of trash produced in the Costa Rican capital on a daily basis, as Contreras Castro's narrator mentions multiple times (12, 20, 42). Much like in "Ultraje," the maritime metaphors with which *Única mirando al mar* opens and that recur throughout the text prime us to see trash not as an uncomplicated series of solid, easily contained objects, but rather as material that is harder to grasp, solids that act like liquids in their slipperiness and leakiness. While Enrigue's story stages the way that trash can defy containment once it is in the hands of waste workers, one of Contreras

Castro's approximations to this theme is to consider what happens when waste workers do not collect the garbage.

A little over halfway through the novel, there are two simultaneous work stoppages: both the municipal sanitation workers and the buzos in Río Azul suspend operations, but they do so for very different reasons. The "informal" waste workers have decided not to work so they can celebrate the wedding of two of their own: Única Oconitrillo and Momboñombo Moñagallo. The two are married in the dump itself in a farcical scene that is characteristic of the novel's humor, from the liturgical malapropisms of the self-ordained buzo priest who performs the ceremony to the scatological moments that elicit great laughter from all the attendees (91–98). This closure of the dump as part of the novel's domestic plot (the consolidation of Única, Momboñombo, and El Bacán as a family unit) enters into contact with what we could call its waste management plot because, at the same time, the city's trash collectors initiate what will be a weeklong strike during which all of San José's trash (800 tons per day) languishes in the streets. As the narrator puts it, "Los trabajadores del servicio de recolección de basura de la Municipalidad de San José suspendieron sus labores el cuatro de enero y demandaron la compra inmediata de diez unidades recolectoras más que al parecer, les habían ofrecido desde febrero del noventa y uno" (The waste collection workers of the City of San José halted their labor on January 4 and demanded the immediate purchase of an additional ten collection units that, it seemed, they had been promised since February of 91) (92–93). The garbage piled up in the streets is not the only thing that mucks up the production of urban spaces amenable to the free flow of consumers: "Durante la semana de la huelga, muchos buzos decidieron lanzarse a las calles de la cuidad [sic] dado que los camiones y la basura, como si de repente un mar abandonara sus playas, se habían ido, y el sustento había que ir a buscarlo donde estuviera. Pero un buzo en las calles de San José es un marinero en tierra: andaban todos mareados" (During the weeklong strike, many buzos decided to go out into the city streets since the trucks and the trash, like a sea suddenly abandoning the beach, were gone, and one had to go looking for sustenance wherever it might have been. But a buzo in the streets of San José is a sailor on land: they were all unsteady on their feet) (98). For passersby, "los buzos llegan a formar una unidad indisoluble con el bote de basura para el que los ve comiendo directamente de la boca de un estañón de basura; los buzos son eso con lo que nadie desea tropezar" (the buzos end up forming an insoluble mass with the trash can for whoever sees them eating straight from the mouth of one; buzos are what no one wants to trip over) (99–100). While the strike eventually ends after the city government provides sanitation workers with more materials, this incident underscores how precarious waste management systems are, especially when implemented in line with neoliberal imperatives to slash budgets. Indeed, whether "formal" waste workers exercise their collective power by not picking up the trash or "informal" pickers process waste in the streets, trash poses challenges to the coherent production of space.

Such a challenge is mounted by trash not only when it is found where it should not be, but also when it ends up right where it belongs (according to the dictates of the management paradigm): the landfill. *Bariloche*, in particular, accounts for the abject quality of this space. One morning, after finishing his route, Rota reaches the landfill and observes it in the morning light: "No sabía qué hacían al cabo de los años con todo aquello, adónde iban a parar los excedentes de la montaña, a qué estómago o a qué garganta. . . . Se le ocurrió imaginar que la mole, una vez digerido su banquete hediondo, excretaba las sobras hacia el corazón de la ciudad, y de allí partían diseminadas a los hogares y a los contenedores de las calles que más tarde volverían a alimentar el basurero, una y otra vez. Era curiosa la cuestión de la mierda y de su itinerario" (He didn't know what they did with all that as the years went by, where that mountain's excess ended up, in what stomach or throat . . . . It occurred to him to imagine that the pile, after digesting its stinking feast, excreted the leftovers toward the heart of the city, and from there they made their way to the homes and street-side containers that would later feed the dump again, over and over. How odd, the matter of shit and its itinerary) (Neuman 1999, 103).

Imagining trash's itinerary as a closed cycle of ingestion and excretion that perpetually increases the size of the landfill serves to underscore the two sides of the connection between trash and the production of space: on the one hand, trash's habitual routes show the connections that tie the city together, but, on the other hand, trash ends up in zones of abjection, places that the vast majority of urban dwellers prefer to ignore. Indeed, one of the implications of the monstrous dump as eater/excreter that Rota imagines is that ignoring those zones of abjection is futile because they are part of all pockets of urban space, even ones that seem to have nothing to do with the landfill, like the home or the comfortable middle-class neighborhood. In this sense, trash has the power to signal the gaps that arise among the vertices of Lefebvre's spatial dialectic in the regime of neocapitalism, enacting both fragmented, deteriorated urban space and the deteriorated mental and emotional states of waste workers.

"Ultraje" features a key moment that echoes the overlapping of the domestic and waste management plots in *Única mirando al mar* that I consider above. Toward the end of the story, Horowitz arrives at his apartment early one morning after passing out drunk in a park only to find that his wife and son are not there. His initial sense of relief at being alone is shattered by the discovery of a series of discards and waste products: he finds a couple of used condoms floating in the toilet, along with a pair of dirty men's underwear and condom wrappers casually tossed aside in his bedroom. Distraught by the implications of these discoveries, he sits on his bed and immediately smells something strange: "No tardó en descubrir en el centro preciso del lecho una caca tan grande que no podía ser producto de mujer" (Enrigue 2005) ("It took him only a few seconds to discover, in the dead center of the bed, a turd so large it could not have been made by a woman") (Riley 2013, 73). This trash tableau is obviously humiliating and emasculating for Horowitz because it is evidence of his wife's affair, but it also reveals something significant about how waste resists management and frustrates notions of pure, uncontaminated spaces. Shit, wrappers, condoms, and unwanted clothing are eminently domestic forms of waste that humans live with, so to speak, more or less constantly. Admittedly, Enrigue stages them in a shocking way in order to produce a specific effect on his story's protagonist, but this staging also allows us to appreciate how unavoidable such forms of waste are in our most intimate spaces (even if we do not tend to find them in exactly the same spots as Horowitz does). In fact, as it concerns the story's plot and the broader consideration of trash works, the waste that Horowitz finds in his apartment is indeed significant. By examining the story through the lens of waste management, it is clear that, whether it is in the streets or in his home, the waste that surrounds this trash worker cannot be managed. Ultimately, that is what triggers Horowitz's violent but unsuccessful bid for freedom.

Bariloche offers a sustained meditation on the unmanageability of waste in the domestic sphere. The most potent indication of the deterioration of space in Neuman's novel is Rota's failure to articulate a representational space that would allow him to develop beneficial spatial practices in Buenos Aires. As an outsider who moves to the capital in his adolescence, he never manages to fit in—to find his place—in the city.[20] His only attempt to imagine a space of his own is his obsessive putting together of jigsaw puzzles with images of his birthplace. While at first blush, these scenic puzzles may not seem to be trash, they are indeed caught up in the novel's engagement with trash in two ways. On a figurative level, they are a waste of time that only serves to maintain Rota in a state of arrested development, unable to cope with the losses he has suffered and the meaninglessness of his life in Buenos Aires. The figurative valence of the puzzles as waste is distilled into the moment when he realizes that the last one he attempts to put together is defective and tries to return it to the store where he bought it (Neuman 1999, 158). This leads to the puzzles' literal instantiation as trash: Rota puts all his puzzles in a backpack, which he wears as he wades into the landfill, effectively throwing himself and his obsessions away (163–68). Bariloche, the hometown that Rota strives to find in these puzzles that are destined for the dump, is always barely out of his reach, just as it lies outside of the narrative fragments that make up the novel. The only place in the text to present an "objective" vision of Rota's birthplace is the space between the novel's epigraphs and the first chapter, where we read what appears to be a fragment taken from a geography manual: "Bariloche: c. emplazada sobre la orilla merid. del lago Nahuel Huapi, prov. de Río Negro, 41° 19' lat. S, 71° 24' long. O. Limítrofe con prov. de Neuquén. Estación sismográfica. Accid. más imp.: cerro Catedral y monte Tronador" (Bariloche: c. located on south. shore of Nahuel Huapi lake, Río Negro prov., 41° 19' S lat., 71° 24' W long. Borders Neuquén prov. Seismic center. Most imp. landforms: Cerro Catedral and Cerro Tronador) (13). The precision of this paratextual description of the space that Rota longs for offers a sharp contrast to his fragmented memories of the place and the fragmentation of the final puzzle he tries to put together, which is missing several pieces, making his imaginary reconstruction of Bariloche impossible (158).

What is more, Rota's insistent attempts at reconstructing the lost space of his childhood are accompanied by the gradual emergence of a crisis within the narrative fabric of the novel, which is composed of about forty-five very brief chapters that present a variety of narrative modes. Most of the chapters are narrated in a fairly conventional fashion: an omniscient voice deftly unravels the plot while subsuming other forms of discourse (like dialogue) into the narration itself by omitting attributions and punctuation that would distinguish these elements from the narration. This narrative mode does the work of advancing the plot, but it is frequently interrupted or fragmented by other modes. There are, for instance, several chapters in which Rota himself recounts memories of his first romantic and sexual experiences in his hometown (39–41, 61), as well as two chapters narrated by Rota's colleague el Negro, who describes Rota's increasingly erratic behavior at work (89–91, 118–19). Even more disruptive are what could be called the novel's lyrical passages, which, unlike the externally or internally focalized passages I have mentioned, seem only to stall the plot of the novel. These fragments are detailed descriptions of wooded landscapes with long sentences full of adjectives and metaphors. At first, they are confined to the heavily lyrical chapters (19, 45), but as the novel progresses, they appear without any explanations or transitions in the middle of the chapters that are replete with narrative (82, 138). While the purpose of these passages is never spelled out, it becomes increasingly clear that they are descriptions of the puzzles that Rota obsessively puts together in his apartment. That these puzzles are ciphers of his frustrated desire to infuse his adult life in Buenos Aires with meaning and are the objects he takes into the dump with him at the end of the novel is key to understanding both the trashing of Rota's subjectivity and Neuman's use of the logic of trash to signal the tension between order and disorder, value and disposal that underlies the structure of *Bariloche*. In other words, trash does not only contaminate and deteriorate Rota's ability to find an appropriate place for himself in the city to such an extreme that he throws himself away.[21] At the same time, the specter of trash suffuses the novel's structure in that the narrative fragments dedicated to describing Rota's puzzles (useless objects that turn out to have always been trash) interrupt, contaminate, and ultimately overtake the narrative modes that propel Neuman's novel forward. In this sense, the narrator's description of the landfill as "un horizonte de fragmentos extrañamente organizados" (a horizon of strangely organized fragments) would also seem to refer to the novel itself (166).

While trash frustrates the trash worker's attempts to manage his own domestic space in "Ultraje" and *Bariloche*, in Aira's novel, the presence of a villa miseria—the place where cirujas take the trash items they pick—in the middle of the city signals a disparity between spatial practices and hegemonic spatial representations: the villa's emergence next to a middle-class neighborhood interferes with the designs of engineers, architects, and city planners for the regimentation of space; as such, it represents a subversion of the attempts made from places of officially sanctioned power to impose coherence on the city. What is more, in *La villa*, Aira portrays how perceptions of space are conditioned by social class.[22] For the middle class, for example, the villa miseria is a place of trash—an *espacio-basura*—not only because the cirujas transport material waste there, but also because it embodies their anxieties about delinquents, immigrants, and other marginalized populations. The fear that Flores's middle-class residents exhibit toward the people in the villa, whom they see as "trash people" (*gente-basura*) is clearly distilled in the letter published in the newspaper *Clarín* by the father of a young girl who dies in a drug-dealing incident just outside the villa (Aira 2001, 34–35; Andrews 2013, 41). But at the same time, the villa's "exotic" squalor makes it a place of spectacle that the middle class can consume from the safety of their living rooms, which is made quite clear by the highly dramatized television broadcast of the police raid on the villa that leads to the novel's denouement, a live broadcast charged with "la expectativa de millones de televidentes enganchados en tiempo real" (147) ("anticipation: millions of viewers were following the events in real time") (Andrews 2013, 140).[23] In fact, the disjointedness of how social space is perceived is bolstered on a formal level by Aira's technique of stitching together a variety of discursive styles throughout the novel that track characters' movements in and around the villa: anthropological discourse (the narrator's description of cartoneros' work), police procedural (Inspector Cabeza's investigation), news media sensationalism (the coverage of the torrential rainstorm and Cabeza's investigation), and government anti-drug discourse (a speech in which a judge condemns drug trafficking at the end of the novel).

If the villa miseria acts as both a place of trash and a place of spectacle from the perspective of the middle class, for its lower-class inhabitants, it is their home: they themselves have built and defined this space and, as such, maintain a strong affective connection to it. The television broadcast of the police raid that serves as a pretext for morbid middle-class pleasure ends up providing Alfredo and Adelita, two of the villa's inhabitants, the opportunity to see their home from a new vantage point. When they see the onscreen images, we read: "Alfredo suspiró: 'Hacía tanto que no la veía, a la Villa . . . .' Adelita le tomó la mano y se la apretó" (Aira 2001, 159–60) ("Alfredo sighed: 'It's such a long time since I saw the old shantytown . . . .' Adelita took his hand and squeezed it") (Andrews 2013, 152). Adelita's gesture communicates an affective bond with the villa that the middle class, with the exception of one character in the novel, is completely unable to comprehend. That exception is Maxi, but we will return to his perception of the villa toward the end of this chapter. For now, it is enough to note that the presence of the shantytown and the activities of its inhabitants in a middle-class neighborhood underscore the link between the waste management paradigm and the disjointed production of space under neoliberalism.

Until this point in our analysis of trash and the production of space, we have seen how waste manages to be unmanageable, even when waste workers supposedly have it under control. This is key to the way that "Ultraje," *Bariloche*, *La villa*, and *Única mirando al mar* represent processes of disturbance and fragmentation of urban space, but those processes reach their zenith in Chejfec's *El aire* and Castellanos Moya's *Baile con serpientes*, novels in which waste is totally out of control. In *El aire*, the production of space breaks down so much that the spaces that surround the protagonist Barroso become completely deteriorated. This is reflected by the steady path he follows toward his demise: the novel ends with him bleeding to death in his apartment. In a way, the Buenos Aires of Barroso's wanderings is a city that is absent of itself, or of a certain conception of itself: Benavente (Barroso's wife, whose name is a clear evocation of Buenos Aires) has fled to Uruguay, and the point of origin of the three letters that she sends her husband instructing him not to chase after her—they come from Carmelo, Colonia, and Montevideo (Chejfec 1992, 18, 122, 151)—mark the increasing distance between the deteriorated Buenos Aires of the novel and the idea of a stable, well-ordered Buenos Aires. So, Barroso wanders through a Buenos Aires shot through with absence in the same way that, as Dianna Niebylski has noted, protagonists in several of Chejfec's novels move through the city without trying to understand it because they simply cannot conceive of an alternative to their meaningless meandering (2012, 20–22).[24]

But to say that in *El aire* the city is marked by absence is not entirely true, because there is a very significant presence that fills Barroso's experience of the city: trash. Contrary to both the dictates of waste management and our presuppositions about marginal urban spaces, waste does not show up in *El aire* where you might expect it to be. For example, there is a route along which Barroso repeatedly walks that leads him to the outskirts of an abandoned area of the city. The first couple of times he passes by this place at night and he cannot see because of the darkness. But one morning Barroso goes to this area and sees by the light of day that it is a vacant area with buildings in ruins that are overgrown with wild plants. However, what is notable is that "[n]o había latas tiradas, vidrios rotos, pedazos de caucho ni piras de desechos humeantes" (there weren't cans that had been thrown out, broken glass, pieces of rubber, or smoldering trash fires) (Chejfec 1992, 60). Explicitly listing the trash that is *not* in this place is significant because it signals the fact that it is not to be found in its proper place. If that is so, then where can the trash be found? The answer the novel provides is that it has invaded the spaces of the middle class and the spatial practices of consumer society. The most obvious evidence of this invasion is the construction of a series of villas miseria by marginalized populations, not on the outskirts of the city or in pockets of unoccupied land between more established residential zones, but rather on top of middle- and upper-middle-class apartment buildings. From the moment that Barroso reads a newspaper article about the "tugurización de las azoteas" (slumification of rooftops), the proliferation of these precarious dwellings begins to worry him, and they become "una confusa amenaza" (a confusing threat) that he never manages to understand (63, 66). The other important facet of the way that trash contaminates space and spatial practices in the novel is the transformation of discarded glass into money. Once again, Barroso discovers this phenomenon in the newspaper, where he reads an ad that says, "VIDRIO ES DINERO" (GLASS IS MONEY) (74). Exactly how and why glass has become common currency is never explained, but what is made clear in the scenes in the novel in which people dig through the trash looking for bottles to pay for the things they need to buy is the fusion of the circuits of capital and the pathways that garbage follows throughout the city.[25] Once again, we see how the circulation of waste problematizes the production of space in the regime of neoliberalism, simultaneously consolidating and deteriorating urban spaces.

Turning now to *Baile con serpientes*, the old yellow Chevrolet that features prominently is key to understanding the relationship between waste (management) and space in Castellanos Moya's novel. Beyond the vehicle's function as a symbol of neoliberal consumption practices and spatial politics (Venkatesh 2012, 63–71), the car itself is framed as trash from the novel's outset. Among the many other cars parked on Eduardo's street:

> El Chevrolet amarillo llamaba la atención por no pocos motivos: se trataba de una carcacha de hacía por lo menos treinta años, con la carrocería descascarada y los cristales tapiados con pedazos de cartón—parecía, pues, una vieja pertenencia sentimental de algún vecino que se negaba a llevarla a la huesera.
>
> Las primeras en descubrir que algo raro pasaba con ese vejestorio fueron las amas de casa y las sirvientas que a media mañana salían de compras a la tienda o simplemente a comadrear. Un hombre canoso, barbado y harapiento, emergía del Chevrolet a aquellas horas con la pinta de quien recién despertaba, de quien había pasado la noche durmiendo en ese cacharro. (Castellanos Moya 2012, 11)

(The yellow Chevrolet attracted attention for a number of reasons. It was a heap that looked at least thirty years old, with a smashed-up body and windows boarded up with pieces of cardboard. It looked like and old wreck that a neighbour wouldn't take to the scrapyard for sentimental reasons.

The first to notice that there was something strange about the car were the housewives and maids who went out in the mornings to go shopping or just to gossip. At that time, a ragged man with grey hair and a beard would emerge from the Chevrolet, looking like someone who'd just woken up after spending the night in his wreck.) (Springer 2009, 9)

Terms like *carcacha* (heap) and *cacharro* (wreck), along with the opinion that the car really belongs in a *huesera* (scrapyard), underscore the Chevrolet's status as a hunk of junk. Indeed, this notion is reinforced by the fact that, following several spectacular acts of violence, Eduardo and the snakes hide the car in a junkyard, where it spends a significant portion of the novel's diegesis until its status as waste is resoundingly confirmed when the police attack the junkyard with flamethrowers and incendiary devices, reducing the car to a mangled mess of metal (Castellanos Moya 2012, 169; Springer 2009, 154–55).

More important than the fact that the yellow Chevrolet is itself a trash object is the role that the vehicle plays in the form of waste management depicted in the novel. The raggedy, unkempt figure that neighborhood housewives and domestic workers spy warily as he exits the car is Jacinto Bustillo, the accountant-cum-scavenger that Eduardo latches onto and kills early in the novel. As Eduardo learns while accompanying him one day, Jacinto roams the city's industrial areas in search of recyclable materials. Subsequently, as Eduardo recounts, "abandonamos la zona inudustrial y fuimos hacia calles atestadas de comercios, de compraventa de chatarra, donde el tipo que decía llamarse Jacinto Bustillo era recibido como un viejo cliente, un apestoso que abría su saco de lona para mostrar el cachivache preciso. Yo me quedaba en la acera, apartado, fumando, solapado entre la turba de transeúntes, virtual guardaespaldas, sin perder detalle de las transacciones que realizaba . . . . 'Es usted un maestro en los negocios, don Jacinto,' le decía, con admiración" (Castellanos Moya 2012, 20–21) ("We left the industrial area and walked to streets crammed with pawnshops, where the foul-smelling man who said his name was Jacinto Bustillo opened his canvas bag to show off his precious junk and was welcomed like a valued customer. I stayed out of the way on the sidewalk, smoking, like a bodyguard hidden behind the crowd of transients. I kept a careful eye on Don Jacinto's dealings . . . . Admiring him, I said, 'You're a master businessman, Don Jacinto'") (Springer 2009, 18).

After murdering Jacinto and taking his car keys, Eduardo enters the yellow Chevrolet, which serves as a sort of warehouse for the junk that Jacinto does not manage to sell. It presents an overpowering "tufo rancio" ("rancid stink") that emanates from the "ringleras de frascos y botes de lata" ("rows of bottles and cans") and "mantas y otros trapos" ("blankets and other rags") (Castellanos Moya 2012, 24; Springer 2009, 21–22).[26] In essence, what Eduardo, the unemployed sociologist, witnesses during his day of perverse participant observation is an important, if sorely unappreciated, form of waste management. By combing through the city's industrial discards and diverting recyclable materials from the waste stream, Jacinto bolsters the waste management framework in two ways: he helps to prolong the useful life of the landfill that, while never mentioned, most certainly exists, and he participates in the generation of revenue streams around waste. In practical terms, Jacinto's car plays a key role in his waste management practices: it is his storage space, his living quarters, and his mode of transportation. On a more figurative level, the yellow Chevrolet helps to underscore the point that Ureta makes regarding the fantasy of the management ethos. In the absence of a depiction of a more conventional storage space for trash (like a landfill), Jacinto's car symbolically stands in for the "ultimate sink," but it plays the part quite poorly. While the the cardboard that covers its windows manages to hide the trash that Jacinto stores inside it (keeping it out of mind, which is waste management's goal), the car's status as a hunk of junk, a piece of trash, cannot help but draw attention and suspicion, as the novel's opening lines make clear.

The fissures in waste management's self-proclaimed ability to neutralize waste and perpetuate the impression of clean, coherent urban space that Jacinto's car underscores are completely laid bare once Eduardo takes command of the vehicle and unleashes the violent, anthropomorphized snakes that live in the Chevrolet and that Jacinto seems to have kept more or less contained. For if the car itself condenses the procedures and shortcomings of the informal brand of waste management that the novel presents, the snakes, whose origins and extremely lethal abilities are never explained or contextualized, beg to be read as metonymic extensions of the trash that the yellow Chevrolet both contains and represents. In this sense, they enact both the ultimate unmanageability of waste and waste's power to disrupt and fracture the production of space. This is made especially evident by the locations that Eduardo and the snakes target on their rampage throughout the city. Before setting off, Eduardo proclaims, "Y ahí íbamos, radiantes, avanzando a toda máquina—el Chevrolet amarillo, las serpientes y yo—, ganosos de llegar a otras zonas de la ciudad, donde iniciaríamos una nueva aventura" (Castellanos Moya 2012, 27) ("And off we went, at full speed, the yellow Chevrolet, the snakes and I, happy and anxious to get to other parts of the city, where we would begin the adventure of our new lives") (Springer 2009, 24). The adventure undertaken by this human-snake-machine assemblage (notice how Eduardo's syntax joins the three together into the "we" that is the sentence's subject) leads them to lay waste to key sites of consumer activity (a mall [Castellanos Moya 2012, 27–32; Springer 2009, 24–29] and a market [Castellanos Moya 2012, 35–37; Springer 2009, 32–33]), state power (the homes of an anti-narcotics police officer [Castellanos Moya 2012, 44–45; Springer 2009, 40–42] and a powerful politician [Castellanos Moya 2012, 49–52; Springer 2009, 45–48]), and the fossil fuel energy regime that facilitates dependence on automobiles (a gas station [Castellanos Moya 2012, 43; Springer 2009, 39–40]). That the investigative hypotheses put forward by the police and the press in the novel's second and third parts in an attempt to make sense of all this mayhem never even begin to approach the absurdity that brings about the attacks only serves to underscore the truly fragile grip that the management paradigm, fully underwritten by neoliberal rationality, has on the trash that, despite waste workers' best efforts, constantly threatens the production of space.

Reading these trash works with an eye toward the way that they represent waste management practices shows both the management paradigm's key role in shaping urban environments in Latin America during the neoliberal era and its limitations when it comes to confronting the material reality of waste. Whether it be through municipal garbage collection or scavenging, waste management is marshaled as part of what Lefebvre would call "conceived space," the practices that allow space to be produced in a way that aligns with hegemonic notions of how a city should work. Characters from almost all the texts I have analyzed here engage in work that helps move trash out of the way, seemingly making it disappear once it is thrown away. At the same time, however, trash works show that the very encounter between waste workers and waste that facilitates that disappearing act also amplifies trash's leakiness, its tendency to be unruly and to escape the methods of capture and neutralization that waste management imposes upon it. In a word, these texts underscore the limits of the waste management paradigm, an approach to materiality that spins a fantasy about where trash goes after we throw it away.

What is more, all of these texts perform this simultaneous representation and critique of waste management through the archetypical figure of a man who has "work issues": he is unsatisfied with his job, he lost his job, he cannot find a job. So, in addition to indexing the limits of waste management as an ideology, trash works also draw our attention to the limits of the individualistic, masculinist framework in telling stories about how to deal with trash. For the most part, the encounter between men, waste, and work staged in these texts results in disaster: Rota and Barroso presumably die, Horowitz and Eduardo unleash violence and chaos, Momboñombo loses the community he had found in Río Azul, and the shantytown that Maxi is drawn to is almost destroyed by police violence and flooding. These calamitous narrative resolutions ought to be read with trash and the challenge it poses to the notion of mastery in mind. When the protagonists of these trash works are confronted with waste in landfills, on the street, and in their homes, they are, by and large, unable to deal with its messiness, its unmanageability, its uncontainability. In this sense, they embody what Braidotti calls "the cultural logic of Humanism," with its focus on mastering the material world, the "negative and specular counterpart" to their whole, autonomous selves (2013, 15). That their stories end in personal disaster is a consequence of their failure to live up to this cultural logic and master the messiness of their surroundings. It is indicative of waste management's inability to accept and live with the posthuman condition, the inescapable fact that humans are "embodied and embedded" in webs of materiality that call for a "strong sense of collectivity, relationality and hence community building" instead of individualistic responses to the challenges that waste poses (49).

Beyond Waste Management: An Ethics of Care

If the waste management paradigm peddles a fantasy that promises permanent, technical, apolitical solutions to the problem of waste produced by humans, it also overshadows other waste-related practices that occur alongside it and escape its ideological underpinnings. As Ureta puts it, "there is much more happening with waste than WM practices. As soon as one starts paying close attention to the practices enacted in and around waste one realizes that many of them do not remotely comply with the tenets of WM programs; rather they emerge and develop in ways completely unexpected by them" (2016, 1534). These unexpected, noncompliant waste practices manifest themselves as different forms of care that Ureta tracks in the way that personnel in a Chilean copper mine deal with the industrial solid waste that is an inevitable by-product of mining. While the context for Ureta's theorization of care as a way of dealing with waste is certainly different from the urban milieu I have examined in this chapter, the questions surrounding municipal solid waste as represented in the trash works resonate with his insights regarding the limits of the management paradigm and the way that care creates an opening for waste practices based on a politics of mutuality, vulnerability, and openness. By way of conclusion, I would like to briefly consider how two trash works in particular—Contreras Castro's *Única mirando al mar* and Aira's *La villa*—enact an ethics of care as an alternative to the waste management practices that are represented in their plots.

Contreras Castro's and Aira's novels are alone among the trash works studied in this chapter in presenting waste workers in community, and, therefore, it comes as no surprise that they have a tendency to show glimpses of forms of mutuality and care that the other texts I have analyzed do not show. (In this sense, they also resonate with the nonfiction portrayals of communities that work with trash that I examine in chapters 2 and 4.) As opposed to protagonists who react to trash's unruliness by withdrawing from social life or by lashing out with violence, Maxi and Momboñombo respond to the challenges of trash by entering into relationships with communities of waste workers. It is precisely their characterization as waste vis-à-vis the norms of neoliberal rationality that underpins those relationships and allows them to develop. Momboñombo, we should recall, is remaindered, tossed aside like a piece of trash, after he tries to blow the whistle on his employer, the Biblioteca General, for selling books by the ton to a toilet paper manufacturer (Contreras Castro 1994, 24–25). He then throws himself into a trash truck in an apparent attempt to end his own life; that act of self-disposal is what gets him to the dump and introduces him to the community of buzos that live and work there (17). As for Maxi, the relationship he develops with the cartoneros (and the other inhabitants of the shantytown thereafter) arises from a different form of waste: the physical strength he has developed as a bodybuilder that allows him to haul the cartoneros' carts of junk with great ease. We must not forget that a bodybuilder is a person who lifts weights not to gain strength for pursuing some other activity, but rather simply to get bigger muscles. In this sense, Maxi's bodybuilding exhibits the essence of the capitalist mode of production: "Accumulation for the sake of accumulation" (Marx 1936, 652). By the same token, however, Maxi also embodies—both physically and symbolically—the idea of waste, which is made even clearer by the fact that he was unsuccessful in school and has no job. As the narrator puts it, he has no "utilidad social" (Aira

2001, 25) ("social function") (Andrews 2013, 20). By submitting his body to the fundamental law of capitalist production—accumulation for its own sake—Maxi reveals the waste that lies at the heart of the capitalist social order's logic: the relentless accumulation of muscle mass is a waste of time and energy. Paradoxically, what allows Maxi to find an alternative kind of usefulness through his relationship with the shantytown's inhabitants is his dedication to waste, the "misuse" of his body and his time, at least in terms of a capitalist system that places a high value on productivity.

How, then, do these two novels engage with notions of care? For Ureta, there are three forms of care that are especially equipped to challenge the assumptions and shortcomings of the notion of waste management: "care as tinkering practices, care as a form of affective entanglement and care as a particular kind of power" (2016, 1534). Tinkering as a form of care can be understood as an alternative to the highly technical solutions of the waste management paradigm that give the impression that waste simply disappears or inexplicably turns into something else (1534–35). It is an open-ended, contingent way of dealing with the material world that "is always experimental and tentative, reflexive of its own presence and limits" (1535). In *La villa* in particular, the notion of tinkering offers a compelling entry point for considering the role that care plays in dealing with waste. Maxi's "misuseful" practices run parallel to those in which the cirujas and other *villeros* engage with trash. I say that they misuse trash because trash is something that, by definition, has lost its usefulness. But, as Bill Brown reminds us, "Misuse frees objects from the systems to which they've been beholden" (1998, 953). It is precisely the villeros' misuse of objects, their ability to tinker with the trash they collect, that fascinates Maxi. As Aira's narrator tells us, "en el fondo de la pobreza, en la radical supresión del dinero, se esbozaban otras formas de riqueza: por ejemplo de habilidades. Ya la manipulación de la electricidad señalaba en esa dirección. Y nadie sabía qué habilidades creativas podía tener gente que provenía de lugares muy distantes del mundo, y las más de las veces no tenía trabajo fijo y disponía de mucho tiempo libre" (2001, 35) ("in the depths of poverty, where money plays no role at all, other kinds of wealth emerge, for example the wealth of skills. This was intimated by the shantytown's wiring system. And there was no knowing what creative skills might have developed among people who had come from faraway places, and who, for the most part, had plenty of free time because they were unemployed") (Andrews 2013, 28). The abilities born of misuse—misuse of objects, of time, and of space—not only fascinate Maxi; they also end up saving his life at the end of the novel when the inhabitants of the villa creatively modify their unique system of street lights in order to fool Inspector Cabezas (Aira 2001, 168; Andrews 2013, 161). This is precisely where the other two forms of care that Ureta mentions link up with the work of tinkering: because of the villeros' experimental, tentative use of materials and space, they are able to express their affective entanglement with Maxi by preparing a safe place for him to rest at the same time that they exercise their power to keep the rogue police inspector from harming him and their community. Aira's novel, then, seems to suggest the possibility of developing a misuse of trash and articulating new social relations around this resignification of waste materials (something that finds a concrete example in the *editoriales cartoneras* that began with Eloísa Cartonera in the wake of Argentina's economic crisis).[27] In this way, approaching trash through a mindset of care can help to lead to a significant ethical and aesthetic reconfiguration of our relationship to the material world.

In *Única mirando al mar*, affective entanglements ground the ethics of care that is evident in the community of buzos in the Río Azul dump, while Única, the novel's titular character, is the key vector for the organization of those entanglements. If "caring for waste necessarily means *living with it*" and recognizing that it "is not going to go away, no matter how much we wanted it or planned it," then Única embodies the notion of care as affective entanglements (Ureta 2016, 1536). This is true of the way that she interacts with the materials that the dump affords, using them to meet both her own needs and those of her fellow buzos, an ethic of mutual aid that she sums up for Momboñombo soon after his arrival: "ya ves, a mí nadie me jode, porque yo trato bien a todo el mundo; yo siempre ando viendo a ver qué le gusta a cada uno y si me lo encuentro voy y se lo doy, aunque sea algo valioso y así, poco a poco la gente va entendiendo que no vale la pena vivir agarrándonos del moño por cualquier cochinadilla, que es mejor compartir" (you see, nobody fucks with me because I treat everyone well; I'm always figuring out what everyone likes, and if I find it I give it to them, even if it's something valuable, and that way, little by little, people start understanding that it's not worth it to rip each other's hair out for some old piece of junk, that it's better to share) (Contreras Castro 1994, 30–31). Ultimately, Única teaches Momboñombo the value of living in community, opening himself to both the risks and the rewards of vulnerability and solidarity, which is an orientation toward waste and waste work that the other protagonists of trash works (with the exception of Maxi) sorely lack.

When he becomes aware of the government's plans to close the dump, Momboñombo makes repeated attempts to organize Río Azul's buzos, to get them to see that they have, in Ureta's words, "a particular kind of power" as key actors in San José's waste management system (Ureta 2016, 1534). That he is ultimately frustrated in his aims to procure government assistance in relocating the buzos probably tells us something about the preeminence of the waste management paradigm and its tendency to make both waste and waste workers invisible. Perhaps, then, the "particular kind of power" that is evident in the novel is the power that it can exercise over readers, getting them to pay attention to what happens to waste and the people who work with it. We should all be paying attention, like Alfonso Reyes's urban observer, even if the encounter between trash and trash workers that we bear witness to does not result in a joyous revelation of the interconnectedness of all matter. Or better yet, *especially* when it does not result in something akin to what Reyes describes, but instead compels us to understand what is at stake and to take steps to address the problem of trash.

4

Cleaning Up

On the Limits of Neoliberal Environmentalism

In 2014, Mexican filmmaker Tayde Vargas's "Los artilugios del Señor Tlacuache" ("Mr. Possum's Contraptions") won the top prize for documentary short film at the EcoFilm Festival, an international event dedicated to showcasing environmentally themed short films that took place annually in Mexico between 2011 and 2020.[1] The film centers on a real-life "Caballero de la Basura," as his compatriot Alfonso Reyes might call him: Jaime Jiménez, a self-proclaimed "fierrero" (scrapman) and "chatarrero" (junkman), is "un viejo que [anda] con su tambache lleno de cachivaches por toda la ciudad" (an old man who goes all around the city with his bundle of trash) (Vargas 2014). He answers to the nickname Señor Tlacuache (Mr. Possum) and makes art objects with the junk, trash, and detritus that he collects in the streets of Mexico City.

Vargas's film shows us Señor Tlacuache at work on a project that turns out to be a sculpture of himself on a motorcycle, made entirely of scavenged items that he has modified and reworked, including fifteen years' worth of his own hair, which he initially decided to keep in order to avoid, as he puts it, throwing himself away. Both visually and sonically, the film emphasizes serenity, contemplation, and the slow, steady work of creative transformation. It opens with a shot of a gray, overcast sky before cutting to a bird's eye view of the rain falling gently on a city street framed by leafy tree branches. We then see a sequence of two shots of a relatively unremarkable slice of Mexico City's skyline featuring a skyscraper under construction and a tower crane, followed by a five-shot sequence that offers different views of the space that serves as Señor Tlacuache's workshop. In a somewhat surprising move, this initial presentation of Jiménez's workspace does not emphasize the trash he stores there, but rather the vegetation that grows in the workshop's patio: we see close-ups of lush, green leaves and red flowers moving rhythmically with the breeze and rain.² These shots are backed by a soothing, stripped-down piece of music played on acoustic guitar and piano that still allows for the rainfall to be heard on the soundtrack.³

This initial sequence of images, ambient sound, and tranquil music works as a sort of "cold open" that begins to suggest the central aim of the film before we see or hear from Señor Tlacuache, its central figure, even before the title card comes into view. The juxtaposition of an urban landscape of buildings under construction and plants (that we very quickly come to understand as inhabitants of Señor Tlacuache's workshop) receiving nourishment in the form of rain presents us with two paradigms for thinking about construction, building, and growth. On the one hand, there is growth in the sense of urban development, large-scale economic and industrial activity, and the imposition of a grandiose human vision on the environment that the shots of the skyline bring to mind. On the other, the plants suggest growth as a project that, in the context of a garden located in a space of human work and habitation, is humbler and more open-ended; it necessarily depends on human ingenuity, natural processes, and the affordances of the environment in order to come to fruition.

As the subsequent footage of Señor Tlacuache at work on his sculpture and his voiceover rumination on trash, scavenging, and making art attest, his own approach to construction, growth, and activity operates between the two paradigms that Vargas's initial shot sequence proposes, drawing certain elements from both. The footage of him working on his project makes it clear that his methods and materials depend on the form of large-scale, industrial production hinted at by large construction projects like the one we catch a glimpse of at the beginning of the film. Vargas's camera shows us a workshop full of scavenged construction materials, like door frames, bathroom fixtures, and windows, as well as tools, engine parts, and a host of other mass-produced items. Señor Tlacuache uses the tools of construction—drills, hammers, and the like—to bring those materials together, pressing them into forms that correspond to his own personal aesthetic vision. On the other hand, his calm, unhurried bearing and the content of his voiceover narration suggest that what he gleans from the plants' approach is an ethos of growth and activity rooted in care and an openness to using what his surroundings afford him.⁴

Addressing the typical revulsion people feel toward trash, he says, "Hay gente que no lo hace, gente que ve la basura y no la quiere tocar, no la quiere ver. Cuando . . . tienes voluntad . . . te agachas y no te importa si te ensucias. Y entonces te agachas, la tomas y tu necesidad de imaginar es la que hace que voltees a ver dónde la pongo. ¿Qué le hago? ¿Para qué la recogí?" (There are people who won't do it, people who see trash and don't want to touch it, don't want to see it. When . . . you're willing . . . you crouch down and you don't care if you get dirty. And so you crouch down, you take the trash and your need to imagine is what makes you look around and ask where will I put this. What will I do with it? Why did I pick it up?) (Vargas 2014). He elaborates on this theme at a different moment as well: "Porque la mugre que te da ese objeto no te va a comer. Al contrario, te va a enriquecer. Cuando ya lo estás trabajando, te comienzas a meter en ese mundo" (Because the muck that object gives you is not going to eat you. On the contrary, it will enrich you. When you get to working with it, you start to enter into that world) (Vargas 2014). The "enrichment" to which Señor Tlacuache refers is certainly not monetary. Instead, it is a richness borne of working with objects and meeting the challenges they present in the process of making something new or different. Here we see not only a recognition of the material reality of trash and its place in life, but also a disposition toward being with trash, relating to it, putting one's will and energies in dialogue with the possibilities trash affords.

This documentary portrayal of a man slowly and thoughtfully cultivating his trash art certainly offers many points of contact with the works of narrative fiction considered in the previous chapter. Señor Tlacuache is a man who makes his living scavenging, and while the work portrayed in the film is a more aesthetic labor than the activities in which almost all of the other waste workers we have come across so far in this book engage, it is work nonetheless. "Los artilugios del Señor Tlacuache" touches on one of the dilemmas of waste work that "trash works" throw into sharp relief—dealing with waste within a management paradigm or through an ethics of care—and clearly offers further reflection on the limits and limitations of the management framework by advocating for the benefits of care. What the film shows us is a man engaged in salvage in a way that emphasizes deliberation, care, and a form of creative expression that recognizes the unavoidable entanglements between humans, waste, and wasting processes. In this sense, as a "character," Señor Tlacuache manages to transcend the representational limits of the trash works from chapter 3 by giving us an even closer, more fine-grained consideration of the ethics of care than what we see in novels like *Única mirando al mar* and *La villa*, not to mention the other texts that stay more firmly entrenched in the mentality of waste management.

I open this chapter with a brief analysis of Vargas's film not only because it allows us to consider the limits of waste management and the possibilities afforded by care beyond literary texts, but also because it very neatly condenses the main concerns I will address in this chapter. It is a documentary that aims both to tell the story of an interesting person and to transmit a message about how to confront environmental problems. This pedagogical aspect of "Los artilugios del Señor Tlacuache" can be broken down into two steps. The first is evident in what I discuss above and basically amounts to showing what Anna Tsing refers to as the "arts of noticing," a form of careful attentiveness and openness to possibilities for world-making and the cultivation of social relations among the ruins of capitalism (2015, 255). Señor Tlacuache models the art of noticing trash: he sees trash, confronts it, and does something about it. The second step is a call for the viewer to follow his lead, to put the lesson he has modeled into practice. This call to active participation becomes clear at the end of the film, when we see Señor Tlacuache framed in a close-up shot, directly addressing the camera. This is the first moment in which what he says is not presented as voiceover, but rather as a message aimed at viewers, which heightens the sense that what he is saying carries weight, that it is the pedagogical heart of the film. He says, "¿Qué vas a hacer? ¿Vas a dejar más basura a tus hijos? ¿Eso quieres para tus hijos? Ya mucha basura hemos tirado todos y si no hay alguien que te diga, 'Oye, tienes que reciclar' . . . . Es obligación de todos. De todos. No de unos cuantos" (What are you going to do? Are you going to leave more trash for your children? We've all already thrown away a lot of trash, and if there's nobody telling you, "Hey, you have to recycle" . . . . It's everyone's duty. Everyone. Not just for a few people) (Vargas 2014). While he does gesture toward a collective group that should take action through the use of *todos* and *nosotros*, it is telling that he directs his message to a singular *tú*, the "you" watching the film, an individual, an audience of one.[5] Clearly, the way the second person singular is used here is a manner of speaking; I am not arguing that either Señor Tlacuache or Vargas have only individual viewers in mind. To the contrary, I think both would hope that this documentary and its message of contemplative engagement with and care for discards contribute to inspiring collective action to address the problem of trash. Nonetheless, the film's focus on a single person's eclectic approach to dealing with waste and the individualized bent of its call to action both highlight neoliberalism's limited horizons for imagining what it means to act environmentally.

Vargas's documentary, in short, is a cultural text that aims to inform, raise consciousness, and inspire viewers to personally commit to doing something to help solve the problems that trash presents. In urging viewers to take notice of waste in ways they are unaccustomed to doing and leaving them with the idea that through small, simple actions (like recycling) they can make a difference, the story it tells about trash and the kinds of actions that can be taken to address it resemble rather closely what we could call the overall story arc of a number of recent depictions of environmental projects and campaigns. It is my aim in this chapter to analyze a few relevant examples that allow us to consider, on the one hand, the limits of an environmental discourse that is very effective at drawing attention and provoking an affective response but that centers individual action and, on the other, the potential for moving beyond those limits. Lucy Walker, João Jardim, and Karen Harley's 2009 documentary feature *Waste Land* (which portrays a social project based on trash art in Brazil) and the advertising and social media campaign for Gallinazo Avisa (a trash cleanup program from 2015 in Peru) adhere closely to the script exemplified by "Los artilugios del Señor Tlacuache" and therefore serve as instructive examples of the promise and pitfalls of a brand of environmentalism that privileges individual action. They ground the "arts of noticing" in the perspective of an interesting individual (or limited group of individuals) and offer up individual action as the horizon of possibility for doing something to address the social, economic, and environmental problems that attend the proliferation of waste. A third example, *RUS. Residuos Urbanos Sólidos. Basura y espacio público en Latinoamérica. 2008–2010*, which was a series of public art projects undertaken by a Spanish environmental collective in many sites throughout Latin America, exhibits a more collective strategy for acting environmentally within the constraints of neoliberalism and will serve as a way to close this book's final chapter with a glimpse beyond the limits of neoliberal environmentalism. But before delving into these examples, in the next section I will explain what I mean by neoliberal environmentalism.

Neoliberal Environmentalism: The Promises and Pitfalls of Individualization

In my consideration of the way trash and work come together in recent examples of Latin American narrative fiction in chapter 3, I considered the effects of neoliberal rationality—the reduction of human activity to purely economic terms, producing what Wendy Brown calls *homo oeconomicus*—on the portrayal of waste workers. If that framework allows us to see the limits of the management paradigm and the real constraints that condition trash work, might it also be useful in considering environmental discourses that currently hold sway? What does neoliberal rationality's subordination of life to supposedly natural market forces show us about projects that people devise to deal with trash not as a form of work but rather as a commitment to environmental values? In his widely read and cited *A Brief History of Neoliberalism*, David Harvey anticipates Brown's formulation of *homo oeconomicus* when he notes that the most recent instantiation of global capitalism "holds that the social good will be maximized by maximizing the reach and frequency of market transactions, and it seeks to bring all human action into the domain of the market" (2005, 3). While parsing out the difference between the classical, laissez-faire brand of economic liberalism that held sway in the period between the French Revolution and the the First World War and neoliberalism, Adam Kotsko notes:

> the most clear-eyed advocates of neoliberalism realized that there could be no simple question of "return" to the laissez-faire model. Rather than simply getting the state "out of the way," they both deployed and transformed state power, including the institutions of the welfare state, to reshape society in accordance with market models. In some cases this meant creating markets where none had previously existed, as in the privatization of education and other public services. In others it took the form of a more general spread of a competitive market ethos into ever more areas of life—so that we are encouraged to think of our reputation as a "brand," for instance, or our social contacts as fodder for "networking." Whereas classical liberalism insisted that capitalism had to be allowed free rein within its sphere, under neoliberalism capitalism no longer has a set sphere. We are always "on the clock," always accruing (or squandering) various forms of financial and social capital. (2018, 5–6)

As Harvey and Kotsko make clear, neoliberalism is an approach to organizing society, and its purported aim is to make society better; in this sense, it is a capacious term that can be applied—and indeed has been applied—in many ways to any number of social formations, as any cursory bibliographical search will confirm. Strictly speaking, neoliberalism refers to a policy model that favors certain types of macroeconomic measures for structuring material relations in a society, including deregulation, privatization, and disinvestment in the welfare state.[6] While the economic policies implemented by states and encouraged by international bodies like the World Bank, the Inter-American Development Bank, and the International

Monetary Fund are undoubtedly central to defining neoliberalism, they will not be my focus here. Those technical policy strategies are a manifestation of a broader ethos, for neoliberalism is "more than simply a formula for economic policy. It aspires to be a complete way of life and a holistic worldview, in a way that previous modes of capitalism did not" (Kotsko 2018, 6). Simply put, "it is a discourse that aims to reshape the world" (7).[7]

As I mention above, one way that this "holistic worldview" manifests itself in Latin American cultural production that engages with trash is through depictions of workers upon whom we depend to manage the waste we produce. The first two chapters of this book also offer a critical perspective on neoliberalism's worldview, with a particular focus on the notion of freedom. One of the core tenets of neoliberal thought is that individual freedom is of paramount value and that the best way to secure individual freedom and human dignity is through unregulated markets and free trade (Harvey 2005, 7). That is, the foundational logic or worldview of neoliberalism maintains that humans must free themselves and their institutions from state interference in order to secure their own personal freedoms; these steps are "both necessary and sufficient for the creation of wealth and therefore for the improved well-being of the population at large" (7).[8] The inexorability of this logical sequence—neoliberalism leads to freedom, which leads to prosperity and social good—is called into question most openly in "Ilha das Flores," which, as chapter 1 makes clear, presents a persistent unraveling of normative notions of the human that leads to an explicit meditation on what freedom means for poor people (especially women and children) in the context of competing for scraps of garbage with pigs. However, all the other works addressed in chapters 1 and 2 share a preoccupation with the experience of marginalization and poverty in light of the disjunct between neoliberalism's promise of freedom, prosperity, and social improvement and the reality that this most recent instantiation of capitalism has delivered.[9]

The questioning of discourses of freedom that connects the stories from and beyond the dump that I have brought together in this book throws into sharp relief the need for a closer consideration of the ideological underpinnings of the neoliberal notion of freedom. (This will also allow me to approach the point of this section, which is to define the contours of neoliberal environmentalism.) Kotsko's take on neoliberalism as a form of political theology illuminates this question quite usefully. In invoking political theology, he does not argue, for instance, that neoliberalism is a religion or that it mimics religious practice; instead, he recognizes that "theology has always been about much more than God" and questions of devotion or religious orthodoxy and that "[e]ven the simplest theological systems have a lot to say about the world we live in, how it came to be the way it is, and how it should be" (2018, 7). In short, he regards "political theology as the study of systems of legitimacy, of the ways that political, social, economic, and religious orders maintain their explanatory power and justify the loyalty of their adherents" (8).[10] His articulation of the basic shape of neoliberalism's political theology serves to flesh out Harvey's point that it seeks to subsume all human activity under the domain of the market: "Overall, then, in neoliberalism an account of human nature where economic competition is the highest value leads to a political theory where the prime duty of the state is to enable, and indeed mandate, such competition, and the result is a world wherein individuals, firms, and states are all continually constrained to express themselves via economic competition. This means that neoliberalism tends to create a world in which neoliberalism is 'true.' A more coherent and self-reinforcing political theology can scarcely be imagined" (38).

For Kotsko, the key component of this worldview is the naturalization of the Christian notion of "free will": all individuals always have the freedom to exercise choice, and individuals alone are responsible for the outcomes of those choices, whether those outcomes are positive or negative (86). Kotsko argues convincingly, however, that this limitless freedom is a ruse, because it creates the illusion that individuals can simply make the right choices in order to improve their own lives and the world in general, when, in fact, the freedom that individuals enjoy is limited to choosing actions that either increase or decrease their market competitiveness (69–96). This illusory form of agency results in a social order in which the socioeconomic position of people is seen as not only a reflection of their financial acumen, but also, and more importantly, a reflection of their moral worth. Market competition inevitably produces winners and losers, both of whom get what they deserve, because the choices that they made of their own volition led them to their station.

The implications of this view of individual freedom for the characters—both fictional and nonfictional—of the works I analyze in the preceding chapters are clear: the fact that they have to live on trash in one way or another is certainly unfortunate, but it is the natural order of things. Neoliberal rationality would seem to lead us to conclude that if they wanted their lives to be different, they could just do something about it. By the same token, the fact that they live in such unfortunate circumstances must be due to some sin (to channel Kotsko's language) or another, whether it be addiction, sloth, or something else. The broader upshot of this form of thought is the naturalization and invisibilization of such poor, unfortunate souls. The mere existence of the texts and films examined so far is a clear demonstration of an effort to push back against neoliberal rationality and its perverse acceptance of the notion that the poor will be and must always be among us.

But what effect does the neoliberal brand of freedom have in the context of maximizing social good or making the world a better place? More concretely, how does neoliberal rationality shape the ways we imagine taking care of the environments we inhabit? Being completely free to choose how and when to act environmentally would seem, at face value, liberating, but if that freedom of choice is actually a function of market logic, the range of choices often ends up being limited to what more or less "green" products we can buy (Maniates 2001, 34). This is, in large part, due to the way that freedom of choice is linked to individual autonomy and responsibility in the neoliberal imaginary. For Michael F. Maniates, the individualization of responsibility is the hallmark of what I am calling neoliberal environmentalism: "it characterizes environmental problems as the consequence of destructive consumer choice" and "asks that individuals imagine themselves as consumers first and citizens second" (34). This is an individual, consumer-based approach to environmentality.[11] It displays the enormous faith in both the logic and the morality of market forces that is so central to neoliberal rationality, for "[i]t embraces the notion that knotty issues of consumption, consumerism, power and responsibility can be resolved neatly and cleanly through enlightened, uncoordinated consumer choice. Education is a critical ingredient in this view—smart consumers will make choices, it's thought, with the larger public good in mind" (33).

Making educated, thoughtful choices about what to buy and considering the impact of one's purchases on the environment is not a bad thing, especially if we bracket off those individual commitments and consider them in a vacuum. In fact, those sorts of individual choices form the basis of ethical commitments between humans and other creatures, as well as the wider world (Liboiron 2014). The problem, however, is that the discursive power of the notion of individual responsibility—which, for me, is clearly linked to the hegemony of neoliberal rationality—crowds out other ways of approaching environmentality. "When responsibility for environmental problems is individualized, there is little room to ponder institutions, the nature and exercise of political power, or ways of collectively changing the distribution of power and influence in society—to, in other words, 'think institutionally'" (Maniates 2001, 33).

When it comes to the problem of waste, Max Liboiron echoes Maniates in arguing that the forms of awareness that promulgate ethical consumer choices ultimately do very little to create change. In their analysis of the shortcomings of the dominant framework for addressing food waste (encouraging individuals to take steps to address the problem), Liboiron notes the difficulty of scaling individual actions to the steps needed for systemic change. It *feels* true to say that if everyone changed their behavior, those small, individual actions would result in a sea change regarding the production and ultimate disposition of waste due to what seems like the unassailable logic of cumulative effects. The apparent and simple elegance of this logic is, however, a fantasy because it sidesteps both the virtual impossibility of actually convincing "everyone" (or simply enough people) to agree that waste is a problem they should actively address and the difficulty in coordinating "everyone's" actions. As Liboiron succinctly puts it, "The premise of awareness campaigns is that individuals are the best unit for change. The individualization of action is a way to fragment it, slow it down, and redirect it to ineffective routes" (Liboiron 2014). In other words, individualization draws attention, thought, and resources away from action that would address broad, systemic problems surrounding trash, like approaching the question of waste at the level of infrastructure, which has two advantages over what Maniates would call "enlightened, uncoordinated consumer choice" (2001, 33): "first, most environmental and other societywide problems are not due to individual intent and behavior to begin with, but rather the social, economic, political, and other systems that make some decisions and behaviors more likely or possible than others. Secondly, focusing on these systems for change actually scales up to the scale of the problem" (Liboiron 2014).[12]

If infrastructural, systemic, and institutional changes are really the key to addressing the problem of waste, and targeting individual behavior is ineffective, why is individualization so seductive when it comes to framing environmentality? Maniates opens the essay I have been citing with a brief meditation on Dr. Seuss's *The Lorax* (a beloved children's book that deals with themes of environmental destruction and greed) that suggestively crystallizes the power of framing environmental action as the domain of autonomous individuals. He notes that the book is "fabulously popular" despite the "dismal and depressing" story it tells: a businessman decimates an ecosystem despite the titular character's best efforts to challenge unchecked capitalism and rampant consumerism, and "[t]he conclusion sees a small boy with no evident training in forestry or community organizing unpromisingly entrusted with the last seed of a critical species. He's told to 'Plant a new Truffula. Treat it with care. Give it clean water. And feed it fresh air. Grow a forest. Protect it from axes that hack. Then the Lorax and all of his friends may come back.' His chances of success are by no means high" (2001, 31–32). For Maniates, the book's ending—the clear, simple charge for a lone individual to plant a tree as the most important response to the bad actions of another individual (the rapacious businessman's despoiling of the forest)—is the main reason that *The Lorax* "has become a beloved organizing touchstone for environmentalists" because it so neatly conforms to the plot of individual action as the explanation for environmental harm and the key to undoing that harm (32). But he also makes passing reference to the book's form and aesthetic qualities as factors that contribute to its popularity, noting that its fun and imaginative illustrations, along with its clever and catchy rhyme schemes, "provide safe passage through a topic we know is out there but would rather avoid" (32). While these aesthetic concerns are not central to Maniates's line of analysis, they strike me as key to understanding the seductive quality of neoliberal environmentalism. The illustrations and formal elements of a Dr. Seuss book make it iconic and memorable; they lay the groundwork for the book's message to be internalized by readers.

While the relationship between aesthetics and didacticism is perhaps more evident in children's literature, the depictions of environmental projects and campaigns that I examine in what follows also need to be analyzed in terms of the way their form shapes the type of environmentality they envision. In other words, how and to what extent do they consider individual behavior as the horizon of possibility for addressing the problems that trash poses? One form of approaching this question is through the way these depictions engage with what Daniel Worden calls "the documentary aesthetic," which he sees as a "signature element" of neoliberal cultural production (2020, 4). The documentary aesthetic, which occurs across a variety of contemporary media forms, anchors the representation of uncomfortable, confusing, and chaotic realities in individual perspectives as a way of making sense of the excessive amount of information and detail that is necessary to understand the impenetrable and inscrutable systems that make up the contemporary world and all but negate individual experience (6).[13] As Worden puts it, "It is perfectly neoliberal that we filter the world through our individual lenses, for that is the normative vantage point of free market economics. Documentary works can make visible the abstractions, detachments, and ironies that constitute our individuated lives. Along with this critical perspective, documentary works can also envision alternative modes of living, beyond the exploitative structures that surround us. It turns out these alternatives are everywhere if you know how to look" (20).

This characterization describes a film like "Los artilugios del Señor Tlacuache" perfectly. Vargas's documentary approaches the difficult-to-grasp structures and systems that produce and manage (or fail to manage) trash through the experience of one man. Señor Tlacuache's philosophy of taking notice of waste and engaging with it as the basis for his creative project is a good expression of an ethics of care that literary depictions of trash work generally lack. It is a portrayal of environmentality that makes sense and models the kind of alternative mode of living that Worden claims as one of the powers that the documentary aesthetic wields. What is more, it explicitly aims not only to make us envision an alternative mode of living, but also to take steps toward making it a reality by linking one individual (Señor Tlacuache) with another (the viewer), the first urging the second to behave like he does. In a word, the film hopes to be inspiring. If we follow Worden's line of thought, I suppose we should conclude that it *is* inspiring and, therefore, that it performs the task of unveiling and disrupting, if only on a very small scale, the logic and power of neoliberalism. I, however, am not as sanguine as Worden about the disruptive power of the documentary aesthetic. There is doubtlessly a rousing, persuasive, seductive quality to framing this type of environmental ethic within the scale of individual action, because it offers a modicum of personal empowerment in a context of seemingly intractable problems. Also, it certainly foregrounds the sort of humble, open relationship to waste that is an essential component of building a nonanthropocentric environmental ethic. Vargas's documentary and the depictions of trash projects that I analyze in the following sections all aim to inspire in one way or another, and they allow us to envision not only possible futures but also current realities that many of us do not want to see or know how to look for, like landfills and other dump sites. That is, they encourage us to imagine a future in which we care about the waste in our environments by bringing the reality of waste into our field of vision, making us aware of it. But is promoting awareness enough? As Heather Houser reminds us, "awareness and response are not coterminous. The same emotions that bring us to awareness might orient response in uninvited ways" (2014, 16). Promoting awareness of the environmental and social problems related to trash and offering potentially inspiring solutions that you, the individual, can imagine taking on yourself is what the neoliberal environmental imaginary has on offer. I now turn to *Waste Land* and Gallinazo Avisa to examine how they exhibit the promises and perils of this approach to environmentality.

Making a Difference in *Waste Land*

Just north of the city of Rio de Janeiro, in a suburb called Duque de Caxias, lies a now-defunct landfill that took its name from the neighborhood in which it was located: Jardim Gramacho. While it closed in 2012 after over thirty-four years of operation, at the height of its life as an active dumping site for the refuse of parts of Rio and several of its suburbs, over 9,000 tons of garbage were dumped in the landfill every day ("Gramacho" 2008). Due to the lack of formal selective waste collection and recycling programs in Rio over that time span, virtually all of the waste thrown away by the inhabitants who were served by Jardim Gramacho ended up in the landfill, whether that waste was potentially recyclable or not. In view of the dire straits in which many of the urban poor found themselves during the severe economic downturn that followed the so-called economic miracle engineered in the first part of the 1970s by the military dictatorship that governed Brazil from 1964 to 1985, the Jardim Gramacho landfill became a chaotic, dangerous worksite in which catadores scavenged the refuse for scrap metal, plastic, cardboard, or any other reusable item that they could sell for cash. Over the years, their numbers grew, and by the middle of the 2000s, over 1,300 catadores were working in twelve-hour shifts to salvage an average of 180 tons of recyclable material per day from the landfill, which, according to local sanitary engineers, is roughly equivalent to the amount of trash that a city of 400,000 inhabitants would produce on a daily basis ("Gramacho" 2008). These staggering figures should be understood in the light of the exceedingly dangerous work environment of the landfill in which, according to sanitary engineer Adacto Ottani, the catadores picked through the trash alongside rats, vultures, and biting flies and were constantly at risk of sustaining severe injuries or contracting diseases that range from digestive maladies to tetanus to hepatitis ("Gramacho" 2008).

The source from which I gathered the foregoing information on Jardim Gramacho is a video report that was produced by the Brazilian news service UOL in November 2008. I make explicit mention of this because I would like to consider that report in tandem with another one that was produced by the same news service in June 2012 and that detailed the closure of the landfill. While the first report feels like an exposé of the landfill and its potential to occasion an imminent ecological and public health disaster, the second report strikes a triumphant tone. In it, we see snippets of the pronouncements made by government officials from the site of the landfill on the occasion of its closure, which is touted as a decisive step in the direction of closing all of Brazil's open-air landfills and replacing them with ones that meet international standards ("Aterro sanitário de Gramacho é fechado" 2012). Additionally, we are informed of a plan for implementing a system that will capture the methane gas produced by the material in the landfill and use it to provide for the energy needs of people in the surrounding communities ("Aterro sanitário de Gramacho é fechado" 2012). As for the catadores, the report assures us that some 1,600 of them have applied for and received an indemnity of 14,000 *reais*. Curiously, though, the report ends with a clip from an interview with an unnamed woman, presumably a catadora, who wonders what she and the other pickers are supposed to do now that they can no longer work in Jardim Gramacho. With an anxious expression on her face and desperation in her voice, she asks, "Como a gente vai viver agora?" (How are we supposed to live now?) ("Aterro sanitário de Gramacho é fechado" 2012). Obviously, her question points to the possibility that, in the face of having to learn a new skill and possibly move to a different part of the city (many catadores lived in the landfill itself or in a favela that grew around it), a government-provided monetary indemnity falls short. Additionally, however, the anonymous catadora's question hints at something more sinister and problematic than the efficacy of the state's indemnity program. The verb "to live" in the question "how are we supposed to live now?" has multiple valences, the most obvious of which, in this context, is economic; that is to say, "how are we supposed to make a living?" would be relevant. But I also detect a social inflection in this woman's question, one that takes into account that the catadores' activity in the landfill was a way of life that had come into being in that place, a way of life that was negated by the closure of Jardim Gramacho.[14]

A series of social structures that extend far into the past led to the creation of the Jardim Gramacho landfill and the way of life that the catadores developed there. Indeed, one only has to think of a figure like Carolina Maria de Jesus, whose diary *Quarto de despejo* (1960) is a wide-ranging reflection on trash and trash-picking in a São Paulo favela, to realize that the issues of class and racial marginalization and economic and environmental precarity that swirl around Jardim Gramacho are not limited to that site alone, nor are they new problems. What is more, the official measures that were taken to close the landfill would seem to do very little to address the long-term environmental and social maladies of uneven, top-down modernization that made possible the scenario depicted in the 2008 UOL news report referred to above. Yet, only four years later, the second news report that I referenced gave the strong impression that the problem had been solved, in part by covering up the landfill. Much like the anonymous catadora's problematic question at the end of the news report, the fundamental question of Jardim Gramacho remains. What can be done to deal with a space like Jardim Gramacho, in both environmental and social terms? Lucy Walker, João Jardim, and Karen Harley's film *Waste Land*—released during the period between the UOL news service's initial lament and the subsequent celebration of the goings on in Jardim Gramacho—would seem to propose an answer to that very question.

Waste Land is, as virtually all the critics who commented on it upon its release noted, a heartwarming, uplifting documentary that combines an ecological theme with a message about art and human dignity.[15] Lucy Walker and her co-directors depict the story of visual artist Vik Muniz's project "Pictures of Garbage."[16] This artistic intervention was a collaborative effort between Muniz and six catadores—Isis, Zumbi, Tião, Irmã, Magna, and Suelem—who were working in Jardim Gramacho salvaging recyclable material. For the project, the New York–based Brazilian artist traveled to Rio, took photographic portraits of each of the six catadores (mainly in the landfill and in poses that mimicked iconic paintings like Jacques-Louis David's *The Death of Marat* and Pablo Picasso's *Woman Ironing*) and, with the help of the subjects of the portraits, recreated the images on a massive scale using materials that the catadores collected from the landfill. Muniz then photographed the recreated portraits and sold them at auction all around the globe, returning the proceeds to the participants and the Associação de Catadores do Aterro Metropolitano de Jardim Gramacho (Association of Recycling Pickers of Jardim Gramacho).[17] All told, the project raised in excess of $250,000 for the association, which, according to the film's postscript, was used to finance the purchase of a truck, other equipment, and the establishment of a learning center for the members of the ACAMJG.[18]

Of all the cultural texts I have gathered together and analyzed in this book, *Waste Land* is undoubtedly the most well-known and widely circulated, and it has been the subject of much praise and critique, both in and out of academic circles. Just to give a sample of some critical readings of the film, I would point to Kathleen M. Millar's consideration of Muniz's project and its portrayal as "especially vivid example[s] of how images of waste tend to oscillate between rendering waste as brutal abjection or transcending garbage by giving it aesthetic value" that "ultimately [compound] the racialization of the mostly nonwhite bodies of the Jardim Gramacho dump" due to their "refusal to actually engage with the materiality of waste and of the labor of *catadores*" (2020, 6). In a somewhat related vein, Joni Hayward Marcum tracks the limits of the film's engagement with garbage aesthetics, arguing that it "simultaneously takes part in and falls short of the political goals of this aesthetic—namely to focus both visual and political attention on the inequalities faced by marginalized people, places, and materials" (2021, 36). These and other interpretations of the film interrogate the ethics of its representation of the Other, the way it understands trash, and the problematics of the relationship between an artist's vision and the work of those who help him realize it. In broad terms, I share the same concerns about the way Walker's film documents the reality of Jardim Gramacho, and these critical perspectives have contributed to my own initial reading of it, which I draw on here (McKay 2016). But one way in which *Waste Land* has not often been read is as a model for fostering environmentalism. Along the lines of "Los artilugios del Señor Tlacuache," *Waste Land* promotes a certain mode of environmentality, what I am calling neoliberal environmentalism. While it is not an environmental campaign that promotes direct action (like Gallinazo Avisa, which I examine in the next section of this chapter) and it does not exhibit the same sort of direct interpellation of the viewer as that of Vargas's film (the deployment of the second person to urge the viewer to stop producing so much trash and start recycling), the film does have a similar didactic thrust that is carefully embedded in its rendering of Muniz's project and the lives of the catadores at the individualistic scale of the documentary aesthetic. This modeling of environmentally friendly behavior is evident in the film itself, as I show in what follows, but considering some of the documentary's para-filmic elements is a useful entry point for understanding how it interpellates viewers, how it attempts to produce effects in the world.[19]

Two such para-filmic elements can be found on the film's website; its URL is listed at the end of the credits. First is the prominently situated trailer, which appears on the site's landing page and features the tagline, "What happens in the world's largest trash city will transform you" (*Waste Land Movie*). Setting aside the question of what exactly a "trash city" is, what is notable about this messaging is the emphasis on the effect the documentary is supposed to have on *you*, the individual viewer. Obviously, the function of a trailer is to advertise the film that it introduces, deploying marketing strategies to entice potential viewers, so it is perhaps unwise to ascribe too much weight to the trailer when it comes to interpreting the film itself. However, the tagline certainly resonates with the film's investment in the notion of transformation (transforming trash into art, catadores into artists with professional options beyond the dump) and suggests something important about the way the filmmakers hope their project is received: as an inspiring piece of cinema that changes the way viewers see the world and, perhaps, how they act. Such a hope for action on the part of viewers who have been transformed by watching *Waste Land* is made manifest by another para-filmic element: the "Get Involved" section of the website, with instructions on how to "spread the word" (on Facebook and Twitter) and make financial contributions via PayPal. This section of the website expands on the information provided in the film's postscript and details the amount of money raised through the sale of the "Pictures of Garbage" portraits ($250,000) and the prize winnings for the film from various festivals ($85,000), indicating that all of this money was donated to ACAMJG, which used it to pay off debt, provide housing for catadores, build a learning center, and buy a new truck, among other things (*Waste Land Movie*). While they are relatively minor and peripheral elements, taken together, these two para-filmic features—the tagline promising personal transformation and the invitation to make a financial contribution to the ACAMJG and its environmental and social efforts—neatly express *Waste Land*'s desire to inspire and motivate action.

I mention above that academic criticism of the film has not often addressed it as a model for fostering environmentality. One exception is a 2014 essay in the *Journal of Macromarketing* by Mark Tadajewski and Kathy Hamilton. Admittedly, business and marketing journals are not typical reading fare for me, but this piece, which analyzes *Waste Land* and the 2010 documentary *Trashed* from the disciplinary perspective of consumer research and macromarketing, is especially instructive in terms of explicating the relationship between Walker's film and the cultivation of an environmental ethic grounded in individualization. They approach *Waste Land* from the perspective of Transformative Consumer Research, an approach to business and marketing scholarship that promotes research aimed at bettering the world by making a difference in the lives of consumers (Davis, Ozanne, and Hill 2016, 159). In its articulation of the social good in terms of the benefits and detriments that accrue to consumer activity, this framework exemplifies neoliberal rationality's market-oriented approach to human activity. This is borne out in Tadajewski and Hamilton's analysis of *Waste Land*, which they see as a film that ably "secure[s] audience attention" by filtering questions of waste management and social exclusion through the experience of individuals (which rings true with Worden's formulation of the documentary aesthetic) (2014, 83). Also, given the film's success at generating a connection with viewers, "enlightening and uplifting" them, it is able to plant seeds for future action by stressing "how we as individuals can make a difference in ensuring that our ecosystems remain vital, healthy and capable of supporting life" (85). Tadajewski and Hamilton conclude their analysis of these two documentaries with the sort of vague platitudes common to the horizon of action envisioned by neoliberal environmentalism: "While it might be a piece-meal form of social change, if we alter our own consumption habits along the lines suggested on the DVD box for *Trashed* (utilize reusable bags; use reusable bottles and filter water at home; reduce food miles, shop locally, form a cooperative with friends and family), the point is that we can do something. Small changes sometimes make dramatic differences" (85). What is more, they make a stronger claim about how films like Walker's can foster environmental commitments when they say that they have "the potential to move us from a state of indifference and apathy toward outrage and demand for social change" (85).

Tadajewski and Hamilton's analysis of the film does not really say anything insightful about its aesthetic qualities or its depiction of the realities of trash work in Brazil, but I bring it to bear here because it is such a clear example of the form of neoliberal environmentality that I have discussed in the previous section. The desired outcome that they express for audiences that contemplate Walker's depiction of Muniz's environmental and artistic project is notable (they say such exposure can make "dramatic differences" and generate "outrage and demand for social change"). But the path toward those big changes is beset by concessions and hedging from the outset (they say that the changes they foresee the documentary inspiring *might* be piecemeal and small but that such small changes *sometimes* lead to more dramatic ones). This is because it is a path shaped by the ideological constraints of individual consumer action. While this important element is one that a reading like Tadajewski and Hamilton's fails to recognize, their essay is valuable because it so clearly articulates how the film purports to operate. In documenting Muniz's "Pictures of Garbage" project and his work with the catadores of Jardim Gramacho, *Waste Land* does not merely want to document reality, but also to transform viewers, to make them socially and environmentally conscious, and to inspire them to make the world a better place.

The question remains: Does *Waste Land* fulfill its promise of transforming viewers into environmentalists? That is, at least in part, what it *wants* to do, but its investment in cultivating audience identification through the individualizing bent of the documentary aesthetic puts a clear limit on its ability to promulgate an environmental ethic that moves beyond the paradigm of neoliberal rationality. To be fair, if we focus on the initial phase of the two-step didactic process of "first enlightening, then inspiring" that depictions of trash projects exhibit, *Waste Land* does succeed to a certain extent at raising awareness, nudging viewers to notice the socioenvironmental realities that are most likely not part of their daily lives. Beyond the achievement of thematizing the work of catadores and allowing international audiences to become aware of it, the film's form also suggests the need to develop a deeper awareness of the way trash operates in urban spaces. Its depiction of Jardim Gramacho's relationship to Rio de Janeiro serves to illustrate this point. While the landfill is located on the very edge of Duque de Caxias, a suburb just north of Rio proper, it also overlooks Guanabara Bay, the same bay that serves as a shoreline for municipalities like Rio de Janeiro, Niterói, and São Gonçalo, glimpses of which can be seen in the background of the footage of Jardim Gramacho in the film. What is more, the landfill's connection to the greater Rio area is driven home with a series of establishing shots shown about ten minutes into the film, a quick sequence of iconic images of Rio that moves from an aerial shot taken from a helicopter hovering over a favela that affords a picturesque view of the shoreline to shots of the Cristo Redentor statue and people sunbathing and swimming at a beautiful beach, finally ending with shots of garbage that is on its way to the landfill in Jardim Gramacho. In this way, Walker asserts that the landfill is as much a part of the urban fabric as quintessentially *carioca* locales like Copacabana, Pão de Açúcar, Tijuca, or a favela. This sequence also illustrates how a landfill is connected to urban space through the flow of material. By showing trash at an intermediate point between the places from which it is discarded and the landfill where it will end up, the film urges viewers to consider the fact that all of the material that makes up Jardim Gramacho came from somewhere else, and, despite the transformation that it undergoes by being discarded, it retains a trace of that provenance, a point that is made somewhat comically later on in the film when a few catadores imagine what kind of people must have thrown certain items away (a shoe that must have belonged to a businesswoman, trash that came from a poor person's house because it was thrown away in small bag, and a letter about a subscription to *Playboy* that elicits a great deal of snickering).

If *Waste Land* can be said to bring a certain modality of trash work, along with its environmental and social implications, to the awareness of viewers and therefore to take a step toward inspiring a form of environmentality that aims to address the problem of trash, it is in the second phase of its didactic process (that of modeling a form of action) that the film reveals the pitfalls of neoliberal environmentalism. Walker's axiographical decision—to invoke documentary theorist Bill Nichols's term for "how values, particularly an ethics of representation, [come] to be known and experienced" in a documentary film (1991, 77)—to organize *Waste Land* around Vik Muniz as its main character and primary focus for generating audience identification is key in this regard. From the film's first frames, the viewer is invited to identify with Muniz's perspective. Before the opening credits roll, we see a clip from an appearance that Muniz made on the *Programa do Jô*, a *Late Show*-style talk show in Brazil. The host, Jô Soares, proclaims his guest as the most important contemporary Brazilian artist, noting that, through his work with materials like dirt, wire, string, and peanut butter, Muniz "dá vida ao lixo" (gives life to trash) (Walker 2009). When Soares asks him how he began working with garbage, the camera quickly cuts to a shot of Muniz looking happily pensive and the opening credits for the film begin to roll. Using this interview from the *Programa do Jô* as a frame for *Waste Land* suggests that the film is an answer to the question that Soares asks Muniz and serves as the first step in a process in which the evolution of Muniz's perspective of the catadores and Jardim Gramacho is established as the central narrative thread that ties the film together.

As Muniz is preparing to travel to Brazil to begin developing his project, his initial conception of the landfill as a gathering place for radical, problematic alterity is evident. While he is making his plans, we see a conversation that Muniz has with his wife Janaína, as he shows her video clips of mountains of trash and flocks of vultures, in addition to images of Jardim Gramacho on Google Earth. He expresses serious concerns about how the project will develop due to unforeseeable safety issues and his idea that the people who work in the landfill will be very difficult to work with, because he imagines them to be violent drug addicts. While these uninformed opinions may be perceived by viewers as harsh, it is not far-fetched to consider them more or less consonant with those that equally uninformed viewers would hold before getting to know some of the waste workers in the landfill further along in the film. Despite his reservations and preconceived notions about the catadores, Vik and his team go to Rio to begin the project. During the first tour that the group takes of the landfill, Walker deftly employs both the camera and editing techniques in order to solidify the viewer's identification with Muniz's perspective, which has been set up by framing the film as Muniz's reflection on his own story as an artist who works with garbage and by demonstrating his lack of knowledge about Jardim Gramacho and the catadores, which, by and large, the viewer shares. As Muniz walks through the vast landfill, a subjective camera is perched over his shoulder, and images of heaps of trash, vultures, and people digging through the refuse are crosscut with medium shots of Muniz as he takes in the scene. In short, not only do we see what he sees, but also we see it how he sees it, and we are, to a certain extent, conditioned to sympathize with his interpretation of what he sees.[20] Thus, when he mentions that things in the landfill are not as bad as he thought they would be and that the catadores, rather than being depressed, seem to enjoy their work, we are perhaps inclined to share his evaluation of the situation. However, some subtle editing work serves to undermine Muniz's (and in turn our) all-too-hasty conclusion: just as Muniz is shown mentioning that the catadores seem happy, Walker cuts to an image of what can only be described as a sudden avalanche of trash that sends catadores scrambling for safety. The dissonance between what Muniz is saying and the image on the screen serves to call into question our assumptions about the situation of the catadores as has been voiced by Muniz thus far. It is a subtle but effective move that signals that Muniz (and therefore the viewer) needs to learn more about the catadores and their work. What he learns and feels about this complex reality, we will in turn also learn and feel, which is characteristic of the juxtapositions of the documentary aesthetic that "[offset] emotion and personal experience with the structures that produce their possibilities" (Worden 2020, 9).

This evolution in Muniz's (and the audience's) opinion about the reality of Jardim Gramacho progresses as he gets to know the catadores better and starts working on his "Pictures of Garbage" project with them. While Muniz's voice, which predominates at the beginning of the film, gives way to the voices of the catadores as the project unfolds, his perspective continues to structure the way that the viewer perceives what goes on in the landfill and the efficacy of his artistic and environmentalist intervention. At one point, for instance, he travels to São Paulo to visit his family, which precipitates a reflection on his part about having grown up in poverty, much like the catadores he is working with. In this sense, the film posits a neutralization of the alterity of catadores and the landfill. It establishes a trajectory that moves from the assumed radical alterity of the catadores to the conclusion that the Others who live and work in Jardim Gramacho are not so different from Muniz, and, by extension, they are not so different from the viewer, since the viewer is constantly invited to identify with Muniz. What marks the difference between the Muniz and the catadores are socioeconomic forces articulated as "chance." In the end, Muniz concludes that, with a few bad breaks along the way, *he* could have ended up as a catador, too. While he does not explicitly articulate the inverse of that hypothesis—that is, with a few good breaks, the catadores could end up becoming *him*—that seems to be exactly the scenario that the film wants to portray, a point that becomes exceedingly clear just before the title credits begin to roll and we see footage of Tião, one of the participants in Muniz's project and the president of ACAMJG, as a guest on the *Programa do Jô*, occupying the very same seat in which we first saw Muniz at the beginning of the film. This bookending of the film with clips from the talk show is emblematic of its deployment of the individualism that is characteristic of the documentary aesthetic. Not only is the messy reality of Jardim Gramacho presented within the framework of an individual's perception of it, but also that individual serves as a link in a chain of identification that runs from the viewer through Muniz to Tião. This erasure of difference is particularly grievous given that Tião's life experience is decidedly *unlike* that of Muniz and, presumably, that of virtually all viewers of the film. Prior to working on the "Pictures of Garbage" project, Tião had a significant family and personal history in labor organizing and politics, but, as Millar notes, "[t]his part of Tião's life history is not presented in the film. Instead, Tião's story is a version of a bootstrapped narrative—one of individual struggle that is eventually triumphant (in part through the help of Muniz who is portrayed as almost 'discovering' Tião)," which leverages "the trope of the poor genius, who is innately talented and through self-education eventually achieves success" (2020, 14).

To return to Nichols's concept of axiographics, he notes that the question spectators are confronted with when watching documentary film "is not what kind of imaginary world the filmmaker has created but how the filmmaker acquitted him- or herself in relation to those segments of the historical world that have become the scene of the film. Where does the filmmaker stand? What space does he or she occupy and what politics or ethics attach themselves to it?" (1991, 79). *Waste Land*'s wager on presenting the segment of the world occupied by the catadores in Jardim Gramacho through the individualistic narrative of success that is projected from

Muniz to Tião pays off in the sense that it fulfills the viewer's desire (or perhaps the desire the film attempts to construct for the viewer) to see one of the film's key transformations (human self-actualization) come to fruition. But any resulting good feelings or uplift from this come at an ethical cost, because the film's investment in individualization and easy identification neutralizes questions of specificity, alterity, and political and structural change. The role of the landfill and its contents is crucial in the depiction of how Muniz comes to identify with the catadores, for it is the very material of which Jardim Gramacho is made that gives life to the portraits and establishes the foundation of a relationship between Muniz and the catadores. This is also the core of what the film proposes as a model for an environmental ethic. On the one hand, both the collaborative art project and the film suggest the possibility of an intriguing ethical stance for the individual to take with respect to the landfill and the problem of trash, one that reaffirms the value of both people and objects that have been discarded. On the other hand, this ethical relationship seems, as Pablo Gonçalo contends, to be cloaked in "uma roupagem contemporânea do paternalismo de outrora" (the contemporary trappings of an erstwhile paternalism) (2011, 101). Not only does Muniz's authorship of and control over the "Pictures of Garbage" project belie his insistence upon the nonhierarchical, collaborative nature of the undertaking,[21] but also the seeming ease with which trash becomes art and art becomes commodity in the film ends up looking like an erasure of the problem of the landfill itself. By the end of the film, the landfill simply seems to fade away, leaving the viewer with the sensation that such a highly problematic space has been completely domesticated by incorporating it into the international art market. Despite the warm feelings Muniz's project might inspire and the undeniable fact that it gave international visibility to a highly marginalized population that does essential work when it comes to confronting the problem of trash, the film's portrayal of his work sanitizes and commodifies the social and environmental issues at stake in Jardim Gramacho.

Instead of exploring the possibility of a renowned artist like Muniz using his connections and clout to shed light on the political and environmental organizing of ACAMJG and suggesting that international audiences pay heed to the lessons that catadores have to offer on taking care of the environment, *Waste Land* opts to tell a story about an individual's good-hearted efforts to help a few other poor, unfortunate individuals. In the process, as such a script dictates, those poor, unfortunate individuals are really the ones who end up helping him, since they teach him that chasing material comforts (that is, consuming and discarding indiscriminately) is not all that it's cracked up to be. And that is the primary lesson that Muniz's project has to teach viewers as well. The film's investment in the individual responsibility of neoliberal environmentalism is strong, ranging from Muniz's private art enterprise to its focus on how that project affects the lives of a handful of individual catadores.[22] In the end, what viewers experience is not, contrary to Tadajewski and Hamilton, a documentary that moves them from "indifference and apathy" to "outrage and demand for social change" (2014, 85). Instead, the film's failure to problematize Muniz's paternalistic, facile identification with the catadores and their milieu neutralizes the need for outrage and further demands. The sense that the viewer walks away with (this viewer, at least) is that the problem has been solved through Muniz's good deeds. Further, because I have been induced to identify with Muniz, I can leave the film almost feeling like I myself had some sort of hand in those good deeds. I am certainly exaggerating here, but, in a sense, the film works as a fantasy for a viewer like me, who can begin viewing in a "state of indifference and apathy" and end feeling quite good about myself, if not for *actually* having done anything to "make the world a better place," then at least for having had the intelligence and ethical clarity to educate myself about catadores. I am transformed, and the world is a better place. Such is the fantasy that neoliberal environmentalism has to offer, and *Waste Land* is an adept expression of its limits.

Gallinazo Avisa: Only *You* Can Prevent Pollution

If *Waste Land*'s portrayal of Jardim Gramacho's catadores brings to mind the communities of trash pickers operating in and out of the dump that I considered in this book's second chapter, the next depiction of an environmental campaign focused on trash is an echo of the human/animal limit that I analyzed in chapter 1, especially as made manifest in Ribeyro's short story "Los gallinazos sin plumas" (but perhaps with much of the pedagogical quality of Salazar Bondy's children's book *El Señor Gallinazo vuelve a Lima*). In 2015, the Ministry of Environment of Peru and the United States Agency for International Development undertook a project called Gallinazo Avisa, an environmental campaign designed to bring attention to the problem of illegal and clandestine trash dumping sites in Lima and to encourage individual citizens and groups to participate in the identification and remediation of these dumping sites.[23] As part of the project, ten vultures were equipped with GPS devices and body cameras in order to track their movements and to record videos of dumps while they would fly around the city in search of food. The videos and other data, presented from the perspective of the vultures, were shared on a variety of social media platforms—including YouTube, Facebook, and Twitter—so that users who followed the project could keep track of the routes the vultures traced throughout the city and share information about illegal dumping sites that they themselves found as they wandered throughout Peru's capital.

I first came across this "ingenious way to attack the problem" of trash piles throughout the city while thumbing through *The Lima Reader*, a recent entry in Duke University Press's series of Latin America readers (Walker 2017, 254). I was in a bookstore in Ann Arbor, Michigan, shortly after giving a paper at the biennial conference of the Association for the Study of Literature and Environment on the social and political struggles of cartoneros in Buenos Aires. The conversations that I had recently experienced about trash, trash workers, and the city, along with the placement of this brief chapter at the very end of a volume that was intended to "provide a sample of Lima's complex history—its glories and traditions, its pleasures and charms, as well as its old and new predicaments and tensions" and offer "a comprehensive and historically informed view of the city's changing physical contours, its ever-shifting populations, and the competing mythologies and imaginaries created around all of them" struck me as indicative of the centrality of waste and waste management in defining those predicaments and tensions now and in the years to come (Aguirre and Walker 2017, 3). As the anthology's final word on Lima, this description of a project that made strange bedfellows of humans, vultures, and high technology suggested to me the possibility of imagining an innovative way both to perceive urban space, the trash, and bodies that flow through it and to work toward dealing with the interface of space, trash, and bodies in a way that addresses both human and nonhuman needs and concerns.

I make explicit mention of the details of how I became aware of Gallinazo Avisa in order to highlight the way that my own disciplinary formation, intellectual interests, and base of operations condition my reaction to the project and my analytical approach to it here. As a scholar of contemporary Latin American cultures, who is based in the United States with a particular interest in cultural representations of trash, my reading of Gallinazo Avisa is mediated in a number of ways, the most obvious of which are time and space. My thoughts on the project come after the fact and are articulated from a distance that represents both cultural difference and privilege. Also, my training as a literary and cultural studies scholar certainly influences my approach, which emphasizes the aesthetic and discursive texture of the main promotional video that was produced for the project, and perhaps this approach comes at the expense of a results-based evaluation that other disciplinary approaches might provide. Such limitations and particularities are, however, an inescapable element of the critical enterprise. What is more, acknowledging and exploring my own situation, however briefly, allow me to emphasize just how seductive an environmental campaign like Gallinazo Avisa can be. It is the type of project that, as I argue below, neatly conforms to the neoliberal environmentalist paradigm of framing environmental problems and solutions as the purview of individuals who use their freedom either to make messes or to clean them up. Charles F. Walker's brief essay on Gallinazo Avisa in *The Lima Reader*, which celebrates its creativity and potential "to contribute to the search for solutions," can be seen as a token of the way that neoliberalism's approach to environmental action tends to be treated without question as a good way of addressing problems like trash, especially in view of the essay's privileged position at the end of the book, which suggests an endorsement of campaigns like this in the future (2017, 256). Lest I come across as unduly critical of the editors of *The Lima Reader*, I feel compelled to confess that my own initial reaction to Gallinazo Avisa tended toward excitement and endorsement to an even greater extent than that of Walker. I gave a conference presentation and wrote a draft of an essay that proposed the environmental campaign as a profoundly ethical undertaking that decentered human needs and perspectives in an attempt to cultivate a form of environmentality that fostered human/nonhuman alliances. Ultimately, I abandoned the essay because the more closely I considered Gallinazo Avisa, the less convinced I became that my initial celebratory reaction was well considered. This is not to say that I find the project's efforts to do something to address Lima's trash problem wrong or unethical. There are far worse things people can do with their time and energy than remove garbage from beaches, abandoned lots, and riverbanks. What I find pernicious about Gallinazo Avisa, much like *Waste Land*, is the way that it presents itself, which a careful reading of the project's advertising will hopefully make clear. While that material is undoubtedly ephemeral, paying attention to it while taking it as seriously as a high-profile cultural text like Walker's film is a worthwhile critical enterprise, for doing so shows that neoliberal environmentalism suffuses portrayals of trash projects both large and small.[24]

There are a number of audiovisual materials associated with Gallinazo Avisa, but I will use the campaign's main promotional video, which can be found on the project's YouTube channel, as the focal point for my reflections ("Gallinazo Avisa").[25] While the project's other social media interventions also offer compelling material for analysis—tweets ranging from reminders to celebrate International Vulture Awareness Day to announcements about vulture-themed merchandise available for purchase, for instance (@GallinazoAvisa, "Humanos, los invito"; @GallinazoAvisa, "Humanos, estamos viendo")—the main promotional video contains all of the basic elements the project puts into play and provides a sense of the way Gallinazo Avisa blurs the lines between advertising and activism. In short, it simultaneously displays the project's more problematic aspects while it suggests the possibility of rethinking the way that animals (both human and nonhuman), trash, and technology come into contact with each other and shape urban environments.

The project's main promotional video, launched on YouTube in 2015, has a relatively brief running time of two minutes and twelve seconds, which would seem to situate it somewhere between commercial advertising and short film. This generic ambiguity is appropriate because the video relies on narrative and formal features central to both commercials and wildlife documentaries. On the one hand, it reads like a commercial in that the entire narrative arc bends toward a climactic "sell job" in which the voiceover narrator directly interpellates viewers, using the imperative to urge them to participate in the project, in a way that echoes Señor Tlacuache's direct address to the viewer in Vargas's documentary short: "¡*Únanse* a nosotros, *entren* en la web, *usen* nuestro mapa!" (*Join* us, *go* to the website, *use* our map!) ("Gallinazo Avisa"; emphasis mine). What is more, the advertising discourse that the video's narrative structure uses is reinforced by propulsive, fast-paced editing and by the deployment of a consistent branding iconography for the project (logo, color schemes, and fonts used for onscreen text), all of which combine to produce a well-packaged, legible pitch with a basic function to convince viewers to buy (into) an environmental project that also seems like a sort of consumer product.

On the other hand, the video also leverages key tropes of wildlife documentaries, like voiceover narration, anthropomorphism, visual displays of animals engaging in everyday activities in their natural habitats, and a general sense of the need to rescue animals from harm (Horak 2006, 473). However, much like the way that the campaign's use of advertising discourse blurs the line between consumer activity and environmental activism, its deployment of these tropes does not quite conform to what viewers might normally expect of a wildlife documentary. The video opens in black and white, with a long shot of a church bell tower, followed by a quick cut to a medium shot of a vulture perched in the same bell tower facing away from the camera. The shadows, framing, and use of black-and-white film make it easy to miss the vulture in spite of its position in the center of the frame. Simultaneous with this sequence of shots, the voiceover narrator begins to tell the story of humanity's relationship with garbage by setting up a dichotomy. On the one hand, pestilence, disease, and filth have emanated from waste for the last 14,000 years (this piece of narration coincides with a quick sequence of close-up shots of a trash dump, including animal carcasses and swarms of flies); on the other, there are humans who produce trash but placidly ignore the threat it poses to order and development (here the voiceover is accompanied by images of crowds of people walking through busy city streets and an aerial shot of the Costa Verde highway that runs between Lima's iconic *barrancos* [cliffs] and the Pacific Ocean).[26] As the narrator puts it, what stands between these two phenomena—trash and humans—is *us*, the vultures. As the narrator reveals himself to be a vulture, there is a low-angle shot of a flock of vultures swarming in the sky, followed by a return to the medium shot of the vulture in the bell tower spreading its wings, then a quick sequence of a close-up of the bird and an extreme close-up of its head. In the brief pause the narrator makes between "us" and "the vultures," the vulture in the bell tower turns and faces the camera directly, effectively breaking the fourth wall at the very moment the voiceover narrator is revealed to be a vulture instead of a human being. This marks an interesting variation on the documentary aesthetic with which the campaign video engages, for while it reflects Worden's formulation of the mode of neoliberal cultural production by presenting a complicated contemporary reality from the standpoint of an individual, the individual in this case is a vulture with whom the viewer is meant to sympathize.

I describe the first thirty seconds of the video in such detail because these small technical elements (voiceover, framing, camera angles, editing) reveal the way the campaign uses the tropes of wildlife or nature documentaries to set up one of the project's key discursive strategies: the supposed decentering of the human perspective. The script followed by the narrator, which proposes a long history of environmental degradation at the hands of human beings, mimics the type of authoritative voiceover that any casual viewer of nature documentaries would recognize. However, this discursive formulation is turned on its head by the fact that the authority on wildlife is, in this case, not a human being but a vulture, a point that is made clear by the highly dramatic way in which the narrator's identity is revealed a quarter of the way into the video. Shifting the locus of authority on matters concerning the "natural" world also raises the question of what type of "wildlife" is being captured by the camera and put on display for viewers. In this sense, the video's discursive strategy suggests that the shots of humans moving through the city are images of wildlife just as much as the ones of vultures are.[27]

The video continues in the vein of the wildlife documentary when the narrator explains how vultures' sharp senses and guts equipped by evolution allow them to protect unwitting humans from the toxicity of waste. The visual material that accompanies this segment of the narration also further destabilizes the perceived form of life on display in the video: a high angle shot of people in a plaza in Lima suggests the perspective of a vulture, and another quick sequence of close-ups of trash, this time with vultures digging for food, frames the vultures as the animals that are captured and documented by the camera. At this point, the video shifts from explaining and documenting the role of vultures in waste management to making the advertising pitch I describe above. The narrator says that while he and his kind continue to work tirelessly, Lima's trash is taking over, a claim that is illustrated by a series of aerial shots (complete with a distorting filter that blurs the edges of the frame to establish what is seen as pertaining to the vultures' point of view) of illegal dump sites in different locations throughout the city: a working-class neighborhood, cliffs by the sea, and the streets of the city center. This gives way to a description of the project Gallinazo Avisa, which the narrator frames as an alliance or collaboration between vultures and humans, followed by the call to action that directly urges viewers to participate in the project by following the vultures on Gallinazo Avisa's social media pages and by identifying illegal dump sites on their own. Throughout this whole sequence, techniques similar to those described above—alternating between high- and low-angle shots, using different filters to produce distortions in the image in the frame—are used in order to differentiate the species-based perspectives deployed in the video.

The sequence of end titles that punctuate the video's conclusion neatly and efficiently condenses the way that this trash remediation project inscribes itself within the bounds of neoliberal environmentalism: text reading "GALLINAZO AVISA" (in all caps) is accompanied by the campaign's logo, a silhouette of a vulture with a bullhorn in its claws, and followed by the terse declaration, "TÚ ACTÚAS," which then gives way to the final end title, WWW.GALLINAZOAVISA.PE, the URL for the project's website.[28] The first two end titles manage to reinstate the clear divide between the human and the nonhuman, a boundary that is deployed in the service of creating a hierarchical relationship that the campaign plays at upending but ultimately subscribes to in full. The vultures' purpose is to gather intelligence for humans on humans' terms, never communicating anything that exceeds or escapes the anthropomorphic projection of the human perspective to which the body cameras and voiceover narration subject them. They are domesticated into the iconography of an advertising campaign logo. It is expected that the autonomous, rational human individuals who come across the campaign video should use the intelligence gathered by the birds as the basis for their decision to take individual action. As the last end title suggests, the primary modality of action that the project envisions is online engagement.

Clearly, Gallinazo Avisa is a relatively minor example of the sort of depictions of creative trash projects that I have considered in this chapter, more akin to the scale of "Los artilugios del Señor Tlacuache" than *Waste Land*. But it shares with those two documentaries the individualized sensibility of neoliberal environmentalism. All three deploy their ecologically themed messages within a framework that places heavy responsibility on the shoulders of individuals to make good choices about consumption, to commit to picking up trash, or to be conscientious about recycling. They do so in a highly attractive way, organizing the stories they tell around compelling individuals (a junk man, an artist, anthropomorphic vultures) who also serve as points of entry for viewers of these cultural texts to begin understanding and caring about the complex social and environmental reality of trash in places like Mexico City, Rio de Janeiro, or Lima. This ideological, structural, and aesthetic emphasis on the role of the individual in dealing with the problem of trash is precisely what makes these depictions of trash projects so compelling and so pernicious. Because we, as individuals, can relate to or understand "characters" like Señor Tlacuache, Vik Muniz, and the vultures, we begin to see what is at stake in paying attention to trash in our own environments. But we are, perhaps, deluded into thinking that individual action related to habits of consumption is the first and best step toward doing something about all that trash.

As I reach the end of this chapter, I want to make it clear that I am not arguing that what I have called neoliberal environmentalism is the most important or dominant form of environmentality in Latin America, either with regard to projects aimed at dealing with waste or with regard to other environmental concerns. What I hope to have shown is that it is powerful and seductive because it *seems* to make so much sense and it *feels* empowering. In the end, however, it is a failure to recognize that we are not really autonomous individuals, but rather entities who only come into being in and through relationality. It is a refusal to engage in what Braidotti calls nomadic thought, which "conceptualizes matter as self-organized and relational in its very structures. This means that each nomadic connection offers at least the possibility of an ethical relation of opening out towards an empowering connection to others" (2011, 3). The depictions of trash projects considered here, especially *Waste Land* and *Gallinazo Avisa*, seem at times to stage these kinds of nomadic connections—with radically different Others, like catadores or vultures, and with trash itself—but the material relations that they enact end up obeying the "master code" of neoliberalism that formats and regulates matter according to the dictates of human exceptionalism and individualism (3). Working with trash has the potential to activate nomadic thinking and connection, so I would like to close this chapter with a brief consideration of another project that might do just that.

Basurama: Beyond Neoliberal Environmentalism?

The multidisciplinary architecture, design, performance, and visual arts collective Basurama was formed in 2001 by a group of students at ETSAM, the Escuela Técnica Superior de Arquitectura de Madrid (Higher Technical School of Architecture of Madrid). Over the last two decades, the group has executed over one hundred artistic and cultural projects in Europe, the Americas, Africa, Asia, and Australia that focus on "los procesos productivos, la generación de desechos que éstos implican y las posibilidades creativas que suscitan estas coyunturas contemporáneas" (the processes of production, the generation of waste that such processes imply, and the creative possibilities caused by these contemporary circumstances) ("Sobre Basurama"). Between 2008 and 2010, Basurama developed and implemented a series of public art projects in Latin America under the title "Residuos Urbanos Sólidos" (Urban Solid Waste), or RUS, the idea of which was to undertake "una reflexión conjunta con respecto al consumo y la reutilización de los residuos y del 'espacio basura' de las ciudades, a través de aproximaciones muy distintas a urbes de características particulares. Todas estas ciudades comparten una serie de conflictos como son, por ejemplo, el consumo masivo, la desigualdad en el acceso a los recursos y la precariedad en el mundo de la gestión de la basura, así como una segregación urbana salvaje, un hipertrofiado y muy rico sector informal, una obsesión por el desarrollo, etc." (a joint reflection on consumption and the reuse of waste and "trash spaces" in cities, through very distinct approaches to urban areas with particular characteristics. All of these cities share a number of conflicts, such as mass consumption, unequal access to resources, and precarity when it comes to the management of trash, as well as brutal urban segregation, an outsized and very rich informal sector, an obsession with development, etc.) (Basurama 2011, 10).[29] A richly detailed log of these projects, their aims and rationale, and careful reflections on the process can be found in the book *RUS. Residuos Urbanos Sólidos. Basura y espacio público en América Latina*, published in 2011 under the collective authorship of Basurama.

When considered alongside the other depictions of creative trash projects that I analyze in the previous sections of this chapter, RUS and the way Basurama presents it strike me as decidedly anti-individualistic and nonhierarchical. Unlike *Waste Land* or Gallinazo Avisa, which rely on the development of individual perspectives to generate audience identification and end up reproducing an individualistic ethos in their elaboration of horizons for possible environmental action, Basurama frames the RUS projects as necessarily collective and collaborative. Beyond the collective authorship of the book that details the ins and outs of Basurama's undertaking—which I see as a subtle formal resistance to the imperatives of the documentary aesthetic—the group's methodological approach emphasizes the ideas of establishing networks with local actors (often community organizers and waste workers) and respecting their knowledge, creativity, and expertise (11). The three general axes around which they organize their projects—the creation of networks, working with trash, and intervening in public space—allow them to approach the specific issues and needs in different communities in a way that both conforms to those particular contexts and makes a clear, consistent statement about the social and environmental problems that trash makes visible and the potential of collective action for addressing those problems (12).

To give just a few examples of Basurama's horizontal, collective methodology in action, it is instructive to consider the group's approach to a recalcitrant problem in contemporary cities: the excessive reliance on individual automobiles in urban transportation. Projects in Mexico City and Lima offer a glimpse of the creative ways trash can be marshaled to call attention to this issue and to open pathways for addressing it. The 2008 project "Haga su propio carrito" (Make your own cart) was undertaken with artisans, industrial designers, and *pepenadores* (Mexico's equivalent to cartoneros and catadores) in Mexico City (36–51). These experts worked together to offer a workshop on how to design and fabricate human-powered carts from scavenged scrap metal, which were meant to recall the kind of carts used by pepenadores and street vendors, but with extravagant elements like gigantic wheels or asymmetrical configurations, in order to call attention to themselves and therefore to remind people of how these forms of transportation, which pollute less than automobiles, are ubiquitous but seemingly invisible. Subsequently, the participants staged a 16.6-kilometer caravan through the city streets to Mexico City's Zócalo as part of a campaign "en contra de la supremacía del automóvil en la ciudad" (against the supremacy of the automobile in the city) (49). In 2009 and 2010, the "Autoparque público de diversiones" (Self-made public playground) approached the problem of transportation in Lima by focusing on a single space: a stretch of elevated platforms that had been constructed for a defunct electric train project (138–51). Basurama worked with local artists, graphic designers, and a collective of architecture students to reclaim this abandoned space by transforming it into a park, a safe place for children and families to play. All the attractions and play structures (swings, climbing areas, and so on.) were made from salvaged car parts and tires "como forma de reflexión paradójica al respecto del transporte público y privado" (as a sort of paradoxical reflection on public and private transportation) (145).

I could give further examples from the RUS series on the intersection between plastic waste and public space, the role of invisibilized forms of labor in managing trash, and more. In fact, I will turn to another of Basurama's interventions in this book's conclusion, but before arriving at that point, I would like to note that in its commitment to relationality and collectivity, Basurama's efforts at addressing the issue of trash show us the possibility of a mode of environmentalism that pushes back against the entrenched mentality of neoliberalism, with its emphasis on the actions of well-intentioned individuals. As Luis I. Prádanos notes, "Basurama does not recycle but reuses; it does not celebrate waste for its potential to become a new market commodity, but repurposes it in socially meaningful ways unmediated by monetary transactions and therefore enjoyable by all; it does not perpetuate the logic of unlimited growth by encouraging endless consumerism, but criticizes the dominant imaginary by embracing alternative ways to relate to community, materiality, and space" (184). This alternative way of relating—to each other, to trash, and the spaces we share with the trash we make—is increasingly necessary because, despite this chapter's title, "cleaning up" our trash is not really as simple as committing ourselves to sorting recyclables from nonrecyclables or picking up garbage we see on the street, at the beach, or in a field. In one way or another, all the depictions of trash projects I have analyzed here allow us to see the impact of trash on bodies and spaces of all kinds. They also throw into sharp relief the limits of the dominant neoliberal imaginary when it comes to cultivating the ability to live with the trash we produce, accepting responsibility for it, and working collectively to shape a world in which its effects are not as noxious as they are in this world.

Conclusion

Trash is shot through with contradictions. It can be so viscerally repulsive as to trigger the gag reflex or so utterly banal that we fail to notice it right in front of our faces. When seen as bits of litter floating on the breeze, it is the essence of the ephemeral, but that litter—much of it plastic—is fusing with rocks, some of the most quintessentially solid and permanent objects on the planet, and making appearances in Earth's most remote corners.[1] As the pat phrase would have it, trash can be both treasure and, well, trash. Trash is many things at the same time, and that multivalence is why it is a material presence in our environment and a symbolic presence in cultural texts that must be looked at, accounted for, and thought about. When we pay careful attention to waste and the contradictions and tensions it enacts, we see that it "is disruptive," that it "creates new networks, makes connections visible, sparks new social relations," and that it "tends to bring other things together" (Amago 2021, 6). This has been borne out in *Trash and Limits in Latin American Culture*. Being mindful of trash's formal and thematic function in "Los gallinazos sin plumas" and "Ilha das Flores" makes visible the connections between economic activity and the exposure of bodies—both human and nonhuman alike—to violence and exclusion. Trash's capacity for sparking new social relations is on display in the stories that Eduardo Coutinho, Alicia Dujovne Ortiz, and Lucy Walker tell about communities that work in landfills, and a project like Gallinazo Avisa suggests the possibility of creating new networks of environmental care, even if it ultimately succumbs to the logic of neoliberal environmentalism. By taking seriously the presence and function of trash in literary fiction about men's experiences of the crises of neoliberalism from such vaunted authors as César Aira, Horacio Castellanos Moya, and Andrés Neuman (to name a few), we can see more clearly what is at stake in the way that waste is managed. In all these cases, trash compels us to contemplate the limits of how we define ourselves as humans, what underpins the formation of communities, our ability to manage the excess we produce, and the notion of individual responsibility in the face of collective environmental crisis. As I draw this book to a close, I would like to consider another of the interdisciplinary collective Basurama's projects, one that was not part of the Residuos Urbanos Sólidos initiative discussed in chapter 4, but that brings home trash's quality as limit and its power as an element of cultural expression.

In Brazil in 2014, Basurama created a sculptural installation called "Luxo é Lixo" (Luxury is Trash) for display on Urca Beach, located at the foot of Pão de Açúcar, one of Rio de Janeiro's most iconic landmarks. The sculpture, a joint project between Basurama and a group of Brazilian university students, was a large-scale representation of the word "LUXO" ("luxury" in Portuguese) made from more than four thousand plastic bags gathered from the trash (*lixo*) by the students participating in the project, residents of the surrounding neighborhood, and local catadores ("Luxo é Lixo"). As the description of the project attests, the sculpture paid homage to Augusto de Campos's 1965 concrete poem "Luxo," which proposes a suggestive, playful dialectic between the words lixo and luxo: the poem consists of the word "lixo" printed in large, block letters made up of the repetition of the word "luxo," printed in a very ornate font; additionally, the poem is printed on a tri-fold piece of paper attached to the page of the book in which it appears (1986, 119).[2]

The point of contact between opulence and waste that Augusto underlines in "Luxo" is what animates Basurama's engagement with the poem, so it would be useful to consider two critical perspectives on the threshold that binds luxo and lixo together: brief reflections on his poem in essays by the renowned critic Roberto Schwarz and Haroldo de Campos (Augusto's brother and fellow *concretista*). Although "Luxo" is not the focal point of analysis for either critic—Schwarz's essay critiques "Póstudo," another of Augusto's poems, while Haroldo argues that a certain poverty of expression is key to understanding the aesthetics of modern Brazilian literature—their tangential readings of the poem directly address the paradoxical connection between trash and art.

Pausing in the middle of his analysis of "Póstudo," Schwarz's attention is drawn to "Luxo," which he disqualifies as aggressively kitschy, lacking in specificity, and intellectually imprecise. For Schwarz, the agressivity of the poem's kitsch is a cheap trick, and the link that it proposes between luxury and trash is no more than "um lugar-comun do moralismo acanhado, que o arranjo gráfico e a semelhança entre as palavras não resgatam" (a bromide of the timid brand of moralism that the poem's graphic arrangement and the similarity of the words cannot overcome) (1987, 60). His evaluation of "Póstudo" seems to be an appropriate summation of his reading of "Luxo" as well: "Sem dúvida é bonito, e banal. Como não temos parâmetros, o que fica é a gesticulação abstrata do desejo de transformar, embalada em tipografia atraente" (It is undoubtedly pretty, and banal. What we are left with is an abstract gesticulation of the desire for transformation, all wrapped in attractive typography) (66). For Schwarz, Augusto's provocation is facile and shallow—note his insistence on the superficiality of the typeface, which is "agressivamente *kitsch*" (aggressively kitsch) and serves as *embalagem*, wrapping, for the poem's (vacuous) content (59). In this sense, "Luxo" is an empty gesture, a waste of time, space, and effort. In other words, it is trash that is not worth much consideration.

While Schwarz dismisses Augusto's poem as a useless object and seems to prefer to relegate it to the literary dustbin, Haroldo de Campos sees in "Luxo" the poetic expression of a discursive stutter, *um estilo gago* that runs through the work of important Brazilian literary figures like Joaquim Maria Machado de Assis, Oswaldo de Andrade, and Graciliano Ramos and that flies in the face of the idea that good writing entails a mastery over language: "Dominar o *logos* é aceder à condição de hominidade. Mas o *logos* despista. O *logos* é minado pelo ideológico. O texto pobre denuncia a retórica bem-falante" (To dominate the *logos* is to accede to the condition of human-ness. But the *logos* misleads. The *logos* is subverted by the ideological. The impoverished text denounces well-spoken rhetoric) (66). Whereas Schwarz remains unconvinced by Augusto's punning, Haroldo hints at a fundamental aspect of puns that Susan Signe Morrison spells out explicitly: "Puns are a form of waste and excess.... Puns interrupt, provoking new lines of thought" (2015, 152–53). The tension between expressibility and inexpressibility, mastery and failure that Haroldo sees as central to what he calls *uma arte pobre* is staged in Augusto's poem in terms of linguistic play and materiality. For Haroldo, "LIXO/LUXO de Augusto é um exemplo frisante dessa dialética de extremidades, que encena na arte mínima de seu 'procedimento menos'... o jogo de suas tensões e mediações, como uma tatuagem intersemiótica. O oxímoro paranomástico 'lixo/luxo' se redobra visualmente numa tipografia desejadamente *kitsch*, enquanto as páginas desdobráveis vão compondo, numa escansão paródica, a luxúria do LUXO de encontro à lixívia do LIXO" (Augusto's LIXO/LUXO is a striking example of this dialectic of extremities, which stages in the minimal art of his "minus procedure" ... the play of its tensions and mediations, like an intersemiotic tattoo. The paronomastic oxymoron "trash/luxury" is visually redoubled in a desirably kitschy typography, while the fold-out pages compose, in a parodic scansion, the lust of LUXO [luxury] against the bleach of LIXO [trash]) (67).

"Luxo," then, asks a series of important questions by displaying the connection between the proliferation and containment of the linguistic sign, both through its aggressively and desirably kitschy typography—note how Haroldo's disposition toward the "superficial" nature of the poem differs from Schwarz's disposition—and through the manipulation of its material support, the folded paper on which the poem is printed that has to be unfolded in order for it to be read. Are the meanings attached to each component of the minimal pair lixo/luxo at odds with each other, or does this oxymoronic pun, as Haroldo calls it, point to the space where meaning loses clarity and signs exceed the limits that are commonly thought to hold them in place? If both trash and luxury can be seen as versions of excess, how do we distinguish between the two? What part does trash play in signifying practices like writing?

All of these tensions, questions, and provocations are inscribed or archived in Basurama's homage to Augusto's poem. While Schwarz dismisses the connection that Augusto makes between opulence and waste as mere timid moralizing, Basurama's reading of the poem, like Haroldo's, takes Augusto's playfulness (and trashiness) more seriously. In fact, Basurama raises the stakes at play in Augusto's poem by opening it up and bringing it into contact with material waste, a presence with contours that remain in the discursive realm in "Luxo." What "Luxo é Lixo" proposes in its materialization of Augusto's poem is a radically literal translation—or perhaps we could call it a *litter-al* translation. But despite this lit(t)eralness, Basurama's translation is also unfaithful to its source material in that it is an inversion, a mirror image of the original: whereas Augusto uses luxo to write the word lixo, the art installation uses lixo to write the word luxo. This inversion makes for a productively unfaithful translation that, read in tandem with Augusto's poem, is suggestive for several reasons. First, it underscores the threshold of undecidability, the limit between the signs lixo and luxo, both at the level of the signifier (the difference between the two rests on a slight shift in the position of the tongue and the shape of the mouth) and at the level of the signified (the way that trash calls into question neat distinctions between seemingly opposing categories). Second, by switching the position of the signs that Augusto deploys in his poem, Basurama inscribes its project more clearly in a discourse that is critical of consumerism and aware of the ineluctably material nature of contemporary regimes of consumption, as well as the threat that such regimes pose to life on this planet. Finally, while "Lixo é Luxo" makes a more overt appeal than "Luxo" to the connection between opulence, environmental degradation, and crisis, this foregrounding of social, political, and environmental stakes does not rule out a sophisticated engagement with Augusto's reflections on writing.

Perhaps it goes without saying that the luxo that amounts to so much trash in Augusto's poem and the luxo whose material condition of possibility is trash itself in Basurama's sculpture can mean many different things, just like all the trash found in the texts analyzed throughout *Trash and Limits in Latin American Culture*. Luxo can stand for an excessive consumer culture, the comforts of one social class that rely on the privations of another, material goods that are inessential and therefore desirable as marks of distinction. However, since both the poem and the sculpture that cites it deal with (and are expressions of) the written word, I would argue that a possible interpretation of luxo revolves around writing as a signifying practice and literature as a specific form of that signifying practice.

If "Luxo" asserts the excessive nature of literature—the proliferation of writing that, as it accumulates, results in the production of garbage—Basurama's "Luxo é Lixo" dislocates, transforms, and supplements Augusto's meditation on writing by inverting the signs that he deploys in his poem. In addition to suggesting that writing ends up being garbage, "Luxo é Lixo" posits that trash is a constitutive element of literature itself. It seems safe to say that the primary aim of the participants in Basurama's project is to provoke reflection on the cultural practices and attitudes that contribute to environmental and social crises; however, by forming letters—the building blocks of the signifier—out of plastic bags scavenged from the trash and by using those letters to write a text that explicitly cites a poet whose work rethinks the way that form, content, and materiality intersect in literature, "Lixo é Luxo" also stands as an emphatic call to reconsider what it is that makes up literary objects and how the stuff of literature comes together to produce meaning, tell stories, and provoke reactions.[3] "Luxo é Lixo," in its engagement with materiality, disposability, and literary culture, signals trash's potential to disrupt received ideas about the transcendence of literary and cultural production as signifying practices. Although it approaches literature through poetry, its reflection on writing, to my mind, is relevant to this study of trash narratives in that it serves as a *litteral* rendering of the idea that certain types of literature (and, by extension, other cultural products) can be trashy. Read in this light, Basurama's project neatly condenses the primary concern that has animated this study: the ways in which writing and storytelling come into contact with refuse.

While trash is a sign of destruction, decomposition, corrosion, and disintegration, it is also an archive of material practices, modes of consumption, and social values. What is more, it is, as Patricia Yaeger notes, "an archive of something that is not yet narratable . . . an archive for something that is not yet a story" (2008, 110). Like "Luxo é Lixo," the texts I have analyzed all use trash to tell stories about the moments and places they were produced. But that trash, which in many cases may outlive those texts and those of us who read and view them, will continue to accumulate, taking on new configurations as it decomposes and telling stories to the future.

Notes

Introduction

1 Dipesh Chakrabarty makes this point, claiming, in fact, that the idea of the Anthropocene reveals that humans do not merely have an interactive relationship with nature, but that human and natural history are so intertwined that the distinction between the two has collapsed (2009, 209).
2 Giles (2014), Hawkins (2001 and 2005), Morrison (2015), Scanlan (2005), and Thompson (1979) all echo Mary Douglas's approach to dirt in their own approaches to trash as "matter out of place" (1984, 37). What these scholars point out as they invoke Douglas's seminal work is that the problem of waste management is fundamentally about creating and maintaining systems of order. Max Liboiron and Josh Lepawsky offer a convincing critique of the tendency of waste scholars to define trash as matter out of place; for them, the value of Douglas's framework is not that it provides a useful definition of waste, but rather that it allows for nuanced analyses of waste management systems as exercises of power (2022, 76–96).
3 See Clapp (2001) for an overview of the flow of toxic waste from OECD (Organisation for Economic Co-operation and Development) to non-OECD countries, which she shows has intensified since the consolidation of neoliberalism in the 1980s and 1990s.
4 Mello and Martins estimate that of the 170,000 tons of trash generated every day in Brazil, only 140,000 are collected (2012, 80).
5 Beyond the specific (and valuable) arguments that Stam and Cisneros make in these essays, published about twenty-five years apart from each other, their existence signals an important fact: more than those of any other country in Latin America, Brazil's literature and film have exhibited a sustained examination of trash over the period that this book covers. From the poetry of Ferreira Gullar and the novels of Ignácio de Loyola Brandão, to films like *Boca de Lixo*, "Ilha das Flores," and *Estamira*, the recurrence of the theme of trash is noteworthy, as Cisneros shows in her essay.

Chapter 1. Excess and Lack

1. The book was first published in 1961 by Ediciones de la Pelota de Trapo. The 2005 edition, published by the Instituto Nacional de Cultura del Perú's Serie Generación del 50, with full-color illustrations by Roberto Pari Varela, is the one I refer to here. I am grateful to Ronny Azuaje for bringing this book to my attention.
2. For a succinct overview of the history of biopolitics and its contemporary theoretical uses, including a careful analysis of competing conceptions of the field, see Lemke (2011). See also Moraña and Sánchez Prado (2014) for a number of different approaches to studying Latin American literature and culture within a biopolitical framework.
3. For a detailed discussion of bare life as it relates to trash, see McKay (2017), where I analyze Ignácio de Loyola Brandão's novel *Zero*. While I do not engage directly with Agamben's writing on sovereignty here, it would be pertinent to address the issues of sovereignty and the law, which are central to Agamben's conceptualization of biopolitics. Sovereignty is a key factor that distinguishes his thinking from that of Foucault (and from those who follow Foucault's notion of biopower more closely than Agamben does), as Lemke points out (2011, 59–60). Lemke also sees Agamben's focus on the juridical framework of power as a significant shortcoming in that it leads him to concentrate on centralized regulation undertaken by formal state apparatuses (like the organization of the Nazi state), and therefore it does not allow him to account for the ways power is exercised outside of the law (60–61). While I see the merit in Lemke's criticisms and I agree that there are limitations inherent to Agamben's focus on juridical power, I think it is possible to read his analysis of sovereign power as a crucial example of the way that the more fundamental category of exclusion works. In other words, my reading of Agamben privileges what I understand to be the underlying logic of exclusion (or banishment or disposal) as the key operation by which a certain type of biopolitics places humans and trash in a threshold, a zone of undecidability.
4. This is the relationship of "inclusive exclusion" or inclusion via exclusion to which Agamben refers throughout *Homo Sacer*, where he argues, for instance, that political life is possible because of (and not in spite of) bare life insofar as the political is defined precisely as that which is not bare life (1998, 12).
5. The critical urge to situate Ribeyro relative to the Boom can be attributed to several factors. First, his literary career covers a span similar to that of most of the authors associated with the Boom (from the 1950s until his death in 1994). Beyond this temporal coincidence, there is a spatial one as well: like Cortázar, García Márquez, and Vargas Llosa, Ribeyro traveled to Europe (most notably Paris) to hone his literary skills. Furthermore, many of the same types of critical appraisals of the Boom writers—that they brought Latin American narrative into modernity and gave it universal import—are brought to bear on Ribeyro, albeit in the more modest context of Peruvian literature. In general terms, he is read as the preeminent portrait artist of the social life of a rapidly—and unevenly—modernizing Lima. For general overviews of Riberyo's work, see Gerdes (1979) and Ortega (1985). For an in-depth

analysis of the importance of urban space in his stories, see Valero Juan (2003). For a recent reappraisal of Ribeyro's oeuvre as an aesthetic counterpart to many Boom authors' projects of totalizing novels, see Choi (2013).

6 Besides some lexical clues—the use of such words as *canillita* for newsboy and *pericote* for rat—that would seem to suggest that the story takes place in Peru or some other South American locale, there are two features of the city described in the story that coincide with Lima. One is the Avenida Pardo, which is one of the main thoroughfares of the Miraflores district of Lima and is mentioned in the first paragraph of the story (Ribeyro 1994, 21). The other is the location of the garbage dump described in the story: it is the result of trash having been dumped over the cliffs that separate parts of the city from the sea (23). Not only has this use of Lima's seaside cliffs as informal trash dumps persisted throughout the city's history, but also it has been portrayed in other works of Peruvian literature, perhaps most notably in the opening and closing scenes of Mario Vargas Llosa's *Historia de Mayta* (1984) and throughout Jorge Eduardo Benavides's *Los años inútiles* (2002).

7 As well as dogs. Notice how the seemingly offhand reference to the canine companions of the gallinazos serves as a subtle suggestion that the line separating dogs from humans starts to blur under the tutelage of destitution. In other words, their relationship with trash acts as a point of convergence in view of the activities they engage in on a daily basis.

8 In this sense, one of the main strains of Ribeyro's work fits within the tradition of urban realism. As Julio Ortega asserts, Ribeyro's stories "desarrollan situaciones críticas de la migración y la vida suburbana, pero también elaboran la dimensión ideológica que la modernización relativa exacerba, así como exploran y postulan algunas versiones del conflicto moral y existencial en una sociedad cambiante, en la que las diferencias sociales y étnicas, la violencia, la frustración y el deterioro forman a las relaciones humanas" (develop scenarios critical of migration and suburban life, but also elaborate on the ideological dimension that relative modernization exacerbates, as well exploring and putting forward versions of the moral and existential conflicts of a changing society in which social and ethnic difference, violence, frustration, and deterioration underlie human relationships) (1985, 128). Eva María Valero Juan identifies "Los gallinazos sin plumas" as Ribeyro's foundational statement regarding the inability of Lima (and Peru as a whole) to face seismic demographic shifts: "En la obra de Ribeyro, la visión evanescente de la sólida ciudad del pasado, 'amurallada física y espiritualmente' y desvanecida en la ciudad de los gallinazos, se constituye en eje de coherencia de toda su narrativa, que . . . construye el sentido de un mundo que avanza a pasos agigantados en un proceso de cambio perpetuo e imparable. En este sentido, su narrativa se inscribe . . . dentro de la experiencia literaria de la modernidad, y en concreto, Ribeyro establece desde 'Los gallinazos sin plumas' la línea principal de su producción: la representación de la ciudad que ingresa en el proceso de la modernidad desprovista de un sistema socioeconómico preparado para asumir y consolidar el cambio" (In Ribeyro's oeuvre, the vision of the solid city of the past, "physically and spiritually walled in," that has faded into one of the city of vultures, constitutes a coherent axis of all of his fiction,

which … constructs the sense of a world advancing at an alarming rate in a process of perpetual, unstoppable change. In this sense, his fiction is inscribed … in the literary experience of modernity, and, concretely, beginning with "Los gallinazos sin plumas," Ribeyro lays down the main through line of his work: the representation of the city entering the process of modernity without an adequate socioeconomic system for taking on and consolidating that change) (2003, 40). Keeping in mind that the population of Lima doubled between 1940 and 1956 and that the number of the city's shantytowns skyrocketed from one to fifty-six over roughly the same period, one can see that "Los gallinazos sin plumas" offers a mordant close-up of the growing pains that Lima suffered in the middle of the twentieth century, but never really grew out of (Spitta 2007, 295).

9 Peter Elmore, for instance, recognizes the trash in "Los gallinazos sin plumas" as one of the elements that show how the story's characters struggle with confronting "la nueva realidad urbana en la forma de los dramas—sórdidos o trágicos, irónicos o patéticos—que les toca vivir," (the new urban reality in the form of the dramas—sordid or tragic, ironic or pathetic—that are their lot), although it is also an important component of Ribeyro's "visión de la Lima contemporánea como tierra baldía o campo minado: la carencia y el conflicto son los signos de la realidad que viven las criaturas de la ficción" (vision of contemporary Lima as a waste land or mine field: lack and conflict being signs of the reality that these fictional creatures live in) (2002, 37, 42). He also quotes Ribeyro as saying that the presence of trash in the story lends it "'un poco más de verosimilitud sicológica'" ("a little more psychological verisimilitude") (138).

10 Addressing the issue of a nostalgic portrayal of Lima's past in Ribeyro's work as a whole, Eunha Choi says, "Even though his stories are peppered with nostalgic expressions, his realist fiction does not deploy nostalgia as a structuring device. Nor does a nostalgic or redemptive gaze frame the depiction of his characters" (2013, 23–24).

11 Furtado is a figure of some note in contemporary Brazilian cinema. Besides his work as a screenwriter and director of shorts and feature-length films alike—"Ilha das Flores" and *O homem que copiava* (2003) are probably his best-known efforts in these respective formats—he is a founding partner of the Casa de Cinema de Porto Alegre, an independent film and television production cooperative with projects that have garnered over 250 prizes at Brazilian and international film festivals. "Ilha das Flores" is among the Casa's most successful productions in terms of international acclaim; it was awarded the Silver Bear for short film at the 1990 Berlin International Film Festival among several other honors. Despite this acclaim and the visibility it brought to the film, "Ilha das Flores" has received little critical attention outside of brief film reviews and cursory mentions in academic works on Brazilian cinema. A recent exception is Axel Pérez Trujillo's essay that analyzes how the film "establishes a critique of current global discourses of the Anthropocene" by focusing on "the intersection between insularity and ecology" (2022, 133). For more on Furtado's oeuvre and the Casa de Cinema de Porto Alegre, see *Casa de Cinema*. For

production details for "Ilha das Flores," including the full text of the film's original screenplay, see "Ilha das Flores" (1989).

12 Among the few academic critics to examine "Ilha das Flores," there is a tendency to misread the film as a documentary short. See Vieira de Jesus (2005), for instance, who treats the film as a documentary and analyzes it according to Bill Nichols's theory of different modes of documentary film. Similarly, in a suggestive (albeit brief) analysis of Furtado's film as a meditation on the more-than-human assemblages in which the story's tomato serves as a critical vector, Gambetta (2009) insists on calling "Ilha das Flores" a documentary. This confusion is almost certainly due to the fact that there really is a place called Ilha das Flores that serves as a garbage dump for much of Porto Alegre's trash and people actually scavenge for food there. Additionally, the film opens with a series of three terse intertitles that read (in caps), "ESTE NÃO É UM FILME DE FICÇÃO. EXISTE UM LUGAR CHAMADO ILHA DAS FLORES. DEUS NÃO EXISTE" (THIS IS NOT A FICTIONAL FILM. A PLACE CALLED ILHA DAS FLORES EXISTS. GOD DOES NOT EXIST). These truth claims are undermined by the closing credits, which state the real identity of the film's characters. The credit for Dona Anete, the woman who buys the tomato, for instance, reads, "Dona Anete na verdade é CICA RECKZIEGEL." (Dona Anete in reality is CICA RECKZIEGEL). Also, the site where the garbage dump scenes were filmed is revealed to be Ilha dos Marinheiros, which is located two kilometers from Ilha das Flores. After admitting to all of the fictional elements in this "documentary," a final credit rolls, once again in caps: "O RESTO É VERDADE" (THE REST IS TRUE). I draw attention to all of this not to quibble over how to classify this film, but because the claim to truth with which the film ends is not one of documenting historical events. Instead, it claims to offer insight into the difficult-to-see truth of the waste stream from the position of imaginative fiction. What is more, interpreting the film as a documentary indicates a failure to see it as a parody of documentary itself, or at least of a certain kind of documentary: highly pedagogical wildlife documentaries, which, as the screenplay points out, serve as a model for the film's structure ("Ilha das Flores").

13 In this sense, sorting and imposing order can be interpreted in light of the concept of exclusion as put forth by Agamben. That is, inclusion tends to produce exclusions as well. For more on the dialectical relationship between order and disorder as it pertains to waste, see Scanlan (2005, 57–80).

14 I should add that the visuals that accompany this bit of narration are a noteworthy example of the way that the film recycles previously seen images. As each of these elements is mentioned (the tomato, Senhor Suzuki, the supermarket, Dona Anete, perfume, and so on), the images that flash across the screen are ones that we have already seen several times over.

15 As the film's end credits indicate, the final sentence that defines "liberty" is extracted (with a very slight reworking) from Cecília Meireles's collection of poems *Romanceiro da Inconfidência* (1953), which tells in verse the history of the captaincy of Minas Gerais from the time of Portuguese colonization through the 1789 Incon-

fidência Mineira, a thwarted separatist movement that, despite its evident failure, would loom large as a symbolic gesture of Brazilian nationalism. The line in question comes from the poem "Romance XXIV ou da bandeira da Inconfidência."

Chapter 2. In and Out of the Dump

1. "Wasted lives" is the well-known term that Zygmunt Bauman coined to designate the seemingly disposable social class that is "an inevitable outcome of modernization, and an inseparable accompaniment of modernity" (2004, 5). For Bauman, the lives in question are undoubtedly and exclusively human: he uses the term interchangeably with "human waste" (not in the sense of the bodily waste humans produce, but rather as the result of a brand of modernization that situates humans themselves as waste). The dogs, pigs, and vultures (and perhaps even the tomatoes) considered in the first chapter of this book offer good reason to expand the term beyond the human.
2. Dujovne Ortiz, a journalist, biographer, and novelist who splits her time between Paris and her native Buenos Aires, is perhaps best known for her books *Maradona soy yo* (1994) and *Eva Perón, la biografía* (1996). For more on her literary trajectory, see Glickman (2000) and Díaz (2007). For a detailed history of solid waste practices in Buenos Aires, including an explanation of the workings of CEAMSE, see Prignano (1998, 321–27).
3. *Ciruja* and *cartonero* are terms used in Argentina for people who make a living salvaging recyclable materials from the garbage. *Catador* is the equivalent in Brazilian Portuguese.
4. Coutinho, who died in 2014, was Brazil's preeminent documentary filmmaker. In addition to making a dozen feature-length documentaries on subjects such as slavery and black identity in Brazil (*O fio da memória*, Coutinho 1991) and the lives of the inhabitants of an old apartment building in Rio (*Edifício Master*, Coutinho 2002), he filmed several documentary shorts and medium-length documentaries (of which *Boca de Lixo* is one). For more on Coutinho's films, see Lins (2007). For an analysis of *Boca de Lixo* in the context of depictions of the urban poor in recent Brazilian cultural production, see Peixoto (2007, 176–78).
5. Just before the end credits roll, the following text appears onscreen: "Filmado no vazadouro de Itaoca, no município de São Gonçalo, a 40 Km do Rio de Janeiro. No Brazil, existem centenas de vazadouros como este, onde trabalham dezenas de milhares de catadores" (Filmed in the Itaoca garbage dump, municipality of São Gonçalo, 40 km from Rio de Janeiro. In Brazil, there are hundreds of dumps like this one, where tens of thousands of catadores work).
6. Born in Tijuana in 1955 and raised in both Mexico and the United States, Urrea is one of the most visible Mexican American writers in the United States literary sphere. The experience of the border and living between cultures that he portrays in *By the Lake of Sleeping Children* are through lines in all of his work, which consists of some sixteen books of fiction, poetry, nonfiction, and memoir.
7. The United States–Mexico border has received a great deal of attention from academics, the media, and cultural agents; giving an adequate summary limited to

recent academic studies of the border exceeds my aims for this chapter. However, I would direct readers' attention to two books that delve into the border's many paradoxes and tensions with great critical intelligence and explanatory aplomb, books that have shaped my analysis of what is as stake in Urrea's portrayal of communities on the border. First, Claire F. Fox's *The Fence and the River* is a study that was undertaken in the years leading up to and just following the implementation of NAFTA; therefore, it offers an analysis of border culture and politics from roughly the same moment as Urrea's book. Fox highlights contradictory discourses on freedom as they are indexed in literature, cinema, photography, video, and performance art (including brief mentions of *By the Lake of Sleeping Children*) in order to show that "the border ... must be understood as polyvalent, as a place where urban and rural, national an international spaces simultaneously coexist, often in complex and contradictory ways" (1999, 2–3). Additionally, in her analysis of the discourses evident in cultural production on the border, she does not lose sight of "the materiality of this 'constructed space' and the power it has to affect and structure the lives of those crossing it and divided by it" (14). A more recent book, Thomas Nail's *Theory of the Border*, underscores the tension between globalization's ideal of unfettered movement and the material constraints that border infrastructure—fences, walls, checkpoints, detention centers, biometric tools—places on bodies (2016, 1). Of particular relevance to the arguments I make here is Nail's theorization of the "in-betweenness" of the border: it is a division that both separates and joins, a conceptual and physical space that simultaneously includes and excludes, and a geopolitical zone of relatively seamless continuity for some and stark division for others (2–5). The border is, in other words, a threshold.

8   For instance, Urrea's focus on an orphanage in the vicinity of the Tijuana *dompe*, his recurring interactions with an Evangelical pastor, and the contingent, fluid family structures that he documents—especially in the book's closing vignette, "A Day in the Life" (1996, 145–87)—all find resonances with elements of *¿Quién mató a Diego Duarte?* and *Boca de Lixo*, which I analyze in this section (such as the prison writing group in Dujovne Ortiz's book and Coutinho's portraits of people who come and go from the dump, developing and dissolving attachments along the way).

Chapter 3. Trash Works

1   "La basura" was published in a posthumous collection of short texts that remained unpublished before Reyes's death in December 1959. The volume, *Vida y ficción*, edited by Ernesto Mejía Sánchez and published by the Fondo de Cultura Económica in 1970, appropriately marked the one hundredth volume of the FCE's "Letras Mexicanas" series that Reyes himself inaugurated with the first volume of his *Obra poética* in 1952. "La basura" is dated 14 August 1959, which means that trash, albeit briefly and tangentially, was among the final themes that occupied Reyes's astounding intellect.

2   Reyes's invocation of the nature of things and what he calls the "velo de átomos" (veil of atoms) (1970, 162) certainly resonates with Jane Bennett's theorization of vital materiality. In particular, "La basura" brings to mind Bennett's consideration

of her own unsettling and generative encounter with a tangle of trash caught in the grate over a storm drain (2010, 4–6). The attention she pays to the thing-power wielded by the particular assemblage of debris she engages with—"[g]love, pollen, rat, cap, stick" (4)—finds a useful complement in Reyes's focus on the labor of those who move assemblages of debris and garbage around social spaces.

3 Here I am referring to Stacy Alaimo's concept of "trans-corporeality," which names "the material interconnections of human corporeality with the more-than-human world" and allows us to trace the "movement across human corporeality and non-human nature" in order to understand that "'the environment' is not located somewhere out there, but is always the very substance of ourselves" (2010, 2–4).

4 Since Brooks's translation is rather free and specific passages from the English and Spanish texts often do not correspond, the translations from Contreras Castro's novel in this chapter are mine, as are the translations from Chejfec's and Neuman's novels. As I completed revisions of this chapter, Robin Myers's English translation of *Bariloche* was still forthcoming from Open Letter, so I was unfortunately not able to consult it here. For Aira, Castellanos Moya, and Enrigue, I use the published English translations.

5 Other texts that could also fit into the category of trash works include novels from Argentina, Brazil, Cuba, and Mexico. The main character in Sergio Busqued's *Bajo este sol tremendo* (2008) is an unemployed loner who spends his days smoking marijuana, eating junk food, and watching trashy television in his late brother's trash-filled house, which he goes to some lengths to clean up. Ignácio de Loyola Brandão's *Zero: romance pré-histórico* (1974) features a protagonist whose employment history includes several waste-related activities, including exterminating and disposing of rats. The titular Rey of Pedro Juan Gutiérrez's *El Rey de La Habana* (2001) is a man who lives on the margins of Cuban society and ultimately ends up dying in a garbage dump. In addition, Eduardo Antonio Parra's *Nostalgia de la sombra* (2002) tells the story of a newspaper copy editor who, after being violently assaulted, wakes up in a trash dump, where he lives for a while before ultimately becoming a hired assassin. For an insightful interpretation of the relationship between masculinity and violence in Parra's novel, see Sánchez Prado (2006, 45–46). For detailed readings of Busqued's and Brandão's protagonists in light of trash and the work they do with it, see Seifert (2017) and McKay (2017), respectively. Although I have chosen not to examine these novels closely here due to questions of space and, in some cases, slight deviations from the temporal and sociopolitical commonalities shared by the other texts (Brandão and Gutiérrez wrote their novels during the 1970s under a military dictatorship in Brazil and under communism in Cuba after the fall of the Soviet Union, respectively), they are still worth mentioning here because they further demonstrate one of the key insights of this chapter: literature's tendency to tell stories about trash and trash work that center masculine crises. In this sense, the trash works that I analyze here should be seen as part of a broader mode of storytelling with critical analysis that exposes the limits of anthropocentrism when it comes to thinking about how we can imagine what it means to live with trash.

6   Critics have read all of these works in light of what they have to say about the experience of neoliberalism in Latin America. Patrick Dove, for instance, situates Aira's *La villa* in the context of the violent impact of neoliberalism on culture, which has resulted in the suspension and exhaustion of fundamental aspects of aesthetic modernity, particularly in terms of the way that Aira portrays the interrelation of literature and mass media (2016, 72–105). Alejandra Laera focuses on the portrayal of money and its circulation in Chejfec's *El aire* as part of a larger argument about literary texts that resort to economic questions in their consideration of the crises and internal contradictions of late capitalism (2014, 37–69). Fernando Aínsa and Iván Pérez Daniel examine Neuman's *Bariloche* and Enrigue's *Hipotermia*, respectively, from the viewpoint of globalization's effects on flows of migration, national identity, and imagined spaces (Aínsa 2010, 35–37; Pérez Daniel 2018, 168–71). For Christian Kroll-Bryce, Castellanos Moya's *Baile con serpientes* is among a number of recent Central American novels that use what he calls "subjetividades alternas" (alternative subjectivities), like unemployed people and nomads, to explore the workings of neoliberal rationality (2016, 615-17). Regarding Contreras Castro's *Única mirando al mar*, Jerry Hoeg (in Rivera-Barnes and Hoeg) sees the novel as a consideration of the ground that traditional values have lost in the face of the rampant consumer culture of neoliberalism (2009, 177–85), while Ana Patricia Rodríguez reads it as one of a number of allegories of the state's failure to protect vulnerable populations in the aftermath of the disintegration of revolutionary projects in Central America in the 1990s (2009, 207–12).

7   I place the terms "formal" and "informal" in quotation marks to call attention to the problematic nature of this distinction as it relates to both labor and the economy, as Kathleen M. Millar contends in her study of the Jardim Gramacho garbage dump in Rio de Janeiro (a locale we will visit in chapter 4 of this book). For Millar, one of the problems "with analyses that [focus] on the articulation between the formal and informal is that these categories are not so much linked as blurred in everyday practice" (2018, 130). Millar takes issue with social scientists' dependence on the formal/informal binary and their invocation of the term "informality," because their invocation of the term "unintentionally lends weight to everyday uses of the term that justify the repression or differential treatment of practices performed by particular social groups" (131). Her contention that formal and informal waste work are two sides of the same coin (and that formal waste management entities simply could not operate without so-called informal trash workers) is convincing and, I think, borne out quite clearly in Aira's and Contreras Castro's novels. So, I use the two terms not to mark a stark difference in the kind of work (or its value) that characters in one or another set of texts engage in; rather, as we will see, the distinction may be useful for showing how different trash works index the "plasticity" of waste work, a term that Millar uses to capture the disruption of dualist frameworks and the relationality that characterizes this kind of labor (132).

8   Neuman, who was born in Argentina and moved with his family to Spain as an adolescent, is probably best known for his Alfaguara Prize–winning *El viajero del*

siglo (2009) and the novel *Fractura* (2018). He merited mention as a finalist for the Herralde Prize for *Bariloche*, his debut novel. It is also worth mentioning that it was this very novel that prompted Roberto Bolaño to proclaim "la literatura del siglo XXI les pertenecerá a Neuman y a unos pocos de sus hermanos de sangre" (Bolaño 2004, 149) ("the literature of the 21st century will belong to Neuman and a few other blood brothers of his") (Wimmer 2011, 160) in a brief text collected in *Entre paréntesis*. This pronouncement has followed Neuman around ever since and functioned as a sort of seal of approval (in marketing terms, at least). Many of his nearly twenty subsequent books, ranging from novels and poetry to short stories and essays, feature Bolaño's proclamation in blurb form on their covers. Initially published by Anagrama in 1999, *Bariloche* was reissued in a slightly revised edition by Alfaguara in 2015. Here I quote from the original Anagrama edition.

9 Enrigue, a Mexican author and academic, has written some ten books of narrative fiction, including the novel *Muerte súbita* (2013), which won both the Premio Herralde and the Premio Iberoamericano de novela Elena Poniatowska, and the short story collection-cum-novel *Hipotermia* (2006), in which "Ultraje" is included. Thematically speaking, Enrigue's works run the gamut from considerations of aesthetic and cultural difference in the early modern world to the genocide of Native Americans and the experience of globalized, postmodern society. *Hipotermia* is exemplary of the latter, insofar as it features a series of characters who experience anxiety, aimlessness, and uprootedness as a result of migration or other experiences that dissolve traditional social bonds. See Pérez Daniel (2018) for a consideration of *Hipotermia* in this light.

10 The Mid-Atlantic United States setting of "Ultraje" runs throughout *Hipotermia*, which reflects an autobiographical element of the collection: in the years leading up to the book's publication, Enrigue was living in the region while pursuing a doctorate at the University of Maryland (Pérez Daniel 2018, 163). One element that makes "Ultraje" stand out, however, is the fact that the story's protagonist is from the United States; in general, the other stories portray the experiences of intellectuals and members of the creative class from Mexico who live in the vicinity of Washington, DC.

11 Originally from Buenos Aires, Chejfec lived for long stints in both Venezuela and New York, where he passed away in 2022, having produced a rich and highly original body of work focused primarily on the novel and essay forms. As is the case with *El aire*, one of the central themes of his work is urban space and the ways his characters move about the city. For a general overview of Chejfec's literary production, see Dianna Niebylski's edited volume *Sergio Chejfec: Trayectorias de una escritura*, an excellent collection of some fifteen critical essays analyzing his work. See also Laera (2012) for a consideration of trash in another of Chejfec's novels, *El llamado de la especie* (1997).

12 Born in Honduras and raised in El Salvador, Castellanos Moya is undoubtedly one of the most significant contemporary Central American authors, and, over the last few decades, he has figured more and more prominently in critical and popular discussions of Latin American and world literature in general. Novels like *Baile con ser-*

Notes to Pages 82–83 · 159

pientes (2012), *El arma en el hombre* (2001), and the controversial *El asco: Thomas Bernhard en San Salvador* (1997) portray the violence and degradation of Central America under the sway of neoliberalism, while works like *Insensatez* (2004) and *Tirana memoria* (2008) excavate twentieth-century Central American history. For an insightful overview of Castellanos Moya's writing and the critical responses it has generated, see Caña Jiménez and Venkatesh (2016).

13 In the first edition of the novel, published in 1996 by the Salvadoran Consejo Nacional para la Cultura y el Arte, the novel takes place in a city called Macrópolis, a fictionalized version of San Salvador. Curiously, the more widely available edition of the novel that I am working with here (published in 2012 as a revised version of the Spanish publisher Tusquet's 2002 reissue of the text) never names the city in which the novel's events take place, and Macrópolis is merely the name of the neighborhood where Eduardo Sosa lives (Castellanos Moya 2012, 74; Springer 2009, 72). For Vinodh Venkatesh (who cites the first edition of the novel), Castellanos Moya's invented city of Macrópolis is of a piece with other Central American authors' deployment of fictionalized cities "as part of a broader trend that evidences writers from distinct countries choosing to write beyond their borders, thereby outlining a common regional corpus of texts" that are "unrestrained by arcane notions of the Nation and 'national literature'" (2012, 64). Castellanos Moya's relationship with Tusquets, which began in the early 2000s and included the reissue of some of his earlier novels, certainly allowed him to transcend notions of national and even regional literature; perhaps the disappearance of any reference to the city of Macrópolis is representative of that shift.

14 Author of some seven works of narrative fiction, Contreras Castro is one of the more salient figures of Costa Rican literature from the last several decades, and, as a whole, his work can be seen as a critical evaluation of "una violencia promovida por las prácticas del programa neoliberal que no es inmediata y/o directamente visible—como podría serlo la de casos de terrorismo o genocidio—sino más bien paulatina en sus efectos y, aparentemente, intangible en su materialización" (a violence promoted by the practices of the neoliberal paradigm that is not immediate and/or directly visible—as it might be in the case of terrorism or genocide—but rather gradual in its effects and, apparently, intangible in its materialization) (Caña Jiménez 2016, 236). While *Única mirando al mar* is a work of fiction, Río Azul was a real landfill that operated in San José between 1972 and 2007 (Díaz 2009). Curiously, the public outcry about the landfill and the continual promises to close down the site that form part of the novel's plot came to fruition in reality after the novel's publication (Mora Chincilla and Mora Amador 2003, 49–55).

15 Even the silliness of Momboñombo's invented name gestures toward notions of disposal, recycling, and masculinity: "The onomastic wordplay is significant. In the first and second names, a total of five letters from the Spanish alphabet are repeated: 6 *o*'s, 4 *m*'s, 2 *ñ*'s, 2 *b*'s, and 2 *a*'s, a repetition of letters that perhaps simulates the guard's recycled status in the dump. While the *g* and *ll* each appear only once in his new last name, Moñagallo, the *ll* stands out as a marker of linguistic and cultural difference, as there is no letter like it outside the Spanish language [one wonders if

this is a typographical error and Rodríguez means to comment on the *ñ*]. The *ll* in Moñagallo, or rather in the word *gallo*, serves as a double phallic symbol, perhaps signifying the emasculation of the old guard as he falls from grace and rank into the dump site, where he virtually has no power. Indeed, the word *gallo* (rooster, cock) coupled with the prefix *moña/o* (woman's hair ribbon) that make up his new name would seem to signal a defaced masculinity by the standards of dominant forms of masculinity within the patriarchal order in the Hispanic world. In renaming himself, Moñagallo seems to ridicule the patriarchal national order that once defined yet rejected him" (Rodríguez 2009, 210).

16 Aira is commonly hailed as one of the most significant voices in contemporary Latin American literature, as is attested by the award of the Prix Formentor in 2021 for the entirety of his work. His substantial output—more than one hundred books including novels, short stories, and essays—defies classification, but most critical assessments of his body of work highlight his relationship to certain strands of the avant-garde and the way he plunders a range of narrative strategies and generic conventions to spin his plots. See Contreras (2002) for a thorough reading of Aira's literary project as a whole. For a more recent analysis of the portrayal of neoliberal urban spaces in a number of Aira's novels (not including *La villa*) see Cisneros (2015).

17 *Única mirando al mar* might seem like an exception, insofar as the titular character is a woman, but I would contend that Momboñombo is the novel's main character. Despite Única's key role, virtually the entire novel is focalized through Momboñombo.

18 I am grateful to Sarah Moody for pointing out that the "works" in "trash works" can be a verb as well as a noun.

19 In one of the few academic studies dedicated to *Bariloche*, Lucy Bell addresses the question of trash's movements not from the perspective of waste management's production of space, as I do here, but rather by attending to the way waste operates as a network (in Bruno Latour's sense of the term) that connects "the 'body' of waste to human and animal bodies" (2015, 1048). In her careful reading of the novel, she mobilizes Stacy Alaimo's concept of transcorporeality to argue that Neuman's portrayal of trash questions neat distinctions between the human and the nonhuman.

20 Fernando Aínsa analyzes *Bariloche* (among other novels written by Neuman) in light of the author's experience as an Argentine living in Spain. For Aínsa, the fact that Rota is a migrant (a *provinciano* in the capital) is key to understanding why he never manages to become integrated into the life of the city (2010, 35–37).

21 Trash's role in (un)grounding Rota's subjectivity is condensed in a series of questions raised by the narrator as Rota enters the landfill at the end of the novel: "¿Qué había realmente dentro de los millones de bolsas? ¿Cuáles serían suyas? ¿Podría rescatarlas?" (What was really inside those millions of bags? Which ones were his? Could he rescue them?) (Neuman 1999, 166).

22 Dánisa Bonacic (2014) analyzes the theme of urban space in *La villa* along these lines by focusing on how the contrast between middle-class spaces and the villa miseria in the novel is indicative of social polarization in Buenos Aires.

23 While a detailed analysis of this aspect of the novel—the villa miseria's portrayal as a commodity produced by mass media and consumed by a middle-class audience—is beyond the scope of this chapter, I should mention that it is another way in which *La villa* critically engages the logic of neoliberalism and notions of management. In an insightful analysis of mass media technics in Aira's novel, Patrick Dove notes, "*La villa* illustrates a powerful imaginary that helps drive mass media technics. Let us call it the fantasy of *complete inclusion* and *complete coverage*, allowing these terms to resonate with a variety of cultural, economic, epistemological and political contexts in the time of late capitalism. Complete inclusion corresponds, for instance, to the technological administering of free choice and unlimited economic opportunity in the market, while complete coverage names the instantaneous dissemination and complete preservation of knowledge through mass media. Total coverage and inclusion are ideological signifiers serving to dissimulate the originary violence, exclusions and divisions that haunt contemporary forms of social organization. *La villa* explores this ideological function by playing with the mediatic notion of full coverage, even to the point of mimicking the media's idiom, while also suggesting that the notion of total visibility also includes its own forms of exclusion" (2009, 16).

24 The sense of absence that is evident in *El aire*'s plot is also apparent in the way that Chejfec deploys language in the text. Throughout the novel, there are unexplained references to a shift in language that has rendered obsolete a series of words that were common currency during Barroso's childhood. For instance, as Barroso wonders about the contents of an envelope that has just been slipped under his door, we read, "Muchos largometrajes—'Cintas,' tradujo *evocando el vocabulario de la infancia*—recurrían al expediente . . . de adelantar algún sobre con el objeto de crear misterio" (Many feature films—"Tapes," he translated, *evoking the vocabulary of his childhood*—resorted to files . . . producing some envelope ahead of time with the objective of creating mystery) (Chejfec 1992, 13-14; emphasis mine). That the narrative voice is consistently interrupted by this kind of focalization that underscores the *uselessness* of certain words is highly suggestive, not only as a gesture that inscribes absence and loss into the language of the novel (words like *cintas* are absent of their former meaning), but also as an indication of the disposable nature of language, the basic material that makes writing possible.

25 Alejandra Laera sees money in *El aire* as "un elemento particularmente capaz de exhibir, de hacer exterior la interiorización, por la vía de la percepción, la sensación, la vivencia de la modernización, es decir, lo que se dio en llamar modernidad" (an element that is particularly capable of exhibiting, bringing forth what is internalized, by means of perception, the sensation, the experience of modernization, that is, what is known as modernity) (2014, 60). Due to the difficulties and inefficiencies that glass presents as a form of currency, Laera argues that its use in Chejfec's narrative is an inscription of what she calls "modernidad en remisión" (modernity in remission), the idea that the crises of contemporary capitalism can be found in the very drivers of capitalism itself (in this case, circulation) (37-69).

26 I have made slight modifications to Springer's translation here.

27 See Bilbija and Celis Carbajal (2009) for a thorough consideration of the context in which cartonera publishing arose, along with manifestos from eight of the first editoriales cartoneras, including Eloísa Cartonera. For a reflection on how Eloísa Cartonera plays with and against the cultural logic of neoliberalism in Argentina, see Bilbija (2014). According to the catalog maintained on Eloísa Cartonera's website, Aira has published three texts with the cartonera publisher: the novellas *Mil gotas* and *El todo que surca la nada* in addition to the short story "El cerebro musical."

Chapter 4. Cleaning Up

1 Organized around a different theme each year, the EcoFilm Festival showcases an impressive array of animated, fiction, and documentary shorts, as well as publicity campaigns, which engage with themes ranging from water and biodiversity to sustainable transportation and food production. In 2014, the year Vargas's film competed, the theme of solid waste attracted some 852 entries in all categories. EcoFilm's YouTube channel, @EcoFilmFestivalMX, is an invaluable resource for anyone interested in researching or teaching environmental film from Mexico and Latin America. Almost all the films and campaigns that were awarded prizes between 2011 and 2020, along with the complete catalog for each edition of the festival, are available on the website.

2 I would claim that the way that Vargas chooses to introduce viewers to Señor Tlacuache's workshop is surprising because confronting viewers with the messy materiality of trash itself is such a common part of the visual language of films that depict trash spaces, especially in the opening shots and scenes of films that offer initial glimpses of dumps and landfills. I think of, for instance, the opening shot of Eduardo Coutinho's *Boca de Lixo*, discussed in chapter 2, which uses a moving close-up of the surface of the dump to great effect, or the scenes from Lucy Walker's *Waste Land* that show Vik Muniz studying Google Earth images of Jardim Gramacho before traveling to Brazil and experiencing the overwhelming nature of the dump firsthand after arriving in Rio de Janeiro. I discuss those scenes from *Waste Land* further along in this chapter. That Vargas initially focuses on the plants found throughout Señor Tlacuache's junk workshop instead of the junk itself both highlights the film's theme of approaching trash with a mindset of cultivation and care and reminds us of a key tenet of the forms of ecological thought that have emerged over the last twenty years, as I point out in the introduction: "nature" and "culture" should not be thought of as separate spheres, but rather as concepts that, from the human point of view, are inextricably intertwined.

3 The end credits list a guitar étude by Italian composer Matteo Carcassi, along with ambient compositions by Elisa A. Portillo Gutiérrez, Miguel Portugal, and Jonathan García, the last of whom also did the sound design and mixing for the film.

4 At one point in the film, Señor Tlacuache directly addresses an aspect of the relationship between the plants in his garden and trash: "El chatarral también es un asilo para plantas y si estamos pensando en el planeta, pues las plantas están en el planeta, ¿no? Sin su oxígeno tronaríamos, no viviríamos. Sin su verde, qué fea sería una ciudad gris" (The junkheap is also an asylum for plants, and if we're talking

about the planet, well, plants are on the planet, right? Without their oxygen, we'd croak, we wouldn't live. Without their greenness, how ugly a gray city would be) (Vargas 2014).

5   This seems like an especially apt form for this message given that the primary way to view Vargas's documentary short is via her website or via platforms like YouTube and Vimeo, which are designed for audiences of one. I, for one, came across this film and watched it in solitude, and when I use it in my teaching, my students watch it alone on their individual devices. I make no claim to say anything new or particularly profound about new media technologies here, but, given the arguments I make throughout this chapter, it strikes me as pertinent to point out that even the conditions for engaging with material that attempts to raise public awareness and perhaps inspire some form of collective action tend to remain within the confines of individual consumption.

6   The bibliography on neoliberalism is truly voluminous. Any attempt I might make at giving a general overview of it, especially given my lack of training in economics, would be woefully inept and incomplete, so I will simply point readers toward a few works that have been helpful to me. David Harvey's *A Brief History of Neoliberalism* and Naomi Klein's *The Shock Doctrine* offer clear, accessible histories of the development and implementation of neoliberal policies throughout the world. Adam Kotsko's *Neoliberalism's Demons* and Wendy Brown's *Undoing the Demos* are engaging theoretical accounts of the ideological underpinnings of neoliberalism and its effects on human freedom and the core institutions of liberal democracy. It bears repeating that in mentioning these particular works, I make no claim to exhaustivity (or objectivity, for that matter—all of these thinkers decry neoliberalism's dangers); rather, my aim is to give a sense of the strains of thought that inform my own characterization of neoliberalism and the way it constrains environmentalism.

7   Economist John Williamson famously synthesized the core policy prescriptions of neoliberal reform in speeches and essays in the late 1980s and early 1990s, when he referred to the tenets of market fundamentalism as the Washington Consensus. His writing gives the sense that neoliberalism is not merely a technical question, but rather a worldview, as the following declaration makes clear: "The superior economic performance of countries that establish and maintain outward-oriented market economies subject to macro-economic discipline is essentially a positive question. The proof may not be quite as conclusive as the proof that the earth is not flat, but it is sufficiently well established as to give sensible people better things to do with their time than challenge its veracity" (1993, 1330). The notion of the Washington Consensus is key to understanding the implementation of neoliberal reforms across Latin America, for the adoption of many of those policy changes was mandatory for countries in the region that sought loans from international economic organizations in order to stave off immediate economic disaster, as Juan Pablo Rodríguez (2021) makes clear in a recent appraisal of the history, achievements, and shortcomings of neoliberalism in the region. He offers a useful synthesis that takes into account factors both external (the weakening of the Keynesian consensus after the Second World War and the oil and debt crises of the 1970s and 1980s) and internal

to Latin America (the crisis of import substitution industrialization) and notes that, in the region, "the rise of neoliberalism took place in a context marked by incomplete democratization, the legacy of colonial power structures, and a reconfigured authoritarianism that consistently favoured market-based policies" (2021, 5).

8 There are two contradictions evident even in these bedrock notions that neoliberalism lays out for itself. First, its purported aim to diminish the role of the state is never really actualized, since the state tends to play a key role in implementing and maintaining neoliberal policies (Harvey 2005, 64–86). Second, neoliberalism's elevation of freedom as the preeminent value is difficult to square with the historical record. Harvey points out, for instance, that the first experiment with neoliberal state formation began in 1973 in Chile as the result of a violent coup d'état led by Augusto Pinochet that overthrew the democratically elected government of Salvador Allende and resulted in the death and disappearance of thousands of Chileans, as well as the suppression of political organizations, social movements, and other forms of popular organization (7–9).

9 Strictly speaking, of course, "Los gallinazos sin plumas" predates the implementation of neoliberal economic policies in Peru and, therefore, is somewhat at odds with this broad characterization. However, Ribeyro's focus on the marginalizing and stratifying effects of capitalist modernization as well as the way the story's final lines juxtapose Efraín and Enrique's escape from their abusive grandfather (an image of freedom) with the animalized city poised to devour them (an image that calls that freedom into question) clearly resonate with the more (or less) explicit critiques of neoliberalism that we find in films like "Ilha das Flores" and *Boca de Lixo*, or in books like *By the Lake of Sleeping Children* and *¿Quién mató a Diego Duarte?*.

10 Kotsko elaborates in detail his own account of political theology in the book's first chapter, "The Political Theology of Late Capital," by discussing both key thinkers in political theology, like Carl Schmitt and Giorgio Agamben, and what he sees as the achievements and blind spots of theorists of neoliberalism, like Harvey and Brown, whose work has informed my own thinking (2018, 11–38).

11 I borrow the term "environmentality" from Lawrence Buell, who uses it to designate the ways that individuals and groups of people think about and express "environmental belonging and citizenship" (2007, 227). Buell argues for the urgency of cultivating a planetary perspective of environmentality, as opposed to a narrower, nation-centered approach, a sentiment that I agree with. But even the notion of planetary environmental belonging can be co-opted by neoliberalism and reduced to an expression of consumer choice, as Maniates's reflection on the truism "think globally, act locally" makes clear: "The slogan . . . has been shaped by global environmentalism to support a consumer-driven, privatized response to transboundary environmental ills: in practice, thinking globally and acting locally means feeling bad and guilty about far-off and mega-environmental destruction, and then traveling down to the corner store to find a 'green' product whose purchase will somehow empower somebody, somewhere, to do good" (2001, 44).

12 Liboiron marshals compelling statistics on waste in order to support the claim that "[g]arbage is infrastructure, not people," noting, for instance, that "98% of all waste

produced in the United States is industrial waste," a form of waste that would be virtually unaffected by even radical shifts in consumer behavior. Perhaps more relevant to the social realities I address here are the statistics that they cite from the United Nations Food and Agriculture Organization on food waste at consumption and pre-consumption stages: in Latin America, about 89 percent of food waste occurs during production and retailing, prior to those products reaching consumers.

13   Worden examines what he calls documentary art and the way it "position[s] personal experience in tense relation to larger structures" in narrative and documentary film, comics, music albums, memoirs, and autobiographies across the Americas (2020, 18–19). The main Latin American work that Worden examines is Patricio Guzmán's self-referential 1997 documentary film *Chile, la memoria obstinada* (65–67).

14   See Millar (2018) for a brilliant ethnography of the Jardim Gramacho landfill. She writes about the catadores' relationship to the dump and the labor they perform there from a perspective that is sensitive to the multivalence of the verb "to live," considering how the catadores' activities, their time spent in and out of the dump, index their life projects in precisely the way I discuss the anonymous catadora's question: as part of their livelihood and their way of life.

15   I take some of this terminology for characterizing the critical response to the film from the page of the review aggregator *Rotten Tomatoes* on *Waste Land*, where terms like "eco-friendly," "life-affirming," and "human spirit" are plentiful.

16   Walker is a British documentary filmmaker who has worked on projects around the globe, including films with environmental themes like the short "The Tsunami and the Cherry Blossom" (2011), which portrays the aftermath of the earthquake and tsunami that led to the meltdown of the Fukushima Daiichi Nuclear Power Plant in Japan. For the sake of simplicity and clarity, I refer to Walker as the film's director rather than repeatedly invoking Walker, Jardim, and Harley, since the latter two are credited with the subordinate role of co-directors. The international bent to Walker's work is evident not only in the subjects she portrays, but also in the audiences she has in mind for her films. *Waste Land*, for instance, "was explicitly made for an international audience" (Allen 2017, 61). Indeed, the film fared quite well globally, garnering an Academy Award nomination in the category of Best Documentary Feature and around twenty-two other prizes (61). The clear projection of an international audience for the film is a significant factor in the form of environmentality that it cultivates.

17   This labor association, known by the acronym ACAMJG, was formed by the pickers of Jardim Gramacho in order to advocate for the rights and recognition that are owed to people who work collecting recyclable materials. The group has continued to function even after the closing of the Jardim Gramacho landfill and is at the forefront of the movement to promote recycling practices in Rio and the rest of Brazil. For more information, see *ACAMJG* and Millar (2018, 156–58).

18   For images of the final product of Muniz and the catadores' project, see "Pictures of Garbage." Although it is not my aim in this chapter to analyze this collaborative art project itself, but rather the film's portrayal of the project, I have found analyses

of Muniz's work to be thought-provoking. See, for instance, Yaeger (2008, 323–25) for a brief discussion of Muniz's work with garbage in general, with some mention of his project in Jardim Gramacho. For a reflection that is centered on "Pictures of Garbage" itself, see Musiol (2013, 163–64), where the author argues that Muniz's use of trash and marginalized people to recreate iconic works of art is a maneuver that reclaims and makes legible the catadores' humanity through a process that she calls "incremental aesthetic humanization."

19 With the term "para-filmic," I refer to the cinematic analog of paratexts, the elements that adorn and accompany written texts without being part of what we would consider to be the "text itself." In the case of *Waste Land*, the film's website and marketing are rich para-filmic elements. I understand paratexts to be, as Gérard Genette argues, "a fringe, always the conveyor of a commentary that is authorial or more or less legitimated by the author, [that] constitutes a zone between text and off-text, a zone not only of transition but also of *transaction*: a privileged place of pragmatics and a strategy, of an influence on the public, an influence that—whether well or poorly understood and achieved—is at the service of a better reception of the text and a more pertinent reading of it" (1997, 2).

20 To appreciate how this type of camerawork and editing align the viewer's perspective with that of Muniz, it is useful to compare the scene of Muniz's initial foray into the landfill to one from later in the film that focuses on Isis, a catadora, as she picks through the garbage in search of recyclable materials. In contrast to the scene that grounds the viewer's perspective in that of Muniz (in which the camera is placed just behind and above his right shoulder), the camera follows Isis at an intermediate distance and films her from a slightly elevated angle, thus suggesting that she is being observed by the viewer, not that the viewer is seeing the landfill through her eyes. Furthermore, this observational shot is not crosscut with shots of Isis's face, shots that would capture her reaction to what she sees as they function in the scene that focuses on Muniz's perspective.

21 That Muniz ultimately has a high degree of control over the direction and outcome of the project is suggested in many ways, like the fact that the "Pictures of Garbage" falls squarely into the aesthetic that he had been developing for several years before beginning the project. But perhaps the best example of the stilted power dynamic between Muniz and the catadores comes when footage of the making of the garbage portraits almost invariably shows Muniz perched atop scaffolding a few stories above the catadores, directing them with a laser pointer as to how they should arrange the garbage on the floor. Despite this type of visual evidence, Walker does not seem interested in exploring this power dynamic in any detail.

22 In terms of messaging, the inclusion of an exchange between catador Valter dos Santos and Muniz while the latter is scouting for participants in his project goes a long way toward crystallizing the film's environmental ethos. Talking in the landfill, dos Santos sums up the environmental importance of the catadores' work by saying, "Uma latinha tem grande importância porque 99 não é 100 e essa uma vai completar" (One can is of great importance because 99 is not 100, and that one will make a difference) (Walker 2009). "99 não é 100" (99 is not 100) becomes something of a

catchphrase that is repeated a few times during the film and, in my view, serves as a sort of echo that condenses and reproduces the individualistic scale of *Waste Land*'s vision for addressing trash.

23 "Gallinazo Avisa" means "Vulture Warns," although most of the English-language materials associated with the project pluralize the titular vultures and call the project Vultures Warn. Gallinazo is the common name throughout much of Spanish-speaking South America for the American black vulture (*Coragyps atratus*). Here, I use the Spanish name for the project.

24 In a way, Gallinazo Avisa could be seen to represent any number of other relatively humble, small-scale environmental campaigns that effectively and creatively call attention to trash but cannot escape the logic of neoliberal environmentalism. To cite just one similarly ephemeral example, I would mention the work of "Marce la Recicladora," the alter ego of Sara Samaniego, a young Colombian influencer who creates and posts videos to social media platforms in which she adopts the persona of a waste worker who provides educational content related to steps that individuals can take to do their part to improve the waste stream (Alonso 2021).

25 As of April 2023, there are nine videos on Gallinazo Avisa's YouTube channel (all posted between 2 December 2015 and 17 June 2016), including the main promotional video that I focus on in this chapter. The others offer variations of the primary facets of the project presented in that video. One video serves as a platform for all the vultures to introduce themselves and explain their role in the project, while others provide brief stretches of raw footage recorded from the vultures' flights throughout Lima. Additionally, there are two videos that focus on the work of a group of *gallinazos tierra* (ground vultures), who are the humans allied with the project, doing environmental education and trash cleanup in Villa María del Triunfo, a district in the southern part of the city.

26 The picturesque image of these cliffs, along with another shot of some of the same cliffs covered in trash at a later point in the video, can be read as a visual reference to Riberyo's "Los gallinazos sin plumas," for the cliffs are the site of the dump where Enrique and Efraín go to scavenge food for themselves and their grandfather's pig Pascual.

27 This play with narrative perspective brings to mind the other key text from chapter 1: Furtado's "Ilha das Flores." While Furtado leverages the tropes of educational wildlife documentaries and pairs them with a seemingly nonhuman perspective in order to pose questions regarding what it means to be human in the context of waste flows, Gallinazo Avisa uses similar techniques in a way that solidifies both the human perspective and the notion that the human individual is the key actor in the environment.

28 As of April 2023, the URL no longer leads to a site related to Gallinazo Avisa, but rather to some sort of portal for online gambling. The project's social media pages (YouTube, Twitter, Facebook), while inactive, still house relevant materials, though.

29 These projects took place in ten cities across the region (Miami, Mexico City, Santo Domingo, San Juan, Guatemala City, Lima, Asunción, Córdoba, Buenos Aires, and Montevideo), in addition to one interurban, international touring project, the Gira

MercoRUS, including the last four of those cities, which are part of the MERCO-SUR trade bloc. RUS was funded by AECID, the Agencia Española de Cooperación Internacional al Desarrollo (Spanish Agency for International Development Cooperation), through its network of cultural centers located throughout Latin America (Basurama 2011, 10).

Conclusion

1 Such "plastic rocks"—which are even being categorized by types like plastiglomerates, pyroplastics, and plastistones that share morphological features with sedimentary, clastic, and igneous rocks, respectively—have been found as far afield as Ilha da Trinidade, a Brazilian island some 680 miles east of the mainland (Berger 2023).
2 The version of the poem that I cite here can be found in Augusto de Campos's collection *VIVA VAIA (POESIA 1949–1979)*. Another version can be found in Hansjörg Mayer's series *Futura*, which is dedicated to typographically experimental literature. Mayer's printing of "Luxo" (1966) does away with the ornate typeface and the uppercase block letters, while it puts a new twist on the poem's engagement with materiality: instead of being printed on a sheet of paper folded into three sections, like a brochure, Mayer's version is a broadside that folds up (and unfolds) like a map.
3 In this sense, "Luxo é Lixo" brings to mind the neologism that Jacques Lacan coined to categorize his own writing: *poubellication*, a conflation of the words *poubelle* (garbage can) and *publication* (publication, written text) that Lacan invoked when speaking about the difficulty that his texts present to readers (1988, 26). On one level, Lacan's use of the term *poubellication* seems to be little more than a self-deprecating joke, but Lacan himself offers another interpretive key in the same lecture when he proclaims, "What is at stake in the analytic discourse is always the following—you give a different reading to the signifiers that are enunciated . . . than what they signify" (37). While it must be noted that Lacan is talking about the activities of reading and interpretation as they relate to a specific discursive situation—psychoanalysis—his way of characterizing the link between trash and writing in his own texts is highly suggestive and serves to illuminate how trash and activities related to waste management are folded into the production of cultural texts.

Works Cited

ACAMJG. Website of the Associação dos Catadores do Aterro Metropolitano de Jardim Gramacho, www.acamjg.blogspot.com. Accessed 12 April 2022.
Adamson, Joni, and Scott Slovic. "The Shoulders We Stand on: An Introduction to Ethnicity and Ecocriticism." *MELUS*, vol. 34, no. 2, 2009, pp. 5–24.
Agamben, Giorgio. *The Coming Community*. Translated by Michael Hardt, University of Minnesota Press, 1993.
———. *Homo Sacer: Sovereign Power and Bare Life*. Translated by Daniel Heller-Roazen, Stanford University Press, 1998.
———. *The Open: Man and Animal*. Translated by Kevin Attell, Stanford University Press, 2004.
Aguirre, Carlos, and Charles F. Walker. "Introduction." *The Lima Reader: History, Culture, Politics*, edited by Carlos Aguirre and Charles F. Walker, Duke University Press, 2017, pp. 1–5.
Aínsa, Fernando. "Palabras nómadas: La patria a la distancia y el imposible regreso." *Letral*, no. 5, 2010, pp. 30–45.
Aira, César. *La villa*. Emecé, 2001.
———. *Shantytown*. Translated by Chris Andrews, New Directions, 2013.
Alaimo, Stacy. *Bodily Natures: Science, Environment, and the Material Self*. Indiana University Press, 2010.
Allen, Alice Louisa. *Shifting Horizons: Urban Space and Social Difference in Contemporary Brazilian Documentary and Photography*. Wiley-Blackwell, 2017.
Alonso, Judit. "Marce La Recicladora, la influencer del reciclaje que arrasa en las redes sociales." *Deutsche Welle*, 12 August 2021, https://www.dw.com/es/marce-la-recicladora-la-influencer-del-reciclaje-que-arrasa-en-las-redes-sociales/a-58848960. Accessed 3 March 2023.
Altamirano, Ignacio Manuel. *El Zarco*. Ediciones Océano, 1986.
Amago, Samuel. *Basura: Cultures of Waste in Contemporary Spain*. University of Virginia Press, 2021.
Appadurai, Arjun. "Mediants, Materiality, Normativity." *Public Culture*, vol. 27, no. 2, 2015, pp. 221–37.
Armiero, Marco. *Wasteocene: Stories from the Global Dump*. Cambridge University Press, 2021.
"Aterro sanitário de Gramacho é fechado no Rio de Janeiro." *UOL Mais*, 3 June 2012.
Azevedo, Aluísio. *O cortiço*. Martins, 1968.

Azuaje, Ronny. "Espacios y subjetividades abyectas en *El Señor Gallinazo vuelve a Lima* de Sebastián Salazar Bondy." 1 May 2021. Spanish American Short Story, University of Alabama, student paper.

Basurama. *RUS. Residuos Urbanos Sólidos. Basura y espacio público en Latinoamérica. 2008–2010*. Editorial Delirio, 2011.

Bauman, Zygmunt. *Wasted Lives: Modernity and its Outcasts*. Polity, 2004.

Bell, Lucy. "Narrative, Nature, Society: The Network of Waste in Andrés Neuman's *Bariloche*." *The Modern Language Review*, vol. 110, no. 4, 2015, pp. 1045–66.

Belli, Gioconda. *Waslala: Memorial del futuro*. Emecé, 1996.

Benavides, Jorge Eduardo. *Los años inútiles*. Alfaguara, 2002.

Bennett, Jane. *Vibrant Matter: A Political Ecology of Things*. Duke University Press, 2010.

Berger, Joshua Howat. "Scientists Make 'Disturbing' Find on Remote Island: Plastic Rocks." *Phys.org*, 21 March 2023, https://phys.org/news/2023-03-scientists-disturbing-remote-island-plastic.html. Accessed 28 March 2023.

Bilbija, Ksenija. "Fiction's Mysterious Ways: Eloísa Cartonera." *Review: Literature and Arts of the Americas*, vol. 47, no. 1, 2014, pp. 13–20.

Bilbija, Ksenija, and Paloma Celis Carbajal, eds. *Akademia Cartonera: A Primer of Latin American Cartonera Publishers*. Parallel Press/University of Wisconsin-Madison Libraries, 2009.

Bolaño, Roberto. *2666*. Anagrama, 2004.

———. "Neuman, tocado por la gracia." *Entre paréntesis*, Anagrama, 2004, p. 149.

———. "Neuman, Touched by Grace." *Between Parenthesis*. Edited by Ignacio Echevarría. Translated by Natasha Wimmer. New Directions, 2011, p. 160.

Bonacic, Dánisa. "Espacio urbano, crisis y convivencia en *La villa* de César Aira." *Revista de Crítica Literaria Latinoamericana*, no. 79, 2014, pp. 359–76.

Braidotti, Rosi. *Nomadic Theory: The Portable Rosi Braidotti*. Columbia University Press, 2011.

———. *The Posthuman*. Polity, 2013.

Brandão, Ignácio de Loyola. *Zero: romance pré-histórico*. 9th ed. Global, 1984.

Brown, Bill. "How to Do Things with Things (A Toy Story)." *Critical Inquiry*, vol. 24, no. 4, 1998, pp. 935–64.

Brown, Wendy. "Neoliberalism and the End of Liberal Democracy." *Edgework: Critical Essays on Knowledge and Politics*, Princeton University Press, 2009, pp. 37–59.

———. *Undoing the Demos: Neoliberalism's Stealth Revolution*. Zone Books, 2015.

Buell, Lawrence. "Ecoglobalist Affects: The Emergence of U.S. Environmental Imagination on a Planetary Scale." *Shades of the Planet: American Literature as World Literature*, edited by Wai Chee Dimock and Lawrence Buell, Princeton University Press, 2007, pp. 227–48.

———. *The Future of Environmental Criticism: Environmental Crisis and Literary Imagination*. Blackwell, 2005.

Buñuel, Luis. *Los olvidados*. Ultramar Films, 1950.

Busqued, Carlos. *Bajo este sol tremendo*. Anagrama, 2008.

Cambaceres, Eugenio. *En la sangre*. Colihue/Hachette, 1980.

Campos, Augusto de. "Luxo." *Futura* 9, 1966.

———. *VIVA VAIA (POESIA 1949–1979)*. Brasiliense, 1986.
Campos, Haroldo de. "Arte pobre, tempo de pobreza, poesia menos." *Novos Estudos Cebrap*, vol. 1, no. 3, 1982, pp. 63–67.
Caña Jiménez, María del Carmen. "Mutantes, monstruos y esperpentos: hacia una nueva concepción de la ciudadanía en la obra de Fernando Contreras Castro." *Chasqui: revista de literatura latinoamericana*, vol. 45, no. 2, 2016, pp. 234–48.
Caña Jiménez, María del Carmen, and Vinodh Venkatesh. "Introducción. Horacio Castellanos Moya: *El diablo en el espejo*." *Horacio Castellanos Moya: El diablo en el espejo*, edited by María del Carmen Caña Jiménez and Vinodh Venkatesh, Albatros Ediciones, 2016, pp. 9–20.
Casa de Cinema de Porto Alegre. Casa de Cinema de Porto Alegre, www.casacinepoa.com.br. Accessed 12 April 2022.
Castellanos Moya, Horacio. *Baile con serpientes*. Tusquets Editores, 2012.
———. *Dance with Snakes*. Translated by Lee Paula Springer. Biblioasis, 2009.
Chakrabarty, Dipesh. "The Climate of History: Four Theses." *Critical Inquiry*, vol. 35, no. 2, 2009, pp. 197–222.
Chejfec, Sergio. *El aire*. 1992. Alfaguara, 2008.
Choi, Eunha. *Gestured Realism in Julio Ramón Ribeyro: Fiction's Fragmented and Contingent Form*. PhD Diss., New York University, 2013.
Cisneros, James. "Dando vueltas por la ciudad neoliberal. Las tramas urbanas de César Aira." *Libro mercado: Literatura y neoliberalismo*, compiled by José Ramón Ruisánchez Serra, Universidad Iberoamericana, 2015, pp. 63–82.
Cisneros, Odile. "The Poetry of Garbage in Contemporary Brazilian Culture." *Literature beyond the Human: Post-Anthropocentric Brazil*, edited by Luca Bacchini and Victoria Saramago, Routledge, 2022, pp. 195–213.
Clapp, Jennifer. *Toxic Exports: The Transfer of Hazardous Wastes from Rich to Poor Countries*. Cornell University Press, 2001.
Congrains Martín, Enrique. *No una sino muchas muertes*. Planeta, 1975.
Contreras, Sandra. *Las vueltas de César Aira*. Beatriz Viterbo, 2002.
Contreras Castro, Fernando. *Única Looking at the Sea*. Translated by Elaine S. Brooks. Diálogos, 2017.
———. *Única mirando al mar*. Ediciones Farben, 1994.
Coole, Dianna, and Samantha Frost. "Introducing the New Materialisms." *New Materialisms: Ontology, Agency, and Politics*, Duke University Press, 2010, pp. 1–43.
Coutinho, Eduardo, dir. *Boca de Lixo*. Centro de Criação de Imagem Popular, 1993.
———. "O cinema documentário e a escuta da alteridade." *Projeto História*, no. 15, 1997, pp. 165–91.
Davis, Brennan, Julie L. Ozanne, and Ronald Paul Hill. "The Transformative Consumer Research Movement." *Journal of Public Policy and Marketing*, vol. 35, no. 2, 2016, pp. 159–69.
Derrida, Jacques. "The Animal That Therefore I Am (More to Follow)." Translated by David Wills. *Critical Inquiry*, vol. 28, no. 2, 2002, pp. 369–418.
Devadas, Vijay, and Jane Mummery. "Community without Community." *borderlands*, vol. 6, no. 1, 2007.

Díaz, Gwendolyn. *Women and Power in Argentine Literature: Stories, Interviews, and Critical Essays*. University of Texas Press, 2007.

Díaz, Luis Eduardo. "Cierre técnico comienza a transformar Río Azul." *La Nación*, 9 November 2009, www.nacion.com/el-pais/servicios/cierre-tecnico-comienza-a-transformar-rio-azul/ALXQ26IAONDMNFTERSFRUHFKAY/story. Accessed 20 October 2021.

Douglas, Mary. *Purity and Danger: An Analysis of the Concepts of Pollution and Taboo*. Ark, 1984.

Dove, Patrick. *Literature and "Interregnum": Globalization, War, and the Crisis of Sovereignty in Latin America*. SUNY Press, 2016.

———. "Mass Media Technics and Post-Politics in César Aira's *La villa*." *Revista de Estudios Hispánicos*, vol. 43, no. 1, 2009, pp. 3–30.

Dujovne Ortiz, Alicia. *¿Quién mató a Diego Duarte? Crónicas de la basura*. Aguilar, 2010.

Echeverría, Esteban. *El matadero/La cautiva*. Edited by Leonor Fleming. Cátedra, 1986.

EcoFilm Festival. www.youtube.com/@EcoFilmFestivalMX. Accessed 11 Sept. 2023.

Edkins, Jenny. "Whatever Politics." *Giorgio Agamben: Sovereignty and Life*, edited by Matthew Calarco and Steven DeCaroli, Stanford University Press, 2007, pp. 70–91.

Elmore, Peter. *El perfil de la palabra: La obra de Julio Ramón Ribeyro*. Fondo Editorial de la Pontificia Universidad Católica del Perú/Fondo de Cultura Económica, 2002.

Eloísa Cartonera. Website of Eloísa Cartonera, www.eloisacartonera.com.ar. Accessed 12 April 2022.

Enrigue, Álvaro. "Outrage." *Hypothermia*, translated by Brendan Riley, Dalkey Archive Press, 2013, pp. 66–78.

———. "Ultraje." *Hipotermia*, 2005. Anagrama, 2013.

Foster, David William. "Metafilmic Devices in Eduardo Coutinho's *Boca de Lixo*." *Revista Científica/FAP*, vol. 4, no. 2, 2009, pp. 155–65.

Foucault, Michel. *The History of Sexuality. Volume I: An Introduction*. Translated by Robert Hurley. Vintage Books, 1990.

Fox, Claire F. *The Fence and the River: Culture and Politics at the U.S.-Mexico Border*. University of Minnesota Press, 1999.

Furtado, Jorge, dir. "Ilha das Flores." Casa de Cinema de Porto Alegre, 1989.

@GallinazoAvisa. "Humanos, estamos viendo la posibilidad de vender polos con el fin de recaudar fondos para el proyecto." *Twitter*, 17 May 2017, twitter.com/GallinazoAvisa/status/864956863024168960?cxt=HHwWgIC86eTr-IAYAAAA.

@GallinazoAvisa. "Humanos, los invito a conocer a mis primos en el taller por el Día Internacional de los Buitres #GallinazoAvisa." *Twitter*, 31 August 2016, twitter.com/GallinazoAvisa/status/771031523583754240?cxt=HHwWgIConb3FoLMVAAAA.

"Gallinazo Avisa, tú actúas." *YouTube*, uploaded by Gallinazo Avisa, 2 December 2015, www.youtube.com/watch?v=YPf_weDJ6aM.

Gambetta, Curt. *Making Waste Public*. Master's thesis, Rice University, 2009.

Genette, Gérard. *Paratexts: Thresholds of Interpretation*. Translated by Jane E. Lewin. Cambridge University Press, 1997.

Gerdes, Dick C. "Julio Ramón Ribeyro: Un análisis de sus cuentos." *Kentucky Romance Quarterly*, vol. 26, no. 1, 1979, pp. 51–65.

Giles, David Boarder. "The Anatomy of a Dumpster: Abject Capital and the Looking Glass of Value." *Social Text*, vol. 32, no. 1, 2014, pp. 93–113.
Glickman, Nora. "Andando se hacen los caminos de Alicia Dujovne Ortiz." *Revista Iberoamericana*, vol. 66, no. 191, 2000, pp. 381–92.
Gonçalo, Pablo. "Ironia, cinismo e pragmatismo nos circuitos de arte: Os documentários de Orson Welles, Banksy e Vik Muniz." *Doc On-Line: Revista Digital de Cinema Documentário*, no. 10, 2011, pp. 72–103.
"Gramacho: A vida no maior aterro sanitário da América Latina." *UOL Mais*, 5 November 2008, www.mais.uol.com.br/view/1575mnadmj5c/gramacho-a-vida-no-maior-aterro-sanitario-da-america-latina-04023170D0C12326?types=A&. Accessed 12 April 2022.
Gutiérrez, Pedro Juan. *El Rey de La Habana*. Anagrama, 1999.
Harvey, David. *A Brief History of Neoliberalism*. Oxford University Press, 2005.
Hawkins, Gay. "Plastic Bags: Living with Rubbish." *International Journal of Cultural Studies*, vol. 4, no. 1, 2001, pp. 5–23.
———. *The Ethics of Waste: How We Relate to Rubbish*. Rowman & Littlefield, 2005.
Heffes, Gisela. *Políticas de la destrucción/Poéticas de la preservación: Apuntes para una lectura (eco)crítica del medio ambiente en América Latina*. Beatriz Viterbo, 2013.
Hernández Adrián, Francisco-J. "Tomás Sánchez on Exhorbitance: Still Lifes of the Tropical Landfill." *The Global South*, vol. 6, no. 1, 2012, pp. 15–37.
Hird, Myra J. "Waste Flows." *Discard Studies*, https://discardstudies.com/discard-studies-compendium/#Wasteflows. Accessed 12 April 2022.
Horak, Jan-Christopher. "Wildlife Documentaries: From Classical Forms to Reality TV." *Film History*, vol. 18, no. 4, 2006, pp. 459–75.
Houser, Heather. *Ecosickness in Contemporary U.S. Fiction: Environment and Affect*. Columbia University Press, 2014.
"Ilha das Flores—roteiro original." *Casa de Cinema de Porto Alegre*, 1 Dec. 1988, www.casacinepoa.com.br/uploads/ilha-das-flores-rot-orig.pdf. Accessed 11 Sept. 2023.
Iovino, Serenella. "The Human Alien. Otherness, Humanism, and the Future of Ecocriticism." *Ecozon@*, vol. 1, no. 1, 2010, pp. 53–61.
Iovino, Serenella, and Serpil Oppermann. "Introduction: Stories Come to Matter." *Material Ecocriticism*, edited by Serenella Iovino and Serpil Oppermann, Indiana University Press, 2014, pp. 1–17.
———. "Material Ecocriticism: Materiality, Agency and Models of Narrativity." *Ecozon@*, vol. 3, no. 1, 2012, pp. 75–91.
———. "Theorizing Material Ecocriticism: A Diptych." *ISLE*, vol. 19, no. 3, 2012, pp. 448–75.
Jesus, Carolina Maria de. *Quarto de despejo: diário de uma favelada*. Livraria Francisco Alves, 1960.
Kennedy, Greg. *An Ontology of Trash*. SUNY Press, 2007.
Klein, Naomi. *The Shock Doctrine: The Rise of Disaster Capitalism*. Picador, 2007.
Kotsko, Adam. *Neoliberalism's Demons: On the Political Theology of Late Capital*. Stanford University Press, 2018.

Kristeva, Julia. *Powers of Horror: An Essay on Abjection*. Translated by Leon S. Roudiez. Columbia University Press, 1982.

Kroll-Bryce, Christian. "Nómadas, desempleados y suicidas: racionalidad neoliberal y subjetividades alternas en la literatura centroamericana de posguerra." *Revista de Estudios Hispánicos*, vol. 50, no. 3, 2016, pp. 605–27.

Lacan, Jacques. *The Seminar of Jacques Lacan, Book XX, Encore 1972–1973*. Edited by Jacques Alain Miller. Translated by Bruce Fink. W. W. Norton & Company, 1988.

Laera, Alejandra. "Bestias, basura, vida (en la narrativa de Sergio Chejfec)." *Cuadernos de Literatura*, no. 31, 2012, pp. 105–17.

———. *Ficciones del dinero: Argentina, 1890–2001*. Fondo de Cultura Económica, 2014.

Lefebvre, Henri. *The Production of Space*. Translated by Donald Nicholson-Smith. Blackwell, 1991.

Lemke, Thomas. *Biopolitics: An Advanced Introduction*. Translated by Eric Frederick Trump. New York University Press, 2011.

Liboiron, Max. "Against Awareness, for Scale: Garbage Is Infrastructure, Not Behavior." *Discard Studies*, 23 January 2014, www.discardstudies.com/2014/01/23/against-awareness-for-scale-garbage-is-infrastructure-not-behavior/. Accessed 30 March 2022.

Liboiron, Max, and Josh Lepawsky. *Discard Studies: Wasting, Systems, and Power*. MIT Press, 2022.

Lins, Consuelo. "The Cinema of Eduardo Coutinho." *Studies in Documentary Film*, vol. 1, no. 3, 2007, pp. 199–206.

Livon-Grosman, Ernesto, dir. *Cartoneros*. Documentary Educational Resources, 2006.

"Luxo é Lixo." *Basurama*, October 2014, www.basurama.org/proyecto/luxo-e-lixo-lujo-es-basura-in-lo3-we-trash. Accessed 12 April 2022.

Maniates, Michael F. "Individualization: Plant a Tree, Buy a Bike, Save the World?" *Global Environmental Politics*, vol. 1, no. 3, 2001, pp. 31–52.

Marcum, Joni Hayward. "Reconsidering the Aesthetics of Garbage in *Waste Land*." *Afterimage*, vol. 48, no. 3, 2021, pp. 35–57.

Marx, Karl. *Capital: A Critique of Political Economy*. Translated by Samuel Moore and Edward Aveling. Modern Library, 1936.

McKay, Micah. "'Deus, salve a América': Ignácio de Loyola Brandão's *Zero* and the Production of Trash." *Chasqui: revista de literatura latinoamericana*, vol. 46, no. 2, 2017, pp. 144–60.

———. "Documenting Jardim Gramacho: *Estamira* (2004) and *Waste Land* (2009)." *Luso-Brazilian Review*, vol. 53, no. 2, 2016, pp. 134–52.

McLoughlin, Daniel. "Threshold." *The Agamben Dictionary*, edited by Alex Murray and Jessica Whyte, Edinburgh University Press, 2011, pp. 189–91.

Meireles, Cecília. *Romanceiro da Inconfidência*. Editora Nova Fronteira, 1989.

Mello, Leonardo Freire de, and Rafael D'Almeida Martins. "Brazil." *Encyclopedia of Consumption and Waste: The Social Science of Garbage*, vol. 1, edited by Carl A. Zimring and William L. Rathje, Sage Publications, 2012, pp. 78–81.

Millar, Kathleen M. "Garbage as Racialization." *Anthropology and Humanism*, vol. 45, no. 1, 2020, pp. 4–24.

———. *Reclaiming the Discarded: Life and Labor on Rio's Garbage Dump*. Duke University Press, 2018.

Mora Chinchilla, Rolando, and Raúl Mora Amador. "Reseña histórica del relleno sanitario de Río Azul y consideraciones sobre los metales pesados tratados en él y los presentes en nuestros hogares." *Reflexiones*, vol. 82, no. 2, 2003, pp. 47–58.

Moraña, Mabel, and Ignacio M. Sánchez Prado, eds. *Heridas abiertas: Biopolítica y representación en América Latina*. Iberoamericana/Vervuert, 2014.

Morrison, Susan Signe. *The Literature of Waste: Material Ecopoetics and Ethical Matter*. Palgrave Macmillan, 2015.

Morton, Timothy. "Guest Column: Queer Ecology." *PMLA*, vol. 125, no. 2, 2010, pp. 273–82.

Muniz, Vik. "Pictures of Garbage." *VikMuniz*, 2014, www.vikmuniz.net/gallery/garbage. Accessed 12 April 2022.

Musiol, Hanna. "Museums of Human Bodies." *College Literature*, vol. 40, no. 3, 2013, pp. 156–75.

Nading, Alex M. "Central America." *Encyclopedia of Consumption and Waste: The Social Science of Garbage*, vol. 1, edited by Carl A. Zimring and William L. Rathje, Sage Publications, 2012, pp. 108–11.

Nail, Thomas. *Theory of the Border*. Oxford University Press, 2016.

Neuman, Andrés. *Bariloche*. Anagrama, 1999.

Nichols, Bill. *Representing Reality: Issues and Concepts in Documentary*. Indiana University Press, 1991.

Niebylski, Dianna C. "Sergio Chejfec: De *Lenta biografía* a *Mis dos mundos*." *Sergio Chejfec: Trayectorias de una escritura. Ensayos críticos*, edited by Dianna C. Niebylski, Instituto Internacional de Literatura Iberoamericana, 2012, pp. 11–29.

———, ed. *Sergio Chejfec: Trayectorias de una escritura. Ensayos críticos*. Instituto Internacional de Literatura Iberoamericana, 2012.

Nixon, Rob. *Slow Violence and the Environmentalism of the Poor*. Harvard University Press, 2011.

Nzeadibe, Thaddeus Chidi, and Ignatius Ani Madu. "Open Dump." *Encyclopedia of Consumption and Waste: The Social Science of Garbage*, vol. 2, edited by Carl A. Zimring and William L. Rathje, Sage Publications, 2012, pp. 631–33.

Oliver, Kelly. "Individual and National Identity." *The Portable Kristeva*, edited by Kelly Oliver, Columbia University Press, 2002, pp. 225–27.

Orlando, Angela. "Mexico." *Encyclopedia of Consumption and Waste: The Social Science of Garbage*, vol. 1, edited by Carl A. Zimring and William L. Rathje, Sage Publications, 2012. 534–36.

Ortega, Julio. "Los cuentos de Ribeyro." *Cuadernos Hispanoamericanos*, no. 417, 1985, pp. 128–45.

Parra, Eduardo Antonio. *Nostalgia de la sombra*. Joaquín Mortiz, 2002.

Peixoto, Marta. "Rio's Favelas in Recent Fiction and Film: Commonplaces of Urban Segregation." *PMLA*, vol. 122, no. 1, 2007, pp. 170–78.

Pérez-Cano, Tania. *Ecopoéticas transatlánticas: Del texto a la acción social*. PhD Diss., University of Iowa, 2013.

Pérez Daniel, Iván. "Narrar después del '*boom*': la clase media y la desnacionalización en *Hipotermia* de Álvaro Enrigue." *Romance Quarterly*, vol. 65, no. 3, 2018, pp. 162–73.

Pérez Trujillo, Axel. "Exposed Insularities: Islands, Capitalism and Waste in Jorge Furtado's *Ilha das Flores* (1989)." *The Film Archipelago: Islands in Latin American Cinema*, edited by Antonio Gómez and Franciso-J. Hernández Adrián, Bloomsbury, 2022, pp. 131–51.

Prádanos, Luis I. *Postgrowth Imaginaries: New Ecologies and Counterhegemonic Culture in Post-2008 Spain*. Liverpool University Press, 2018.

Prignano, Ángel O. *Crónica de la basura porteña: Del fogón indígena al cinturón ecológico*. Junta de Estudios Históricos de San José de Flores, 1998.

Pye, Gillian. "Introduction: Trash as Cultural Category." *Trash Culture: Objects and Obsolescence in Cultural Perspective*, edited by Gillian Pye, Peter Lang, 2010, pp. 1–13.

The Radiological Accident in Goiânia. International Atomic Energy Agency, 1988.

Reyes, Alfonso. "La basura." *Vida y ficción*, edited by Ernesto Mejía Sánchez, Fondo de Cultura Económica, 1970, p. 162.

Ribeyro, Julio Ramón. "Los gallinazos sin plumas." *Cuentos completos*, Alfaguara, 1994, pp. 21–29.

Rivera-Barnes, Beatriz, and Jerry Hoeg. *Reading and Writing the Latin American Landscape*. Palgrave Macmillan, 2009.

Rodríguez, Ana Patricia. *Dividing the Isthmus: Central American Transnational Histories, Literatures, and Cultures*. University of Texas Press, 2009.

Rodríguez, Juan Pablo. "The Politics of Neoliberalism in Latin America: Dynamics of Resilience and Contestation." *Sociology Compass*, vol. 15, no. 3, e12854, 2021, pp. 1–13.

Salazar Bondy, Sebastián. *El Señor Gallinazo vuelve a Lima*. Instituto Nacional de Cultura del Perú, 2005.

———. *Lima la horrible*. Ediciones ERA, 1964.

Sánchez Prado, Ignacio M. "*Amores perros*: Exotic Violence and Neoliberal Fear." *Journal of Latin American Cultural Studies*, vol. 15, no. 1, 2006, pp. 39–57.

Scanlan, John. *On Garbage*. Reaktion Books, 2005.

Schwarz, Roberto. *Que horas são?* Companhia das Letras, 1987.

Seifert, Marcos. "Restos de vida en *Bajo este sol tremendo* de Carlos Busqued." *Perífrasis*, vol. 8, no. 16, 2017, pp. 82–96.

"Sobre Basurama." *Basurama*, www.basurama.org/basurama. Accessed 12 April 2022.

Soper, Kate. *What Is Nature? Culture, Politics and the Non-Human*. Blackwell, 1995.

Spitta, Silvia. "Lima the Horrible: The Cultural Politics of Theft." *PMLA*, vol. 122, no. 1, 2007, pp. 294–300.

Stam, Robert. "Palimpsestic Aesthetics: A Meditation on Hybridity and Garbage." *Performing Hybridity*, edited by May Joseph and Jennifer Natalya Fink, University of Minnesota Press, 1999, pp. 59–78.

Sullivan, Heather I. "Dirt Theory and Material Ecocriticism." *ISLE*, vol. 19, no. 3, 2012, pp. 515–31.

Tadajewski, Mark, and Kathy Hamilton. "Waste, Art, and Social Change: Transformative Consumer Research outside of the Academy?" *Journal of Macromarketing*, vol. 34, no. 1, 2014, pp. 80–86.

Taylor, Erin B. "South America." *Encyclopedia of Consumption and Waste: The Social Science of Garbage*, vol. 2, edited by Carl A. Zimring and William L. Rathje, Sage Publications, 2012, pp. 844–48.

Thompson, Michael. *Rubbish Theory: The Creation and Destruction of Value*. Oxford University Press, 1979.

Tsing, Anna Lowenhaupt. *The Mushroom at the End of the World: On the Possibility of Life in Capitalist Ruins*. Princeton University Press, 2015.

Ureta, Sebestián. "Caring for Waste: Handling Tailings in a Chilean Copper Mine." *Environment and Planning A*, vol. 48, no. 8, 2016, pp. 1532–48.

Urrea, Luis Alberto. *By the Lake of Sleeping Children: The Secret Life of the Mexican Border*. Anchor Books, 1996.

Valero Juan, Eva María. *La ciudad en la obra de Julio Ramón Ribeyro*. Universidad de Alicante, 2003.

Vargas, Tayde, dir. "Los artilugios del Señor Tlachuache." Philocaptio, 2014, www.vimeo.com/196334651. Accessed 11 Sept. 2023.

Vargas Llosa, Mario. *Historia de Mayta*. Seix Barral, 1984.

Venkatesh, Vinodh. "Towards a Poetics of the Automobile in Contemporary Central American Fiction." *Letras Hispanas*, vol. 8, no. 2, 2012, pp. 62–76.

Verbitsky, Bernardo. *Villa miseria también es América*. Editorial Sudamericana, 2003.

Vieira de Jesus, Rosane Meire. "*Ilha das Flores:* o documentarista em primeiro plano." *O Olho da História*, no. 8, 2005.

Walker, Charles F. "Green Vultures." *The Lima Reader: History, Culture, Politics*, edited by Carlos Aguirre and Charles F. Walker, Duke University Press, 2017, pp. 254–56.

Walker, Lucy, João Jardim, and Karen Harley, dirs. *Waste Land*. Almega Projects and O2 Filmes, 2009.

"Waste Land." *Rotten Tomatoes*, www.rottentomatoes.com/m/waste-land. Accessed 13 April 2022.

Waste Land Movie. Almega Projects, www.wastelandmovie.com. Accessed 18 April 2022.

Williamson, John. "Democracy and the 'Washington Consensus.'" *World Development*, vol. 21, no. 8, 1993, pp. 1329–36.

Wolfe, Cary. "Human, All Too Human: 'Animal Studies' and the Humanities." *PMLA*, vol. 124, no. 2, 2009, pp. 564–75.

Worden, Daniel. *Neoliberal Nonfictions: The Documentary Aesthetic from Joan Didion to Jay-Z*. University of Virginia Press, 2020.

Yaeger, Patricia. "Editor's Column: The Death of Nature and the Apotheosis of Trash; or, Rubbish Ecology." *PMLA*, vol. 123, no. 2, 2008, pp. 321–39.

Ziarek, Ewa Plonowska. "Bare Life." *Impasses of the Global: Theory in the Era of Climate Change, Vol. 2*, edited by Henry Sussman, Open Humanities Press, 2012, pp. 194–211.

Zubiaurre, Maite. *Talking Trash: Cultural Uses of Waste*. Vanderbilt University Press, 2019.

Index

actants, 27
aesthetics-didacticism relationship, 118–20
Agamben, Giorgio, 27, 53–54
Air, The. See *aire, El* (Chejfec)
Aira, César, 77, 143, 160n16
aire, El (Chejfec), 77; money in, 161n23; sense of absence, 161n24; space in, 98–100; as trash work, 80–81, 85–88
Alaimo, Stacy, 86, 156n3, 160n19
Altamirano, Ignacio Manuel, 15
Amago, Samuel, 18
animal-human threshold, 29–31
años inútiles, Los (Benavides), 151n6
Anthropocene, 4–10
anthropological machine, 29–31, 53
Appadurai, Arjun, 26–27
argentinidad, ritual, 64
"artilugios del Señor Tlacuache, Los" (film), 109–13, 138; characterization of, 119–21; comparison to *Waste Land*, 124
arts of noticing, 112
asado, 69–70
Associação de Catadores do Aterro Metropolitano de Jardim Gramacho (ACAMJG), 123, 125, 165n17
Association for the Study of Literature and Environment, 133
Azevedo, Aluísio, 15
Azuaje, Ronny, 24

backwardness, 10
Baile con serpientes (Castellanos Moya), 77; Chevrolet as trash object in, 100–102; space in, 100–104; as trash work, 81–83, 85–88
Bajo este sol tremendo (Busqued), 156n5
Banegas, Cristina, 1

Bariloche (Neuman), 77; space in, 89–90, 94–98; as trash work, 78, 85–88
Barroso. See *aire, El* (Chejfec)
"basura, La" (Reyes), 73–76; basic features of trash works in, 77–88
Basurama, 139–42; "Luxo é Lixo" (Luxury is Trash), 144–48
Belli, Gioconda, 16
Bennett, Jane, 27, 86, 155n2
Berni, Antonio, 17
biocrítica, 25–26
bioecocrítica, 26
bioecocriticism, 25
biopolítica global, 26
biopolitical impulses, 29
Boca de Lixo (film), 55–56, 162n2; defining trash in, 59–60; fixed identity in, 65–66; representing unrepresentable, 66–72
Bolaño, Roberto, 16, 158n8
Braidotti, Rosi, 76, 86, 104, 139
Brazil, 11–12, 20–21, 29, 42, 47, 113, 121, 126, 128, 144
Brief History of Neoliberalism, A (Harvey), 114
Brown, Bill, 106
Brown, Wendy, 84, 113, 163n6
Buell, Lawrence, 26, 164n11
Buenos Aires, 1–4, 15–16, 55, 63–69, 79, 81, 84, 89, 96–99, 133
Buñuel, Luis, 16
buzo (garbage picker), 83–84
By the Lake of Sleeping Children (Urrea), 55; *basura* fault line in, 60–61; defining trash in, 60–61; representing unrepresentable, 66–72

cacharro (wreck), 100–101
Cambaceres, Eugenio, 15

Campos, Augusto de, 144–47
Campos, Haroldo de, 144–46
carcacha (heap), term, 100–101
care: concept, 78–88; notions of, 104–8
cartonero, 1–3, 92, 133, 141, 154n3; in *¿Quién mató a Diego Duarte?* (Dujovne Ortiz), 55, 62–63, 67; in *La villa* (Aira), 84, 89, 98, 105
Cartoneros (film), 1–3
Castellanos Moya, Horacio, 77, 143
catador, 56, 65–67, 70–71, 92, 121–32, 139, 140, 144
CEAMSE (Coordinación Ecológica Área Metropolitana Sociedad del Estado), 55, 58–59
Chejfec, Sergio, 77
Chevrolet, as trash object, 100–102
ciruja, 55, 62, 67, 84, 89, 92, 97, 106, 154n3
Cisneros, Odile, 18
Coming Community, The (Agamben), 27–28, 54
common, conceptualization of, 54
community, limits of, 53–57; fixed identity, 61–66; representing unrepresentable, 66–72; trash thresholds, 57–61
community without community, 61–66
conceived space, 103
Congrains Martín, Enrique, 16
Contreras Castro, Fernando, 77
Coutinho, Eduardo, 55–56, 71, 143, 154n4
critical posthuman subject, 76
crónicas (literary nonfiction), 14
cultural texts, trash in, 13–19

Dance with Snakes. See *Baile con serpientes* (Castellanos Moya)
Derrida, Jacques, 4
detritus. *See* trash
dirt, approaches to, 149n2
disposability, ethos of, 6–7
disposal, 4, 6, 12–13, 25, 29, 31, 40, 42, 49–50, 97, 105
dividuality, humans, 27
documentary aesthetic, 119–20; Basurama's resistance to, 140; Gallinazo Avisa's variation on, 136; *Waste Land* and, 124, 126–27, 129–30
dogs, 151n7
Dove, Patrick, 157n6, 161n23
Dujovne Ortiz, Alicia, 55–59, 143, 154n2

Echeverría, Esteban, 14–15
Edkins, Jenny, 54–55
Efraín. *See* "gallinazos sin plumas, Los" (Ribeyro)
Elmore, Peter, 34, 152n9
En la sangre (Cambaceres), 15
Enrigue, Álvaro, 77
Enrique. *See* "gallinazos sin plumas, Los" (Ribeyro)
enterprise, 12, 34, 55, 132, 134
environmentality, term, 164n11
escenas porteñas (Buenos Aires scenes), 2
espejismo, 70
Estamira (film), 16

film, trash in, 13–19
fixed identity, communities, 61–66
Foster, David William, 59, 71
Foucault, Michel, 27
free will, naturalization of, 116–18
Fukushima Daiichi Nuclear Power Plant, 165n16
Furtado, Jorge, 29–31

Gallinazo Avisa, 132–39, 143; name meaning, 167n23; representation by, 167n24; YouTube channel of, 167n25
"gallinazos sin plumas, Los" (Ribeyro): character struggles in, 152n9; foundational statement of, 151n8–9; physical sustenance in, 29–31; predating neoliberalism, 164n9; primary trash use in, 31–41
gallinazos sin plumas. *See* "gallinazos sin plumas, Los" (Ribeyro)
garbage. *See* trash
Gerdes, Dick, 38–39
González, Alicia, 68, 70

Hamilton, Kathy, 125–27
Haraway, Donna, 27
Hardt, Michael, 54
Harley, Karen, 113
Harvey, David, 114, 163n6
Hawkins, Gay, 6–7
Heffes, Gisela, 17, 25
Heidegger, Martin, 8

Hernández Adrián, Francisco-J., 17
Hipotermia (Enrigue), 158n9
Hird, Myra, 6
Historia de Mayta (Vargas Llosa), 151n6
homo oeconomicus, 84–85, 113–14
homo sacer, 85
Homo Sacer (Agamben), 28, 53–54, 150n4
Horowitz, Drake. *See* "Ultraje" (Enrigue)
huesera (scrapyard), 100–101
humans, limits of, 22–25; defining in "Ilha das Flores" (Furtado), 41–52; human/animal threshold, 29–31; trash as threshold, 25–29

"Ilha das Flores" (Furtado): acclaim of, 152n11; defining human in, 41–52; lack in, 50–52; misreading film as documentary, 153n12; narrative-visual dialectic, 42–45; nuclear annihilation in, 44; physical sustenance in, 29–31; plot summary of, 42; recycled phrasing/imagery in, 43–44; satire in, 41–52; tomato waste-stream journey, 45–50
imaginaries, trash, 13–19
inclusive exclusion, 150n4
individualization, promises/pitfalls of, 113–21
Inter-American Development Bank, 114
International Monetary Fund, 114–15
International Vulture Awareness Day, 135
"Intestino grosso" (Fonseca), 33–34
Iovino, Serenella, 72

Jardim, João, 113
Jardim Gramacho, 121–23. *See also Waste Land* (film)
Jesus, Carolina Maria de, 122
Jiménez, Jaime. *See* Señor Tlacuache
José León Suárez, 55, 58–59, 62–64
Journal of Macromarketing, 125

Kennedy, Greg, 8
Kotsko, Adam, 114–7, 163n6
Kristeva, Julia, 8

Lacan, Jacques, 168n3
lack, "Los gallinazos sin plumas," 31–41
Lady Standing at a Virginal (Vermeer), 45
Latin America, 3, 21, 79, 85, 91, 103, 113, 133, 138–39; human limits in, 22–52; trash imaginaries in, 13–19; trash realities in, 10–13
Latour, Bruno, 27
Lefebvre, Henri, 88
liberty, defining, 153n15–16
Liboiron, Max, 118, 149n2
Lima, Peru, creative trash project regarding, 132–39
Lima la horrible (Salazar Bondy), 22–25
Lima Reader, The, 133–34
limitrophy, 4
limits: community, 53–72; humans, 22–52; neoliberal environmentalism, 109–42; waste management, 73–108
linguistic turn of twentieth-century Western philosophy, 5
literature, trash in, 13–19
Livon-Grosman, Ernesto, 1–3
lixões, 12
Lorax, The (Dr. Seuss), 118–19
lugar sin culpa, El (Merino), 33–34
"Luxo" (Augusto de Campos), 144–47
"Luxo é Lixo" (Luxury is Trash), 144–48

Madu, Ignatius Ani, 12
maja desnuda, La (Goya), 45
management, concept, 78–88
Maniates, Michael F., 117–19
Marcum, Joni Hayward, 124
Martins, Rafael D'Almeida, 12
matadero, El (Echeverría), 14–15
material ecocriticism, 18
material turn, 5
Maxi. *See villa, La* (Aira)
McLoughlin, Daniel, 28
mediants, 27
Mello, Leonardo Freire de, 12
Millar, Kathleen M., 123–24, 157n7
Ministry of Environment of Peru, 132
mise en abîme, 71
Moñagallo, Momboñombo. *See Única mirando al mar* (Contreras Castro)
Morton, Timothy, 75
muladar, 32–33
municipal waste workers, portrayal of, 79–80
Muniz, Vik, 123, 128–32

National Geographic, 91
neocapitalism, 88–89
neoliberal environmentalism, limits of, 109–13; Basurama, 139–42; bibliography, 163n6; echoing human/animal limit, 132–39; making differences, 121–32; promises/pitfalls, 113–21
Neuman, Andrés, 77, 143, 157n8–9
Nichols, Bill, 128, 130–31
Nixon, Rob, 10–11
Nostalgia de la sombra (Parra), 156n5
No una sino muchas muertes (Congrains Martín), 16
nuclear annihilation, 44
Nzeadibe, Thaddeus Chidi, 12

Oconitrillo, Única. See *Única mirando al mar* (Contreras Castro)
O cortiço (Azevedo), 15
olvidados, Los (film), 16
Open: Man and Animal, The (Agamben), 30–31
Organisation for Economic Co-operation and Development (OECD), 149n3
Orlando, Angela, 12
Ortega, Julio, 151n8
Other, 8, 14, 29, 43, 67, 124
Ottani, Adacto, 121

para-filmic, term, 166n19
Pascual the pig. See "gallinazos sin plumas, Los" (Ribeyro)
Pérez-Cano, Tania, 33–34
"Pictures of Garbage," project, 123
pig-feeding operation. See "gallinazos sin plumas, Los" (Ribeyro)
Políticas de la destrucción/Poéticas de la preservación (Heffes), 17, 25
Portrait of a Cardinal (Raphael), 45
"Póstudo" (poem), 144–45
practices, waste management, 104–8
Prádanos, Luis I., 141
Prado, Marcos, 16
pre-texts, 3–4
Production of Space, The (Lefebvre), 88
Programa do Jô, 128
proxidina (drug), 84

Quarto de despejo (Jesus), 122
¿Quién mató a Diego Duarte? (Dujovne Ortiz), 24, 55; defining trash in, 58–59; fixed identity in, 61–65; representing unrepresentable, 66–72

realities, trash, 10–13
representation. See unrepresentable, representing
"Residuos Urbanos Sólidos" (Urban Solid Waste) (RUS). See Basurama
Reyes, Alfonso, 73, 109
Ribeyro, Julio Ramón, 29–31
Rodríguez, Juan Pablo, 163–64n7
Roig, Alexandre, 58
Rota, Demetrio. See *Bariloche* (Neuman)
RUS. *Residuos Urbanos Sólidos. Basura y espacio público en Latinoamerica, 2008–2010*, 113, 140

Salazar Bondy, Sebastián, 22–24, 29, 53, 57, 132
Sánchez, Tomás, 17
Santos, Valter dos, 166n22
São Gonçalo, 56, 66–67, 127
satire, in "Ilha das Flores," 41–52
Scanlan, John, 28–29
Señor Gallinazo vuelve a Lima, El (Salazar Bondy), 22–25, 29
Señor Tlacuache, 109–13
Shantytown. See *villa, La* (Aira)
slow violence, 10–12
Soares, Jô, 128
social media, 21, 113, 133, 135, 137, 167n24
Soper, Kate, 40–41
Sorge, 8
Sosa, Eduardo. See *Baile con serpientes* (Castellanos Moya)
space, trash and, 88–104
Spitta, Silvia, 22
Stam, Robert, 18
State of Exception (Agamben), 54
suarenses, 58, 62, 69

Tadajewski, Mark, 125–27
thresholds: human/animal, 29–31; terminology, 57–58; trash as, 25–29, 57–61

Tijuana, 56–57, 60, 66–67, 154n6
tomatoes. *See* "Ilha das Flores" (Furtado): tomato waste-stream journey
trans-corporeality, 156n3
Transformative Consumer Research, 125
trash: accumulation of, 8–10; anthropological machine and, 29–31; in *Cartoneros*, 1–4; central role of, 6; characterization of, 8–9; contradictions of, 143–48; definition, 7–8; fundamentally ambiguous nature of, 36–37; generation of, 149n4; imaginaries of, 13–19; and limits of community, 53–72; limits of humans, 22–52; living in age of, 4–10; realities of, 10–13; sustained examination of, 149n5; thoughtful cultivating, 109–13; as threshold, 25–29, 57–61; waste management limits, 73–108
"trash people" (*gente-basura*), 97–98
trash works: common language, consensus, and code of, 88–89; literary texts as, 77–84; neoliberal rationality and, 84–86; representing waste management in, 103–4; symptomatic readings of, 86
Tsing, Anna, 112
2666 (Bolaño), 16

"Ultraje" (Enrigue), 77, 158n9; space in, 90–92, 95, 97–98; as trash work, 78–79, 85–88
Única Looking at the Sea. *See Única mirando al mar* (Contreras Castro)
Única mirando al mar (Contreras Castro), 77, 159n15; space in, 92–95, 98–99; as trash work, 83–88; WM practices, 105–8
United States Agency for International Development, 132
unrepresentable, representing, 66–72
Ureta, Sebastián, 78, 86–88, 102, 104–8
Urrea, Luis Alberto, 55–57

Vargas, Tayde, 109–13
Venkatesh, Vinodh, 159n13
Verbitsky, Bernardo, 16
villa, La (Aira), 77; portrayal of villa miseria in, 161n23; space in, 89–90, 98–99; as trash work, 84–88; and violent impact of neoliberalism, 157n6; WM practices, 105–8
villa miseria, 84, 97–98, 160n22
Villa miseria también es América (Verbitsky), 16
vultures, 31–41, 132–38
vultures without feathers. *See* "gallinazos sin plumas, Los" (Ribeyro)

Walker, Charles F., 134
Walker, Lucy, 113, 123, 143
Washington Consensus, 163n7–8
Waslala (Belli), 16–17
wasted lives, term, 154n1
Waste Land (film), 113, 162n2, 165n16; academic criticism of, 125–27; comparison to "Los artilugios del Señor Tlacuache," 124; fulfilling promise of transforming viewers, 127–28; fulfilling viewer desires, 130–32; making a difference in, 121–32; and modality of trash work, 128–30; website of, 124–25
waste management, limits of, 73–77; definition, 86–88; establishing space, 88–104; practices, 104–8; trash works, 77–88
Waste Management (journal), 86–87
wastescapes, 17
wilderness zones, 72
wildlife documentary. *See* Gallinazo Avisa
Williamson, John, 163n7
Wolfe, Cary, 30
Worden, Daniel, 119
work, term, 77
World Bank, 114

Xochimancas, 15

YouTube, Gallinazo Avisa on, 135–39

Zarco, El (Altamirano), 15–16
Zero: romance pré-histórico (Brandão), 156n5
Ziarek, Ewa Plonowska, 53, 55
Zubiaurre, Maite, 17–18

Micah McKay is assistant professor of Spanish at the University of Alabama. He is coeditor of *Environmental Cultural Studies Through Time: The Luso-Hispanic World* (*Hispanic Issues On Line*).

www.ingramcontent.com/pod-product-compliance
Lightning Source LLC
Chambersburg PA
CBHW030827230426
43667CB00008B/1410